# Exposed

A volume in the series

**Cornell Modern Indonesia Project**

Edited by Eric Tagliacozzo and Thomas B. Pepinsky

A list of titles in this series is available at cornellpress.cornell.edu.

# Exposed

## A Visual History of the Destruction of the Indonesian Left

GEOFFREY ROBINSON AND DOUGLAS KAMMEN

Southeast Asia Program Publications
an imprint of Cornell University Press
Ithaca and London

Publication of this book was made possible with generous grants from the University of California, Los Angeles, and the National University of Singapore.



First published 2025 by Cornell University Press

Printed in the United States of America
Design and composition by Chris Crochetière, BW&A Books, Inc.

Library of Congress Cataloging-in-Publication Data
Names: Robinson, Geoffrey, 1957– author | Kammen, Douglas Anton author
Title: Exposed : a visual history of the destruction of the Indonesian left / Geoffrey Robinson and Douglas Kammen.
Description: Ithaca [New York] : Southeast Asia Program Publications, an imprint of Cornell University Press, 2025. | Series: Cornell modern Indonesia project | Includes bibliographical references and index.
Identifiers: LCCN 2025001699 | ISBN 9781501780592 hardcover
Subjects: LCSH: Political violence—Indonesia—History—20th century | Indonesia—History—Coup d'état, 1965 | Indonesia—Politics and government—1950–1966
Classification: LCC DS644.32 .R63 2025 | DDC 959.803/5—dc23/eng/20250313
LC record available at https://lccn.loc.gov/2025001699

Yes, the dead do speak, but in their own way and in their own time. Buchenwald, Ravensbruck, Dachau, Auschwitz, and all the other human slaughterhouses, even those in Indonesia, cannot silence the dead.

Pramoedya Ananta Toer, *The Mute's Soliloquy*

# Contents

# Acknowledgments

Over the course of six years, many people and institutions have provided us with assistance, information, and encouragement. We are especially grateful to David Jenkins, who wisely declined our invitation to participate in this project but offered moral support and very kindly allowed us to reproduce several of his photographs. A number of other journalists also provided invaluable assistance. Carol Gonzales granted us access to Beryl Bernay's extraordinary collection of photographs, documents, and ephemera from the years 1964–67. Carol (Goldstein) Abaya answered questions about her experience as a reporter in Jakarta in 1965. Peter Schumacher gave us permission to use his photographs from prison camps in West Kalimantan and Buru Island. The Moelyono family allowed us to reproduce some of the photographs he had taken while embedded with the Indonesian Army in late 1965. Other individuals generously granted us permission to reproduce personal documents and works of art. They included I Dewa Putu Ngurah Djenawi, Elisabeth Ida Mulyani and Derek Bacon, Andreas Iswinarto, Yayak Yatmaka, Joshua Oppenheimer, and Dadang Christanto.

We also wish to extend our special thanks to the many people who assisted us with research. Elisabeth Ida Mulyani offered invaluable research and design assistance during her stay in Los Angeles as a Fulbright scholar; Dahlia Setiyawan helped us to assess and select images from Beryl Bernay's collection; Karen Strassler shared the transcripts of her valuable interviews with the photographers Moelyono and Djoko Pekik; and I Wayan Natar Susila provided a personal account of political imprisonment in Bali. In addition, a great many individuals helped us with research on specific images, journalists, and photographers, including Albertus Harimurti, Nita Karianipurwanti, Wayne Forest, Bonnie Triyana, Purwani Diyah Prabandari, Stanley Adi Prasetyo, Ben Abel, Grace Leksana, Frank Palmos, Salim Said, Hilmar Farid Setiadi, Made Tony Supriatma, Nicole Iturriaga, Diyah Larasati, Tatiana Sulovska, and Jafar Suryomenggolo.

Staff at the following photo agencies patiently answered our questions and assisted with the sometimes exasperating work of licensing: Alamy, Antara, AFP, ANP, AP, Camera Press, Getty Images, Magnum, Redux, Tempo, Topfoto, and UPI. The staff at the photography section of the National Library of Indonesia (Perpustakaan Nasional Republik Indonesia) went above and beyond in answering our questions and providing high-quality reproductions of images in their collection. We are especially grateful to Bapak Teguh Purwanto, the head of the Library and Information Services Center (Kepala Pusat Jasa Perpustakaan dan Informasi), who assisted our research and granted us permission to use a number of those images at no cost.

Needless to say, this book would not have been possible without institutional funding and administrative support. At the National University of Singapore (NUS), we would like to thank Dean Lionel Wee for providing us with a FASS book grant and the Isaac Manasseh Meyer Visiting Fellowship, which allowed Robinson to visit NUS for a stretch of intensive planning at an early stage of the project. At UCLA, the Department of History provided crucial research funding and administrative support. Special thanks are owed to Mahea Oyoso-Sadsad for helping us to navigate UCLA's arcane financial management system.

At Cornell University Press, our editor, Sarah Grossman, expertly guided the project from proposal through production. Jackie Teoh kindly assisted with the logistics. Susan Specter and Eric Levy thoughtfully oversaw the production of the volume.

Finally, we are deeply grateful to Djati for his input on many topics, to Lovisa for her painstaking editing of the entire manuscript, and to other members of our families for their patience and understanding as this project extended far beyond its planned sell-by date.

# Abbreviations and Terms

aksi sepihak: "unilateral actions" by the PKI and affiliated organizations to implement land-reform legislation

Ansor: Nahdlatul Ulama–affiliated youth organization

ASEAN: Association of Southeast Asian Nations

Banser: Barisan Ansor Serbaguna (Ansor Multipurpose Front)

Baperki: Badan Permusyawaratan Kewarganegaraan Indonesia (Deliberative Association for Indonesian Citizenship)

BPS: Badan Pendukung Sukarnoisme (Body to Support Sukarnoism)

BTI: Barisan Tani Indonesia (Indonesian Peasants' Front)

CGMI: Consentrasi Gerakan Mahasiswa Indonesia (Unified Movement of Indonesian University Students)

Dewan Jendral: Council of Generals

Dewan Revolusi: Revolutionary Council

Dwikomando Rakyat: People's Dual Command to crush Malaysia and defend the Revolution

Ganjang Malaysia: Crush Malaysia

Gerwani: Gerakan Wanita Indonesia (Indonesian Women's Movement)

Gestapu: Gerakan September Tiga Puluh (army acronym for September 30th Movement)

Gestok: Gerakan Satu Oktober (October 1st Movement)

G30S: Gerakan 30 September (September 30th Movement)

Hansip: Pertahanan Sipil (Civil Defense)

HMI: Himpunan Mahasiswa Islam (Islamic University Students' Association)

ICRC: International Committee of the Red Cross

IPKI: Ikatan Pendukung Kemerdekaan Indonesia (League of Upholders of Indonesian Freedom)

KAMI: Kesatuan Aksi Mahasiswa Indonesia (Indonesian University Students' Action Front)

KAP-Gestapu: Komando Aksi Pengganyangan Gerakan September Tiga Puluh (Action Command to Crush Gestapu)

KAPPI: Kesatuan Aksi Pemuda Pelajar Indonesia (Indonesian Youth and Student Action Front)

KOGAM: Komando Ganjang Malaysia (Crush Malaysia Command)

Konfrontasi: Confrontation (campaign to oppose the formation of Malaysia, 1963–66)

Kopkamtib: Komando Operasi Pemulihan Keamanan dan Ketertiban (Operations Command for the Restoration of Security and Order)

Kostrad: Komando Cadangan Strategis Angkatan Darat (Army Strategic Reserve Command)

KOTI: Komando Operasi Tertinggi (Supreme Operations Command)

LEKRA: Lembaga Kebudayaan Rakyat (People's Cultural Institute)

Mahmillub: Mahkamah Militer Luar Biasa (Extraordinary Military Tribunal)

Masyumi: Majelis Syuro Muslimin Indonesia (Consultative Council of Indonesian Muslims)

MPRS: Majelis Permusyawaratan Rakyat Sementara (Provisional People's Consultative Assembly)

NU: Nahdlatul Ulama (Council of Islamic Scholars)

Pancasila: Five Principles (Indonesian state ideology)

Paraku: Pasukan Rakyat Kalimantan Utara (North Kalimantan People's Force)

Partai Katolik: Catholic Party

Pemuda Katolik: Catholic Youth

Pemuda Marhaenis: Marhaenist Youth

Pemuda Pancasila: Pancasila Youth

Pemuda Rakyat: People's Youth

PGRS: Pasukan Gerilya Rakyat Sarawak (Sarawak People's Guerrilla Force)

PKI: Partai Komunis Indonesia (Indonesian Communist Party)

PKI Malam: Nighttime PKI (army term for Communist underground)

PNI: Partai Nasional Indonesia (Indonesian Nationalist Party)

PSI: Partai Sosialis Indonesia (Indonesian Socialist Party)

RPKAD: Resimen Para Komando Angkatan Darat (Army Paracommando Regiment)

Supersemar: Surat Perintah Sebelas Maret (Order of March 11, 1966)

Tameng Marhaenis: Marhaenist Shield

Tjakrabirawa Regiment: Presidential guard

Wanra: Perlawanan Rakyat (People's Resistance)

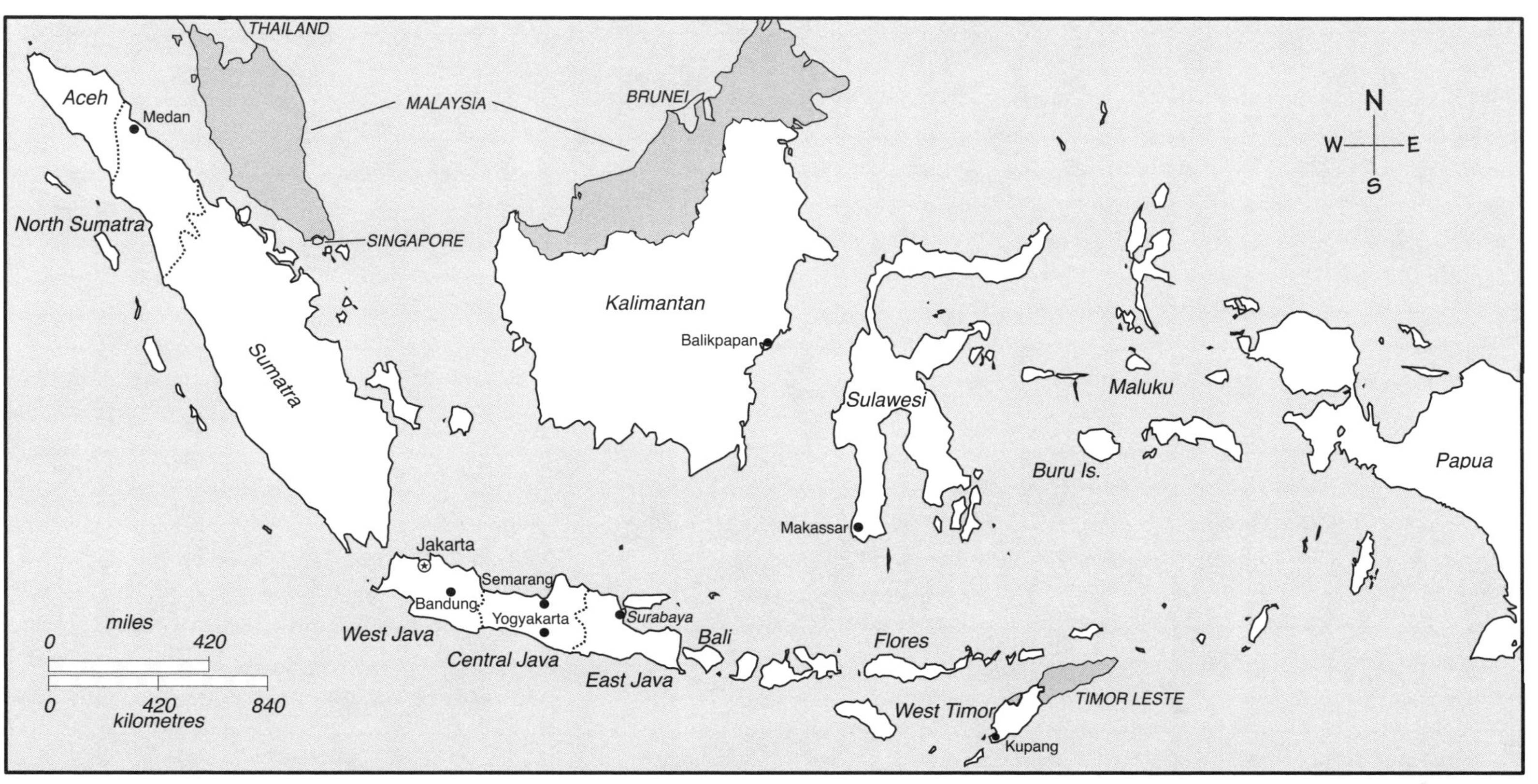


Map of Indonesia

# Exposed

## INTRODUCTION

# Images and the Destruction of the Indonesian Left

> *Some information about the past can be provided only by visual images.*
>
> — Hayden White, "Historiography and Historiophoty"

October 1, 1965, marked the beginning of the end for the Indonesian Left and a major turning point in the Cold War. Over a period of just a few months, something like half a million leftists were killed and a million more were detained in an orchestrated campaign of violence, and there were further arrests and killings over the next several years. In the decade before that violence, the Left had emerged as a vital political and social force in Indonesia, and the left-nationalist President Sukarno, leader of the country's independence movement and a staunch critic of imperialism, had become a leading figure in the global non-aligned movement. By early 1967, all of that had been swept away, and the country had embarked on a period of military-backed authoritarian rule whose legacies continue to reverberate today.

In marked contrast to most other instances of mass violence and momentous political change in the past century—most notably the Holocaust and the genocides in Armenia, Cambodia, and Rwanda—the visual record of the violence against the Left in Indonesia is woefully sparse and incomplete. That shortcoming has contributed, we believe, to the relative obscurity and serious misunderstanding of those events. This book aims to remedy both of these problems through what we call a visual history. Combining some three hundred rare and iconic images—mainly photographs but also political cartoons, posters, graffiti, official documents, and works of art—with brief historical texts, it tells the story of the mass violence of 1965–67 and the destruction of the Indonesian Left that was its purpose and consequence. By highlighting photographs and other images and locating them historically, the book fills a yawning gap in the historical record. It also poses a challenge to the distorted official narratives that have shaped social memory for more than half a century and establishes a basis on which new social memories and interpretations might be formed.

The pioneering photographer Corky Lee, who documented Chinese American lives at the height of the US civil rights movement, believed that photography could perform vital historical and political work—not simply by documenting lives lived but as a corrective to forgotten, marginalized, or suppressed histories. "I'd like to think," he said, "that every time I take my camera out of my bag it's like drawing a sword to combat indifference, injustice and discrimination, trying to get rid of stereotypes." One writer noted that Lee's photographs "helped generations of Chinese-Americans see themselves as part of a larger community . . . during a time when Asian-Americans felt invisible."[1] This book is written in that spirit: to render visible what has been obscured, and to open the possibility of richer historical understanding and possibly even justice.

## The Story and the Problem

The campaign of mass killings and incarceration of the Indonesian Left followed an alleged coup attempt on October 1, 1965, led by a group calling itself the September 30th Movement (Gerakan 30 September). In the course of the movement's bungled operation early that morning, six top army generals were killed. Claiming that the action had been orchestrated by the Indonesian Communist Party (Partai Komunis Indonesia, or PKI) as part of a plot to seize power, the army instigated a campaign to destroy the party and its allies "down to the very roots."[2] The campaign was led by Major General Suharto, who inexplicably had not been targeted by the movement. Then, through a series of political maneuvers, and riding the mass violence he had set in motion, Suharto gradually wrested power from President Sukarno. In March 1966, Sukarno granted Suharto executive authority, and in 1967 Suharto was named acting president. The following year, Suharto became president.

Through this campaign of violence, the army crushed the largest nongoverning Communist party in the world and swept aside President Sukarno, ushering in more than three decades of military-backed authoritarian rule. The campaign meant the silencing, whether by killing, imprisonment, or censorship, of a generation of politicians and intellectuals, writers, and artists associated with the Left, a fact that profoundly altered the course of Indonesian cultural and intellectual life. And it meant the brutalization of the entire society through the regime's conscious deployment of fear, terror, and vigilantism to control public life, and through the culture of terror and impunity that was permitted to develop inside the Indonesian armed forces.

The events of 1965–67 also signaled a pivotal moment in the Cold War, bringing an end to a powerful nonaligned movement that had its origins in the Asian-African Conference held in Bandung in 1955, partly under Indonesian leadership. The decimation of the Left was encouraged and facilitated by the United States and its allies, who had viewed Indonesia's leftward drift in the early 1960s with increasing alarm. Moreover, through their stalwart support for Suharto's "New Order" military regime that came to power in the wake of those crimes, and through their deliberate silence about the violence, these governments and many others effectively shielded Indonesian authorities from exposure and prevented the proper investigation and prosecution of what, by any measure, were among the worst crimes of the twentieth century.

In short, the domestic and international political significance of the horrors of 1965–67 in Indonesia were profound. And yet, more than half a century later, the causes, course, and consequences of these events remain virtually unknown outside Indonesia. That is equally true within the country, where most Indonesians have a very poor understanding of what happened, let alone why. In contrast to other major mass killings of the twentieth century, moreover, the violence against the political Left in Indonesia has never been punished or even properly investigated, and there have been no serious calls for any such action by international bodies or states.

One key reason for the relative obscurity of the violence and terror, we believe, is the absence of a compelling or even remotely complete visual record. What we have instead is a highly sanitized record, created and shaped by the perpetrators of the violence. This record depicts PKI members as depraved, treacherous, faceless, and inhuman, and the army as heroic defenders of national stability, security, and order. That misleading portrait was set in motion by the army within days of the alleged coup and has been reinforced for more than half a century—through controls on the mass media, show trials, state rituals honoring the fallen army "heroes," and both formal and informal limitations on artistic expression and journalistic freedom. The resulting visual record has helped to embed the perverse official version of the alleged coup and its aftermath deeply in Indonesian society and has hindered the emergence of alternative social memories and historical narratives. It has also concealed the most basic human dimension of this history—the murder and detention of hundreds of thousands of leftists—effectively rendering the violence invisible and depriving successive generations of any sense of what it meant, what it felt like, to millions of ordinary people.

A related problem has been the misidentification and decontextualization of the photographs that do exist. In online discussions and even some published works, images from other places and times are sometimes said to show the treatment of PKI detainees in 1965–67. One of the most common cases of this kind is a series of photographs from 1948 in Madiun, East Java, where Indonesian troops crushed what the army described as a PKI uprising, killing thousands. The photos taken at that time—of a bloodied PKI prisoner with a rope around his neck, and a group of detainees being stabbed with a bayonet while in a ditch—frequently appear in blogs and on posters about the events of 1965–67. Presumably these images are used because they are in some ways more dramatic, more obviously violent, than those that exist from the destruction of the Left in the mid-1960s. Whatever the reason, their use undermines or distorts our understanding of what happened after the failed coup on October 1, 1965.

A more amusing, but equally problematic, case of misidentification is a photograph of very young children engaged in an anti-imperialist street rally in Jakarta in the months before October 1, 1965. The image, which is published with some frequency in online posts—and was for a time a candidate for inclusion in this book—is visually compelling and appears to capture the spirit of the times. The problem is that the photo is actually a still from a demonstration that was staged for a 1982 feature film about Indonesia, *The Year of Living Dangerously*, starring Sigourney Weaver and Mel Gibson. This photograph is a reminder that, despite their popular reputation for objectivity, pictures rarely speak for themselves. They can mislead in many ways and must therefore be read critically and with attention to the context and conditions of their production.

Further complicating our understanding of the visual record is the matter of captions. In some cases, like those noted above, the texts attached to photographs from this period are simply wrong. More often, they mislead or misdirect the reader, intentionally or not. Captions accompanying official photographs of leftist political detainees in 1965–67, for example, tend to reinforce quite heavy-handedly the army's narrative of PKI treachery and the army's own heroism. The captions in a photo book published by the army in 1979 are a prime example. The text accompanying a photograph of September 30th Movement leader Lieutenant Colonel Untung reads as follows: "Here is the leader of the counterrevolutionary G30S/PKI . . . whose victims are numberless and which is a black page in Indonesian history."[3] Meanwhile, as described below, the captions that appear alongside photographs taken by foreign journalists in this period tend to reflect the prevailing—often anti-Communist—political views and cultural assumptions of the media outlets for which they worked. In both cases, the captions direct the reader as to how the photograph should be read, and with a few exceptions they tend to reinforce the army's tendentious narrative.

These problems—the absence of an adequate visual record, the misidentification of the record that does exist, and the misdirection introduced through captions and other mechanisms—have yet to be squarely addressed by scholars. Indeed, of the two dozen or so excellent scholarly works published on the events of 1965–67 in the past decade, most include only a handful of images, and many contain none at all. Nor do they tackle the significance of visual images in the production of violence or in the construction of social memory about those events. This is a notable absence. In our view, it has contributed to the historical amnesia that now prevails concerning the mass violence in Indonesia, to the continued dominance of the official state narrative, and to the indifference of the world community to the crimes that were committed. Our hope is that by creating a broad archive of images, properly contextualized, this book will help to alleviate that amnesia and open new ways of understanding these crucial historical events. By highlighting images, moreover, we also draw attention to aspects of the history that have eluded standard narratives and shift the focus beyond the mechanisms by which violence was produced to a wider history of regime change and counterrevolution.

## Aims and Limitations

Against that backdrop, this book makes three related contributions. First, and most simply, we believe it will establish the first reasonably comprehensive visual record of events that have been intentionally distorted or rendered invisible for more than half a century. In that way, it will help create the conditions for a new social memory—a basis on which to challenge official narratives and open new ways of seeing and understanding. Our premise here is that the capacity for memory, and for greater historical understanding, depends powerfully on the existence of visual markers or reminders, such as photographs, memorials, and works of art. Where these visual markers have been controlled by a state intent on erasing all but the official historical narrative, social memory and historical truth are necessarily compromised. Creating a collection of images, and properly contextualizing them, offers one possible avenue for rendering the invisible visible and laying the foundation for a new social memory and a more complex historical understanding.

Second, by combining a rich visual record with brief texts, the book provides a basis for a fresh analysis of the historically important period of 1965–67 and the longer-term consequences for its victims. We recognize that photographs and other visual images are not always reliable as evidence, and that there is a great deal more that can be learned from them than simply "proof" of "what happened." Still, viewing these images as historians, we see them as potential evidence of long-obscured or poorly documented historical events and trends. We believe that, when located in their proper context, and with attention to the conditions of their production, they can remind us of what has been omitted from conventional narratives and highlight dimensions of the history that have been deliberately obscured. Notably, the photographic record from the period before 1965 serves as a reminder of the vibrancy of the Indonesian Left and Indonesia's place in the wider world. Meanwhile, the contextualized visual record from the period after the alleged coup highlights the remarkable complexity of the political struggle of that time, a complexity too often overlooked in accounts that focus either on how violence was produced or teleologically on the ultimate victory of the army. For while the army and its allies did eventually succeed in annihilating the Left, the photographs of the period remind us that that victory was by no means a foregone conclusion.

Finally, we hope this book will serve as an open visual archive of sorts. While recognizing their evidentiary value, we view these images as historical artifacts whose meaning and significance are open to different kinds of analysis and interpretation. On that basis, the book invites readers to view the collected images critically, to see what else they might tell us—what they conceal, what they unintentionally reveal, what they make us feel. Experts in visual culture, for instance, will undoubtedly see in them dimensions and meanings that we have not seen. Similarly, political activists, or those seeking justice for the victims of the violence, may find in this collection evidence or clues to assist them in their cause. In short, far from seeking to provide a definitive interpretation of events, or even a definitive collection of images, we hope this book will serve as a springboard that will encourage others to offer new and different interpretations. We also hope that it will stimulate the collection, exhibition, sharing, and discussion of other images from this period.

Needless to say, this book has limitations, and these are worth spelling out here to avoid any misunderstanding or disappointment. Perhaps most important, it does not include photographs or other visual representations of what was most common: vast numbers of people in villages, towns, and cities, hiding indoors, windows shuttered, making as little noise as possible. Waiting. Nor does it include images of militiamen and soldiers yelling and brandishing weapons as they stormed neighborhoods and villages. There are no images of prisoners being tortured or sexually assaulted, or of their nighttime removal from detention centers and transport to killing fields. And with two notable exceptions, there are no photographs of dead bodies here: no images of corpses dumped in rivers, down wells, into shallow graves, or into the sea. As discussed below, the absence of these images stems primarily from the gaps in the available visual record.

Some readers will also notice that there is no section devoted exclusively to the experience of women, or to the question of gender-based violence. That was a deliberate choice. Rather than treating women as a separate subject, we have sought to locate their experiences within the larger story of political change and violence during these years. For while women and girls were indeed subjected to terrible sexualized violence, and while the army and its allies employed misogynist language and imagery to ignite hatred against the Left, Indonesian women were always much more than victims. As the images in this volume reveal, women were actively engaged in the political and social struggles of the times: they were leaders, thinkers, and innovators, they took to the streets to protest injustice, and they took up arms as part of the broad militarization of society. In other words, in addition to being victims of propaganda and violence, women played an important role in virtually every aspect of the political and social life of the country. Indeed, it was because of their active role in the politics of the time that women were subjected to such vilification and violence after October 1, 1965. By treating their experience as part of these larger patterns, we seek not to minimize the role of women but rather to highlight it, and to make clear that women were not only victims of violence but agents of Indonesian history.

It should also be noted that this is not a definitive history of the events of 1965–67 or their aftermath. Other works, including some of our own, offer more sustained and detailed historical treatments of the period.[4] The book's focus on the visual, as well as its language and organization, is designed for a different purpose: to bring these critical historical events to life, to make an obscure history accessible to a wider audience, and to render visible a story that has been obscured for more than half a century. Nor can this book claim to provide comprehensive geographical coverage. Most of the images printed here are from the capital city of Jakarta and the most populous islands, Java and Bali, with a smaller number from Kalimantan and the prison island of Buru in the Moluccas, fewer still from Sumatra and Sulawesi, and none at all from the islands east of Bali. This unevenness reflects the enormous logistical obstacles faced by private citizens and photographers, foreign and domestic, at the time, and the real dangers of publishing and storing photographs from that period.

Finally, we need to make clear that we are not experts in visual analysis and culture. For that reason, the book leans in the direction of presenting a widely representative body of images and providing a rich historical and political context in the form of brief commentaries rather than close readings of the aesthetics or structure of the images themselves. Indeed, as noted above, among our goals is that this book will serve as a stepping stone—a kind of open archive—to be subjected to analysis and interpretation by scholars and commentators with other kinds of expertise and different interests. In short, far from claiming to offer a definitive analysis of the images, we have a more modest goal: namely, to bring them into the public sphere, where they can form the basis of debate, discussion, and interpretation.

## Conditions of Production

Several features of the official photographic record are especially noteworthy. First, in marked contrast to typical "atrocity photographs" that aim to evoke empathy for the victims of violence and revulsion toward its perpetrators, photographs produced by and for the Indonesian Army typically depict the victims as treacherous and violent, or faceless and abject, and the perpetrators as heroic (and nonviolent) defenders of law and order. Second, unlike the photographs that have emerged from other instances of mass violence and genocide, the official images of Indonesia during the mid-1960s almost never depict the widespread and extreme violence committed by the main perpetrators—that is, the army and its civilian allies. Third, in many of the photographs, the army and its allies pose arrogantly, as though to mark or enact their victory for posterity.[5] By contrast, most political detainees appear hapless, dejected, and defeated, perhaps because they see no way out, or possibly because they have been warned by their captors not to reveal their emotions. Finally, in contrast to most other instances of mass violence, many of the photographs from this period are of women. We see women marching in demonstrations and parades, drilling in military and police formation, and providing food and drink to soldiers and prisoners, but also languishing in places of detention.

The obvious question is why the photographic record looks the way it does. The answer lies in what we call the "conditions of production" of these images—the social, political, and technological conditions that shaped their creation and dissemination. In large part, the distinctive features of the photographic record from 1965–67 stem from the fact that much of it was produced by the army itself, especially its Army Information Center (Pusat Penerangan Angkatan Darat), and by photographers—both domestic and foreign—working under its direct supervision. That is to say, its distinctive features are a reflection of the army's deliberate effort to create a record that would underscore and embed in popular consciousness their version of events.

The photographs taken by the Indonesian photojournalist Moelyono are a case in point. They include an unusual picture of the bodies of two young boys lying face down in the mud (see figure 128). The photo was taken while Moelyono was embedded with the notorious Army Paracommando Regiment (Resimen Para Komando Angkatan Darat, or RPKAD) on its sweep through Central Java in late 1965. As Moelyono later told the scholar Karen Strassler, his army minders placed strict limits on what he could photograph and dictated which images were ultimately published. Significantly, they forbade him to photograph soldiers committing acts of violence. He was also forbidden from showing the faces of dead PKI members, so bodies had to be arranged before being photographed.[6] These conditions help to explain the odd position of the corpses in that photo, their apparent anonymity, and the curious lack of blood at the scene. Even in this most visceral image, one of only a handful showing a dead body, the army's heavy editorial hand is evident.

But there is another reason the visual record appears as it does. In contrast to many other instances of mass violence in modern times, very few if any photographs taken by private individuals have surfaced. The reasons for that absence are worth considering. In the period after October 1, 1965, the army effectively controlled who could take photos and what could be published. Furthermore, cameras and film were expensive and rare in Indonesia at the time. In contrast to the situation today, when digital phones and cameras are ubiquitous, photography in Indonesia in the 1960s was a technology limited to a tiny fraction of the population, including professional photographers and a few members of the social elite. Among that small group, moreover, there was a general reluctance, rooted in legitimate fear, to take photos or to hold on to any images that might cause them trouble with the authorities.

As the renowned Indonesian artist and sometime photographer Djoko Pekik told a researcher years later, when the anti-Left campaign began in 1965 he destroyed the photographs he had taken of political rallies, lest they be seen as evidence of his leftist sympathies.[7] For somewhat different reasons, before he died, the American scholar Roger Paget destroyed the extensive collection of flyers and ephemera he had gathered while conducting his PhD research in Indonesia in 1965–66. When asked why he had done so, he said that the archive felt like a "psychological burden."[8] While it is possible, even likely, that additional photographs and other visual artifacts of this period will surface, for now we are left with the official photographic record and with images created by local and foreign journalists restricted to particular geographic regions and operating within strict limits on what they depicted.

## Official Photographs and Images

Whether they were created by army photographers or by civilians acting under their supervision, it is safe to say that many, though of course not all, of the images we now have were carefully curated to support the army's narrative: that the

PKI was brutal and treacherous, that the violence against its members was the inevitable and spontaneous result of popular anger, and that the army acted heroically, and without apparent resort to violence, to restore law and order and save the nation from disaster.

From the outset, army authorities made skillful use of photographs and other images to construct and disseminate that false narrative. In the days immediately after the alleged coup of October 1, for example, the army-controlled press was filled with emotionally charged photographs that effectively seared the story of PKI brutality and army martyrdom into the collective memory. These included photos of the six generals' decomposing bodies being exhumed (see figure 66), which were presented as "evidence" that the generals had been tortured by their PKI captors, thereby fueling the narrative of PKI brutality, and popular anger. The day after the exhumations, the army-controlled (and foreign) press published images of the grandiose funeral procession for the generals—images that helped to imprint the idea that they were national heroes and martyrs (see figures 64 and 65). At the same time, to emphasize the army's popular legitimacy, official media began to publish images of crowds happily cheering the army and riding on tanks.

A crucial element of the army's propaganda campaign, set in motion within days of the alleged coup, was the false claim that members of the leftist Indonesian Women's Movement (Gerakan Wanita Indonesia, or Gerwani), had danced naked, engaged in an orgy, and then sliced the generals with razor blades. These fabrications were buttressed with photographs and film footage of the accused women, who were often very young, confessing to their evil deeds while in detention. The story of Gerwani depravity also became fodder for cartoonists who depicted them as scantily clad witches cruelly torturing the generals. These false claims were part of a wider campaign against women and the Left, apparently driven by a concern among the army and its allies that politically active women posed an existential threat to their power and to patriarchal norms more generally. That preoccupation goes some way toward explaining why so many women were detained and ill treated after 1965.

Starting in late 1965, authorities began to disseminate photographs showing political detainees under police and military guard or in detention facilities. While some of these images were taken by army photographers, many were the work of local and international photojournalists who had been invited by the army to specially staged publicity events. These include the now-iconic photographs (and film footage) of a man at gunpoint late at night at Salemba Prison in Jakarta in November 1965 (see figures 143–44). Those photographs were taken during a visit by the Jakarta regional military commander, which members of the press were invited to cover. There are also numerous images of political detainees, both men and women, held in detention centers around the country. The fact that these photographs were taken in the context of army-organized visits makes clear their political purpose: through them, the army sought to underscore visually the criminality of the PKI and to show that the army was restoring law and order.

Photographs also became a vital technology in the state's effort to dominate and control the Left. Soon after the alleged October 1 coup, citizens were required to carry official identity cards, complete with a photograph, to prove they were not members of leftist organizations. Paradoxically, photographers became entangled in this system of control. Djoko Pekik, the leftist artist and photographer who destroyed his old photographs to avoid suspicion of pro-PKI sympathies, fled from Jakarta to a city in Central Java, where, to avoid arrest, he posed as "a commercial photographer—shooting the identity photos the authorities required of citizens as they carried out their antileft 'cleansing.'"[9]

From late 1965 through 1967, the Army Information Center also disseminated images of political show trials in which PKI leaders, such as PKI general secretary Sudisman, and Sukarno loyalists, such as Foreign Minister Subandrio, were sentenced to long prison terms or death for their alleged involvement in the murder of the six generals (see figures 181, 182, 249, 250, 258, 259). The authorities made sure that local and foreign journalists were on hand to photograph these court proceedings. Like the trials themselves, the resulting images, published widely inside Indonesia and abroad, had a clear political purpose: to depict the army's seizure of power as a legitimate exercise of the rule of law and to show previously powerful men as criminals deserving severe punishment.

In addition to photographs, the army and its allies made effective (if crude) use of political cartoons and graffiti to drive home their preferred narrative and to mobilize the population against the PKI. In the absence of any photographs of actual PKI violence, cartoons and graffiti filled an important gap in the army's visual account. Predictably, they portrayed the September 30th Movement and the PKI as treacherous and brutal and, closely following the army's language, called for them to be "hung," "destroyed down to the very roots," and "annihilated." Significantly, the cartoons commonly employed iconography common to genocides and mass violence, depicting the army's enemies as inhuman—as rats, snakes, or devils (see figures 77, 134, 135). Portraying the PKI in this way served to obfuscate the real terror committed by the army and its allies. The clear intention was to inflame popular passions against the PKI and its allies and to encourage acts of violence against them.

As the political struggle unfolded in 1966, photography and other visual imagery also served to celebrate and promote the interests of the various groups that opposed the PKI and sought to topple President Sukarno. The anti-Communist "action fronts" organized public exhibitions of photographs and other art forms glorifying their own role. In April 1966, for example, the Indonesian University Students' Action Front (Kesatuan Aksi Mahasiswa Indonesia, or KAMI) and the Association of Indonesian Journalists (Perserikatan Wartawan Indonesia) organized an exhibition titled "The Rise of the Young Generation."

The opening in Jakarta was attended by Suharto and the widows of the slain generals; the exhibit then traveled to Bandung, where the military governor lent his approval. Three months later, in Jakarta, an exhibition opened that featured political caricatures by art students, including critiques of the "Old Order" policies against hairstyles—both Beatle cuts and long hair—that Sukarno and the PKI had viewed as expressions of Western decadence. On the first anniversary of the alleged October 1 coup, the Indonesian Youth and Student Action Front (Kesatuan Aksi Pemuda Pelajar Indonesia) in Medan, North Sumatra, sponsored an exhibition of photographs of Lubang Buaya, where the generals' bodies had been buried, with the aim of "increasing the awareness of the people toward the cruelty of G30S." In these and other exhibits, photography simultaneously served as documentation and celebration.

Photographs and other visual images continued to be a favored medium of official propaganda well after the mass killings had abated. In the 1970s, for instance, the Army History Service issued the first in a series of official photo books, whose explicit purpose was to present photographs as "evidence" of the PKI's treachery and brutality and to celebrate the army's role in saving the nation from the Communist menace.[10] The captions appended to the photos make the book's objective abundantly clear. For example, the caption for a photograph of alleged victims of the PKI reads, "Just how brutal the PKI are is proven in this photograph—the PKI does not value human life at all!" Another exclaims, "What more can we say about the PKI but 'savage, sadistic, and inhumane!'"

The authorities also used photographs to combat mounting international pressure for the release of political detainees in the late 1970s. Official photographs taken inside a long-term detention center for women in Central Java, for example, depict groups of prisoners smiling uncomfortably as they stand next to army officials. A photograph taken at Plantungan sometime in 1978 bears an official stamp reading "vetted" or "approved" (see figure 303).

The unique power of images, and the regime's deliberate deployment of that power, was highlighted in an even more dramatic way in the army's official propaganda film about 1965—*Destruction of the Treacherous G30S/PKI* (see figure 317). The film depicts the PKI's supposed treachery and brutality in the most gruesome detail. From the time it was released in 1984 until 1998, the film was mandatory viewing for all schoolchildren, and for many Indonesians it was the sole source of their knowledge about the alleged coup and its aftermath. In fact, according to a public opinion poll conducted in 1999, some 85 percent of the population said this film was their main source of information about the events of 1965. Through this film, the army underscored its false visual record of the events. That record has shaped and dictated social memory ever since.[11]

## Reexamining the Official Record

Taken together, then, these official and officially sanctioned photographs, cartoons, and images have gone a long way toward decimating the Indonesian Left and embedding the army's official version of history in Indonesian social memory. At the same time, we believe the existing visual record has the potential to tell a new story that subverts the army's political intentions and opens the possibility of new historical interpretation. That potential rests above all on the careful contextualization of the images, on consideration of the conditions of their production, and on a willingness to view them with a critical eye.

For example, the photographs of the slain generals' decomposing bodies, which were intended to provide evidence of PKI brutality, take on a very different meaning when we understand that the generals showed no signs of torture and that this fact was well known to the army command at the time.[12] In that light, the photographs appear not so much as evidence of PKI brutality as of an officially sanctioned disinformation and propaganda campaign designed to incite the population to violence against the PKI.

Likewise, on closer examination, the photographic record presented here undercuts the persistent army claim that the violence against the PKI was spontaneous. The officially sanctioned photographs of late-night arrests in Jakarta and anti-PKI roundups in Central Java highlight the close cooperation between the army and local militia forces. In some, too, we can see a senior army officer holding a piece of paper, very likely a list of suspects. Eyewitness accounts of mass detention and killing frequently mention such lists, and historians have argued that their use highlights the significant degree of army planning involved in the detentions. While they were clearly intended to demonstrate the army's authority, then, these photographs inadvertently provide evidence of the systematic nature of its campaign of violence.

Other images unintentionally depict or hint at the arbitrary treatment of and violence committed against PKI members. These include dozens of photographs taken by the official Fact-Finding Commission tasked by Sukarno to investigate the violence in late 1965. Among other things, the commission's images show vast crowds of ordinary people, including very young children, in detention at the palace in Solo and in a field near Klaten, Central Java (see figures 162–65, 170–72). Significantly, these images were not included in the commission's official report.[13] They were discovered in the Indonesian National Library collection—and even there they appeared only on contact sheets (each image about one square inch), apparently never even enlarged. The collection at the National Library also contains a series of photos taken during a roundup of villagers by soldiers and militiamen on the slopes of Mount Merapi in Central Java. That series includes several of an elderly farmer with blood trickling down his face, a reminder of the violence that attended the military operation (see figure 125).

Another set of officially sanctioned photos shows more than twenty alleged PKI members crouching in a long trench, surrounded by armed soldiers and militia members (see figures 122–23). Like the images of late-night arrests in Jakarta and elsewhere, these photographs were apparently taken as part of an army-coordinated photo opportunity for foreign and domestic journalists in late 1965. The intention appears to have been to demonstrate the army's success in rounding up PKI traitors, without resort to violence. Properly contextualized, however, the images hint strongly at the possibility of violence. While we cannot say with any certainty what happened to the men in this photograph, we know from other sources that PKI members were often forced into trenches before being shot or hacked to death. Likewise, a handful of blurry photographs of PKI chairman D. N. Aidit, bound and blindfolded, taken in November 1965, show no obvious signs of violence (see figures 129–30). Yet we know from other sources that shortly after they were taken, Aidit was summarily executed by the army. These images and others like them strongly suggest violence and in that way tend to subvert the political purpose or intentions of their creators.

The potential for images to subvert the original intentions of their creators can also be seen in the way those pictures have been repurposed in recent years by critical artists, journalists, and others. One example of such repurposing was the use of an officially sanctioned photograph on the cover of a special publication on the confessions of executioners (*algojo*) from 1965–67. The image, published by the Indonesian news weekly *Tempo* in 2012, shows a woman cowering in fear while being surrounded by armed soldiers (see figure 322). While its original intent may have been to demonstrate the army's authority, the photo takes on a very different meaning when it is viewed years later alongside an exposé on mass killings. Similarly, when they were displayed in prodemocracy photo exhibitions in 2006, the official photographs of women political detainees at Plantungan Prison were understood not as evidence of the army's legitimacy or authority but as "false portraits" designed to conceal the regime's arbitrary and unjust treatment of political detainees.[14] In short, when they are viewed in new contexts, and with a more critical framing, the official images have the potential to take on radically new meanings.

## Photojournalists and Artists

In addition to the images created and distributed under direct army supervision, a significant part of the surviving visual record is the work of journalists and photographers. Their work warrants special mention because, as noted above, so few of the photographs taken by private Indonesian civilians appear to have survived. These images are also important because they capture dimensions of the history, both before and after October 1, that are largely absent, or have been expunged, from the official record.

One of the most intriguing examples is a photograph taken by the Indonesian photojournalist Moelyono before the onset of violence. The photo of a festive PKI rally in Yogyakarta sometime in 1965 was shown at a 1999 photo exhibition attended by many young prodemocracy students and activists (see figure 43).[15] Karen Strassler provides a fascinating analysis of the photo, highlighting the way in which it captured the attention and evoked feelings of empathy among the young people who viewed it more than thirty years after it was taken:

> Yet one photograph by Moelyono at the exhibition seemed to draw students' attention. It was a picture taken before the eruption of violence in 1965, showing a group of young people at a mass rally for the Indonesian Communist Party on the *alun-alun* (the large square green in front of the *Keraton* [palace]) in Yogyakarta. The orator is outside the frame; one sees only the crowds of seated listeners who appear to be casually enjoying themselves. In the center of the photograph is a young woman who has turned her head slightly so that she happens to face the camera. She is laughing and girlishly hugging her knees to her chest. Her hair is well-combed. The punctum of the image, her lovely smile is an arresting detail that "pricks" the viewer, making one think about her "whole life external to the portrait." One could not look at her face without wondering what fate had befallen her—even, perhaps, precisely because she had had the misfortune to appear in this photograph. Throughout the exhibition, the flow of viewers always seemed to clot around this picture. People murmured to their companions, "They look so young," "They're just teenagers." Several reached up a finger as if to stroke the girl's face.[16]

Also important is a series of photographs taken in the city of Surakarta in late 1965 by the local photojournalist Sutarto. These include photographs of house-to-house searches by RPKAD troops, images of massive flooding at the height of the anti-Communist campaign, and a grisly image of a severed head and captured weapons apparently displayed by local authorities.[17]

A handful of foreign photojournalists present in 1965, as well as others who made short visits in 1966 and 1967, greatly enriched the visual record of the period. They included the Austrian-Canadian freelance photographer Harry Redl and Michel Le Tac, a photographer for *Paris Match*. Also on hand for brief periods were photographers better known for their iconic images of the Vietnam War, such as the Dutch journalist Co Rentmeester, who took time off from his Saigon posting to visit Indonesia in May 1966, and the German war photographer Horst Faas, who followed in June of that year.[18] In the 1970s, the Dutch photographer Peter Schumacher and the Australian journalist David Jenkins took rare and moving photographs in prison camps, and the British Vietnam War photographer Larry Burrows took an iconic photo of Suharto and his family firing weapons at a shooting range (see figure 318).

There were also several less well-known stringers and photojournalists who were present in Indonesia and are worthy of special consideration. They included two young women whose photographs are among the most revealing and striking of the period. One was Beryl Bernay, a New Yorker who had learned about Indonesia while studying with Margaret Mead as an undergraduate at Columbia University. Bernay arrived in Jakarta in July 1965 as a stringer for ABC and quickly made connections with powerful figures, including President

Sukarno, whom she interviewed on camera just days before the alleged coup of October 1. The second was Carol Goldstein (later Abaya), another young American fascinated by the dramatic political changes unfolding around the world in the early 1960s. During her first visit to Indonesia in 1963, she got to know then Colonel Sabur, who was serving in the Presidential Guard. She arrived back in Jakarta in September 1965, and over the next several months she documented what she could of the drama. Their high-level connections enabled both women to be on the scene at a number of crucial moments.

The images created by this small band of foreign journalists and photographers offer an invaluable complement to the official photographic record. For one thing, like Moelyono's photograph described above, they capture the mood of political and social life in Indonesia before the crisis of October 1965. These images—of Sukarno in private conversation and addressing mass rallies, of boisterous but peaceful PKI marches and demonstrations, of anti-imperialist slogans and banners—serve as reminders of a period shortly before the PKI's annihilation when the Indonesian Left was vibrant, widely popular, and completely legitimate. As such, they tend to subvert the official portrait of the PKI as either treacherous and aggressive or abject and defeated. Photographs taken by foreign journalists also highlight elements of the story after October 1 that are largely absent from the official record. Their images of anti-PKI and anti-Sukarno graffiti, of the physical destruction of PKI properties, of the burning of Chinese offices and schools, and of attacks on the private homes of PKI leaders all provide hints of the real violence that official photographs typically elide or obscure.

Of course, the photographs taken by foreign journalists were limited in some important respects. Few of them reflect the situation outside Jakarta. For the most part, they depict the demonstrations of middle-class students and the maneuvers of government and military officials in Jakarta and, on occasion, in the nearby city of Bandung. These limitations were in some sense unavoidable. From early 1965 onward, foreign journalists were operating in a highly constrained political environment, closely monitored by the government and military authorities and subject to sudden expulsion from the country. In January 1966, for example, American journalists from the *New York Times*, United Press International, and the Associated Press were all expelled from Indonesia. Even those who avoided expulsion were severely restricted in their physical movements and the kinds of photographs they could take. In late 1965, a handful of foreign journalists were permitted to travel to the countryside, but even then, they were always under close military supervision, which made it difficult to take photographs not approved by their minders. In fact, as noted earlier, a number of the images of political detainees in Central Java, published in the foreign press, appear to have been staged by the army for the benefit of a traveling entourage of foreign journalists.

Beyond these externally imposed restrictions, the work of foreign journalists and photographers was shaped by a pervasive anti-Communist ethos within the mainstream Western media at the time. In July 1966, for example, the *New York Times* referred to the events in Indonesia as "a gleam of light in Asia," and *Time* magazine described the annihilation of the PKI as "the best news for years in Asia."[19] That Cold War ethos was reinforced by a steady stream of anti-PKI and anti-Sukarno propaganda fed to journalists in press briefings by Indonesian authorities and by the journalists' own embassy officials. As a result, even the most independent among the foreign correspondents appeared to accept, and even embrace, the army's narrative that the PKI was responsible for killing the generals, and that in seeking to decimate the party and sideline Sukarno, the army was acting responsibly and in the country's best interests. Nevertheless, the photographs by local and foreign photojournalists often reveal as much as they conceal. And when they are stripped of their original captions, when the conditions of their production are understood, when they are viewed in historical context and alongside other evidence, they add important details to the visual record and have the potential to upend the official historical narrative.

## Organization, Sources, and Methods

Finally, it may be useful to say a few words about organization, sources, and methods. This book is divided into eight parts, organized thematically but in rough chronological order. Opening with a portrait of Indonesian political life in the early 1960s, it then traces in turn the alleged coup of October 1, the campaign of violence that immediately followed, the Fact-Finding Commission set up by President Sukarno in late 1965, the struggle for political power between the allies of President Sukarno and those of General Suharto in 1966, the toppling of Sukarno and emergence of the army's New Order regime in 1967, and the fate of long-term political detainees. A brief epilogue highlights the continuing reverberations of these events in Indonesia today.

Each of the book's parts is made up of several topics, consisting of selected images alongside brief historical texts. The texts draw on written materials we have gathered over many years, including secondary materials, Indonesian military manuals, reports, and political trial records, as well as declassified US, British, Canadian, and Swedish government documents. They also include interviews we have conducted with a wide range of people involved in the events in question, including photographers, journalists, and military officers as well as former political prisoners and survivors and the family members of those who did not survive. Our research has also benefited from a rich body of Indonesian-language materials about the events of 1965–67—including prison memoirs, documentary films, oral histories, investigative media accounts, blogs, and scholarly works—that have appeared in the past several years.

While the brief texts rest on sources that are familiar to scholars, they do so in a way that is intended to be meaningful to the nonexpert as well as the expert reader. That is, they are designed primarily to provide essential historical and political context for the images.

Some also offer insights into the images themselves, including the identity of the subjects and the photographer or artist, the conditions under which they were produced and distributed, their contemporary significance or impact, and the later interpretations and meanings that have adhered to them. For the most part, however, we have restricted ourselves to providing the kind of historical context that will facilitate, without dictating, the reader's interpretation and understanding of the images.

Likewise, the captions accompanying the images are deliberately minimalist. They provide essential information—identifying the people or events depicted and, where possible, the place, date, and provenance of the image—but refrain from offering further commentary. Our aim in adopting this approach is to encourage readers to examine and interpret the images on their own terms—to look for details of content, form, expression, or composition that the authors may not see. That approach seemed to us most likely to avoid dictating how the images ought to be read, and thereby to generate new and interesting insights and interpretations.

In addition to photographs, which make up the bulk of the collection, the images include political cartoons, street graffiti, a few secret government documents, and selected works of art. The images are drawn from a wide variety of sources, both official and unofficial, Indonesian and foreign. As noted above, a substantial number of the photographs and cartoons were originally produced by, or under the supervision of, Indonesian Army officials. Some were created by official photographers but never made public and were only recently discovered in the Indonesian National Library. Other images were the work of foreign journalists and photographers. Some of their photographs were distributed by media wire services and published in international newspapers. Others appear never to have been printed and, to our knowledge, are being published here for the first time.

The process of gathering and selecting the photos that appear in this book unfolded over several years. In seeking suitable images, we explored the collections of the major photographic and media agencies. We also searched the collections of Indonesia's National Library and a variety of Indonesian and foreign newspapers from the period, including *Angkatan Bersendjata*, *Berita Yudha*, *KAMI*, *Tempo*, *Kompas*, the *New York Times*, the *Washington Post*, the *Los Angeles Times*, *Paris Match*, *The Times* (London), *Dagens Nyheter*, and *Weekly World Report* (*Sekai Shūhō*). Among our most valuable sources were the personal photo archives of journalists and photographers who were in Indonesia at the time. These included Beryl Bernay, Carol Goldstein/Abaya, David Jenkins, Peter Schumacher, and Moelyono, all of whom kindly made their collections available to us. From these various sources we unearthed well over a thousand images, from which we selected the three hundred or so that appear here.

While the subject of the book is the annihilation of the PKI, the emergence of a new authoritarian regime, and the plight of long-term detainees, it needs to be stressed that the images here are not atrocity photos. As noted above, there are no photos of torture victims and only two of human corpses. That is mainly because few such images exist, but it is also a matter of choice. Our purpose in this book is not to shock readers by confronting them with vile images. To do so is to risk replicating the perpetrator's visual language of violence. Nor have the images been selected primarily because of their unusual artistic merit or their dramatic visual qualities. While many of the images are indeed striking, and often chilling, they have been chosen mainly because they highlight a critical historical moment or capture something of the feeling of the times.

Taken together, the images and commentaries tell a story, and evoke a feeling, not easily conveyed by a handful of images or thousands of words. In that sense, this book is modeled on Orhan Pamuk's wonderful memoir, *Istanbul,* a moving elegy to the city that combines historical text with hundreds of black-and-white photographs.[20] The point of these images, Pamuk explains, is not to document a specific event or to identify family members but to evoke the mood of the city of his youth, and give life to a memory.

# I. Sukarno's Indonesia

Figure 2. Sukarno with Chairman Mao Zedong, during a state visit to China in 1956. (Keystone)

## 1. Sukarno and the Dream of Non-alignment

An ardent critic of colonialism since his youth, Sukarno led the Indonesian nationalist movement against Dutch rule before and during the Second World War and became the country's first president in 1945. Following his declaration of Indonesia's independence on August 17, 1945, he presided over a tumultuous four years of social upheaval, armed struggle, and negotiation as the Dutch sought unsuccessfully to reclaim their former colony. After Indonesia finally gained its independence in 1949, Sukarno became a leading figure in the Third World and hosted its first major gathering, the 1955 Asian-African Conference in Bandung. Although Western powers saw non-alignment as a Trojan horse for the advance of Communism, Sukarno's commitment to national sovereignty and self-sufficiency was genuine, and it guided his foreign policy throughout his two decades as president.

For much of the 1950s, Sukarno sought a middle path between the two Cold War blocs, pursuing friendly relations and aid deals with the United States, the Soviet Union, China, and their respective allies. In 1956, he undertook state visits to all three countries and set in motion substantial economic and military assistance agreements that bolstered the Indonesian economy and armed forces. Aid from the Soviet Union was especially beneficial to the navy and air force, while US aid flowed mainly to the army.

But the magic of non-alignment did not last, as Indonesian politics and foreign policy gradually succumbed to the polarizing logic of the Cold War. Concerned by the success of the Indonesian Communist Party (Partai Komunis Indonesia, or PKI) in national and regional elections (in 1955 and 1957, respectively) and convinced that Sukarno posed a threat to Western interests, the United States sought to weaken or remove him from power. In a brazen covert operation

Figure 3. Sukarno inspecting sailors from the cruiser *Kutuzov*, at Sukhumi, on the Black Sea, 1956. Soviet aid particularly benefited the Indonesian Navy and Air Force.

Figure 4. Sukarno with Premier Nikita Khrushchev during Khrushchev's ten-day state visit to Indonesia in February 1960.

Figure 5. Sukarno with US president John F. Kennedy at the White House, September 13, 1961. (William Allen/ Associated Press)

that was later exposed, the CIA provided direct military and financial assistance to regional rebellions in Sumatra and Sulawesi in 1957–58. The rebellions, and the CIA's support for them, formed the backdrop for Sukarno's decision to impose martial law in 1957 and marked an important shift in his attitude toward the West. While maintaining a veneer of friendship toward the United States, and even visiting President Kennedy at the White House in 1961, Sukarno justifiably grew ever more suspicious of US intentions.

Over the same period, Indonesian relations with China and the Soviet Union remained cordial, and the Soviet share of military assistance grew substantially. During a lively ten-day visit to Indonesia by Premier Nikita Khrushchev in February 1960, for example, Sukarno gladly accepted $250 million in Soviet economic and military credits. By 1961, when Sukarno paid another state visit to Moscow, Soviet military aid to Indonesia totaled roughly $1 billion, a figure vastly greater than the $60 million provided by the United States by that date. The discrepancy was so substantial that US officials worried that Soviet aid "might well lead to Indonesia's early domination by the [Communist] Bloc."[1]

## 2. "Go to Hell with Your Aid!"

Sukarno's relations with the West deteriorated dramatically in the early 1960s. Increasingly frustrated by the Netherlands' insistence that West Irian (the western half of the island of Papua) should be granted independence, in 1962 he launched a military and political campaign for its incorporation by Indonesia. The following year, he sought to prevent British plans to create the new state of Malaysia from its former colonial possessions in the region, through a policy he called Confrontation (Konfrontasi). While the United States claimed to be a neutral party in that dispute, Sukarno was convinced that it was supporting the British position. And when, in March 1964, Secretary of State Dean Rusk threatened that US aid might

Figure 6. Sukarno with aide Lieutenant Colonel Sabur at the United Nations, September 30, 1960. (Associated Press)

be stopped if Indonesia did not end its campaign, Sukarno famously retorted that the United States should "go to hell with your aid!"[2]

Sukarno was also disturbed by the growing frequency of US intervention in the affairs of smaller states around the world. The failed attempt to overthrow Fidel Castro by means of an invasion by paramilitary forces at the Bay of Pigs in 1961, US involvement in the arrest and subsequent murder of Congo's prime minister Patrice Lumumba in 1960–61, and the landing of twenty thousand US marines in the Dominican Republic in April 1965 were all examples, in Sukarno's eyes, of a dangerous American neocolonialism. But it was US intervention in Vietnam that became the central focus of Sukarno's vitriol. In 1964, he infuriated the United States by recognizing the government of North Vietnam and expressing Indonesia's strong support thereafter for its struggle for self-determination.

In 1965, Sukarno's rhetorical hostility to the United States and its allies reached new heights. In January, he abruptly announced that he was withdrawing Indonesia from the United Nations (UN) after it voted to admit Malaysia as a member. In a meeting with the US presidential envoy Ambassador Ellsworth Bunker in April 1965, he described US actions in Malaysia and elsewhere in the Afro-Asian world as "burning, irritating obstacles" to the restoration of good relations between the two countries.[3] In May, he addressed huge rallies celebrating May Day and the PKI's forty-fifth anniversary, where he denounced imperialists of all stripes. And at the credentials ceremony for the new US ambassador, Marshall Green,

Figure 7. Cartoon that originally bore the caption "Indonesia's interior decorator," showing Sukarno painting the room "Chinese Red." (*Philadelphia Inquirer*)

in July, he harangued the United States over its neocolonial policies in Malaysia and Vietnam. His speech was followed by weeks of angry demonstrations against US diplomatic installations, with crowds calling for Green to be thrown out of the country. Then, in his August 17 Independence Day speech, the president launched a blistering attack on the United States and other neocolonial powers.

As relations with the West soured, Indonesia drew ever closer to China. At a meeting with Indonesian foreign minister Subandrio in January 1965, Chinese premier Chou Enlai expressed support for the idea of a Fifth Force of armed workers and peasants. China also applauded Indonesia's decision to withdraw from the UN. Later, Chou and other officials offered to supply Indonesia with one hundred thousand light arms and promised to share its expertise to help Indonesia develop a nuclear weapon. Finally, beginning in late 1964, Chinese doctors sent by Beijing provided medical care to Sukarno, who had come to mistrust the Western doctors he had previously consulted. In short, by 1965, China was probably Indonesia's closest and most reliable ally, while Indonesian hostility toward the United States and its allies had reached unprecedented levels.

## 3. The Indonesian Communist Party and Chairman Aidit

Founded in 1920, the PKI was one stream within a diverse early nationalist movement. Following a poorly planned PKI uprising in 1926, however, the Netherlands Indies government banned the party and imprisoned thousands of its members. Some leaders fled overseas, where they remained until the Second World War. The PKI enjoyed a revival under the Japanese occupation (1942–45) and grew quickly during the revolutionary struggle for independence (1945–49). As Dutch military operations against the Republic intensified, the young national army, devoutly Muslim forces, Communists, and civilians retreated into an increasingly narrow area in Central Java, where ideological differences and competition for resources became intense. In September 1948, the PKI leaders staged an uprising in Madiun, East Java, intended to challenge the policy of negotiation adopted by President Sukarno and steer the revolution to the left. Sukarno responded by ordering the national army to crush the uprising, at significant cost in lives.

Following the achievement of independence in 1949, a new generation of young Javanese leaders revived the PKI by adopting a parliamentary strategy. A key figure in the party's revival was its chairman, Dipa Nusantara Aidit. Although excluded from the shifting governments of the early 1950s, the party grew rapidly and earned the fourth-highest vote tally in the 1955 elections. In the regional elections held in Java in 1957–58, the PKI polled first. The party's swift rise was a tribute to its dynamic leaders, effective organizing, and popular social programs. It also benefited from its good relationship with Sukarno, whose anti-imperialist and nationalist positions the PKI strongly supported.

Figure 8. Indonesian Communist Party chairman Aidit campaigning in 1955. (Howard Sochurek/Getty)

In 1959, frustrated by squabbling among political parties and angered by regional rebellions, Sukarno called for an end to "liberal democracy" and established a new system that he called "Guided Democracy." This change strengthened the president's position as the absolute arbiter of national politics. The absence of elections, however, had

Figure 9. Hammer-and-sickle symbol painted on a palace wall in Central Java. (Keystone)

Figure 10. Temporary PKI statue of a schoolteacher in Javanese dress erected as part of the campaign for the 1958 city council election in Jakarta. (Sam Waagemaar/Camera)

the unforeseen consequence of fueling hyperpoliticization as the parties competed around the clock to attract members to their mass organizations. The PKI was particularly adept at mass mobilization, and, by 1965, it claimed to have 3.5 million members and another 20 million in its affiliated unions, peasants' front, and associations representing youth, women, and artists.

The growth of the party's women's affiliate is particularly revealing. Founded as the Aware Women's Movement (Gerakan Wanita Sedar) in 1950 with 500 members, the organization had expanded to 80,000 members by 1954, when the name was changed to the Indonesian Women's Movement (Gerakan Wanita Indonesia, or Gerwani), signaling a shift to a mass-based organization. By 1957 it claimed more than 660,000 members. Despite internal factional divides, over the next few years Gerwani increasingly aligned its policies with those of the PKI. At the 1961 Gerwani congress, several PKI party members were elected to top positions: Umi Sardjono (a candidate for membership in the PKI Central Committee) as chairwoman and Suharti Suwarto (a PKI Central Committee member) and Sulami as vice chairwomen. Three years later, Gerwani leaders declared that the organization intended to affiliate itself formally with the PKI, though this plan was never carried out. Nevertheless, in May 1965, in an address about the party's membership, PKI chairman Aidit proudly announced that Gerwani had 3,000,000 members.

## 4. The Fight over West Irian

In 1949, in order to secure a final agreement with the Netherlands on independence, Indonesian leaders acceded to Dutch demands that the status of West Irian would be resolved at a later date. Indonesia had insisted that, as part of the Netherlands East Indies, the territory should be included in newly independent Indonesia. The Netherlands, on the other hand, was intent on retaining this vast area rich in natural resources and, in 1952, renamed it Netherlands New Guinea. After five years of unsuccessful bilateral efforts, in 1955, Indonesia secured a resolution in support of its position at the first Asian-African Conference in Bandung before bringing its case before the United Nations. But in multiple votes in the General Assembly, Indonesia failed to secure a two-thirds majority.

West Irian was not simply a point of national pride; for Sukarno, it was also an example of the global struggle to oppose neocolonialism and imperialism, which became a central tenet of his foreign policy. But in 1961, the Netherlands established an elected parliament in West Irian, a move that implied a degree of self-rule and hence a possible stepping stone toward eventual independence. For Sukarno, this was the last straw.

Sukarno responded in December 1961 by announcing the formation of a People's Triple Command (Tri Komando Rakyat, or Trikora) to mobilize mass support for the campaign to "liberate" West Irian. On the military side, Sukarno established a High Command for the Liberation of West Irian, under which a new theater command, called Mandala, was tasked with spearheading operations. Brigadier General Suharto, who later led the campaign to crush the PKI, was appointed commander. Mandala's forward headquarters were in South Sulawesi, where troops drilled and put

Figure 11. Army troops arrive in Hollandia (now Jayapura), West Irian, as part of the formal transfer of the territory to Indonesia, April 1963.

Figure 12. Sukarno inspecting the 454th Airborne Battalion after it returned from the campaign to retake West Irian. Behind Sukarno, from left: Major Untung, commander of the 454th Airborne Battalion; Brigadier General Sabur, commander of the Tjakrabirawa Regiment; and Brigadier General Suharto, commander of the Trikora Operation. (Indonesian Press Photo Service)

on displays for the media. One of the battalions involved in the operation, the 454th Airborne Battalion from Central Java, was commanded by Major Untung Syamsuri, who was decorated for his service and, in 1965, was appointed to the Tjakrabirawa Regiment. Less than a year later, now Lieutenant Colonel Untung emerged as a key figure in the September 30th Movement (Gerakan 30 September, or G30S)

Concerned that the issue of West Irian would drive Sukarno even closer to the Soviet Union and China, President Kennedy finally brought pressure on the Netherlands, which consented to relinquish the territory. The final agreement, signed in New York in 1962, called for the transfer of West Irian to the Republic of Indonesia and, after a seven-year period, a referendum to determine the will of the population.

## 5. "Confrontation" and the "Crush Malaysia" Campaign

The Federation of Malaya gained independence in 1957, but the long-term status of Singapore and three territories in northern Borneo (Sarawak, Sabah, and Brunei) had yet to be resolved. In 1961, as part of its "grand design," the British government and Malayan prime minister Tunku Abdul Rahman agreed on a plan whereby Singapore, Sarawak, and Sabah would join in a federated state of Malaysia (while Brunei would remain a British protectorate). August 31, 1963, was set as the date for the merger.

Opposition to the plan emerged from the leftist Sarawak United People's Party, which was founded in 1959 to consolidate opposition to the failure of Britain to adequately address local aspirations for self-governance. Sukarno soon lent his voice in opposition to the planned merger as well. Sukarno criticized the British plan on the grounds that it failed to allow the people of Sarawak and Sabah an opportunity to express their own desires and have a say in their future. The creation of Malaysia, Sukarno argued, was a neo-imperial plot by which London intended to maintain its interests in Southeast Asia and perhaps also contain a rising Indonesia.

Figure 13. Women march in support of Sukarno's campaign against Malaysia, April 1964. At the time, Sukarno declared, "If you send ten soldiers into Indonesia, I'll send one hundred. If you send one thousand, I'll send ten thousand." (United Press International)

Figure 14. A student dressed as the Malaysian prime minister holds a sign showing that he is a "tool of neo-imperialism," with Uncle Sam bankrolling him from behind. (National Library of Indonesia)

Figure 15. Members of the Indonesian Nationalist Party jab bamboo spears into an effigy of Malaysian prime minister Tunku Abdul Rahman. (United Press International)

Figure 16. Indonesian "volunteers" with bamboo spears, Jakarta, November 1964. (United Press International)

Figure 17. Former sex workers put through basic military drills in Jakarta as part of the national mobilization to support the Confrontation campaign against Malaysia, December 1964. (TopFoto)

Figure 18. Malaysian political cartoon of Sukarno declaring that Malaysia will be crushed before the start of 1965. (Arsib Negara)

Sukarno called for Indonesia to "confront" the British, leading to a series of political and military moves known as Confrontation. In adopting this strategy, Sukarno was emboldened by Indonesia's recent success in West Irian. But the policy was also intended to appeal to the two strongest domestic forces below the president. On the one hand, Confrontation received ready support from the PKI, which eagerly mobilized its supporters to participate in mass rallies and, in early 1965, called for mobilizing peasants and workers into a "Fifth Force." On the other hand, Sukarno's opposition to the formation of Malaysia promised a central role for the armed forces, including new hardware and increased funding. Yet while the air force was supportive, the army viewed Confrontation with suspicion. Senior army officers were concerned that it would cause a further deterioration in relations with the United States, which they looked to for military supplies and training, and would draw troops away from Java, where the PKI was strongest. As a result, the campaign to "Crush Malaysia" contributed to an atmosphere in which politics became increasingly polarized.

Confrontation involved military and civilian mobilization. On the military side, the Mandala Command, which had been established in the context of the West Irian campaign, was extended to cover Sumatra and Kalimantan (the Indonesian part of Borneo). Combat units were sent to border areas, and the civilian auxiliaries were mobilized. The army also brought several thousand "volunteers" (mainly members of the Sarawak Communist Party) to West Java for basic military training. By 1964, special forces units, often operating together with "volunteers," engaged in cross-border raids into Sarawak and carried out a few small-scale landings on peninsular Malaya, the most dramatic of which resulted in the use of explosives at the iconic McDonald House office building in Singapore. British troops, including combat troops and Gurkhas, provided an effective deterrent, and actual combat was limited.

Figure 19. Members of the Indonesian Peasants' Front (BTI) marching in Java, n.d. (Nugraha Bookstore/ Facebook)

## 6. Land Seizures through "Unilateral Actions"

While much of the political action in the early 1960s played out on the streets of Indonesia's cities and towns, some of the most bitter conflicts took place in the countryside, where more than 90 percent of the population lived. There, disputes over land reform became lightning rods for clashes between the followers of different political parties and laid the foundation for violence after October 1, 1965. On one side of the issue was the PKI and its peasant organization, the Indonesian Peasants' Front (Barisan Tani Indonesia, or BTI). On the other side were the Indonesian Nationalist Party (Partai Nasional Indonesia, or PNI) and the Council of Islamic Scholars (Nahdlatul Ulama, or NU) and their peasant organizations.

With support from the major political parties, in 1960, Sukarno promulgated a Basic Agrarian Law to replace colonial-era regulations. Among other things, the new law stipulated that land holdings above a certain size should be redistributed to peasants with little or no land. A separate law established more favorable terms of tenancy for tenant farmers and sharecroppers. These laws were popular with poor farmers but faced stiff resistance from more prosperous landowners and their political backers. As a result, by mid-1963 there had been little progress in implementing the proposed reforms.

Against that backdrop, in late 1963, the PKI began to push for the full implementation of the laws. Embracing the party's rural campaign against the "seven village devils," local PKI and BTI leaders adopted ever more militant tactics. The most contentious of these were the so-called "unilateral actions" (*aksi sepihak*), in which BTI members seized land they believed they were entitled to by law. Unsurprisingly, these actions were furiously resisted by landowners and their followers and sometimes resulted in violence. On both sides, organizers staged rallies and marches in enemy territory, carrying banners and flags, shouting slogans, and singing songs. One marching song sung by PKI/BTI members went like this:

> We swear an oath of equality
> Poverty will surely end
> Farmers and workers will all have work
> A new world will surely come
> Come, come take action now
> Freedom is already ours
> Our flag is red
> And red is the color of the blood of the people
> Red is the color of the blood of the people[4]

While the BTI position was the more radical, the political conflict over land was fueled by both sides. As a local leader of the PNI farmers' organization in Bali later recalled, "One time the BTI leader said to me, 'Why don't we sit down and negotiate?' I said, 'Forget it! Denpasar [the provincial capital] is the place for negotiations. Here we fight to see who wins!'"[5] By late 1964 the BTI was moving more aggressively than even the PKI's national leaders wished, and in December the party joined Sukarno and the PNI in disavowing the unilateral actions campaign altogether. But the land seizures and the clashes continued, and in some areas the BTI succeeded in forcing land transfers. It was in part in retaliation for that success that conservative parties struck back at the PKI and BTI with such violence after October 1965.

## 7. Opposition to Western Imperialism

Following independence in 1949, Indonesia developed a "free and active" foreign policy, independent of the global powers and committed to actively opposing all forms of colonialism and imperialism. In a speech to the UN General Assembly in September 1960, he threw down the gauntlet to the West, calling for the people of Asia and Africa "to build the world anew." While his challenges to the global powers raised alarm, Sukarno could also charm. On a state visit to the United States in 1961, he beamed for photographs with President Kennedy. His iconoclastic thinking challenged staid bipolar norms. In his autobiography, he explained, "To me, both the Declaration of Independence and the Communist Manifesto contain undying truths, but the West doesn't permit a middle road. They manipulate you so you're no longer able to stay independent. To President Roosevelt's four freedoms, I had a fifth: The freedom to be free! The West keeps threatening, 'Do you want to be dominated by the Communists?' We answer, 'No, . . . but neither do we want to be dominated by you!'"[6]

Yet US support for regional rebellions in 1957–58, CIA assassination attempts, and foot dragging over the return of West Irian created mistrust. Concerned that the United States was still intent on having him killed, Sukarno established

Figure 20. Demonstration opposing US ambassador Howard Jones, Jakarta, August 19, 1964. (Bettman-Corbis Collection/Getty)

Figure 21. Demonstrator at the US embassy with sign reading, "Kick Out Jones." (Thomas Hoepker/Magnum)

Figure 22. Protesters demand the expulsion of foreign military bases from Southeast Asia, Jakarta, early 1965. (John Bulmer and Harry Redl/*Illustrated London News*)

a new presidential guard, the Tjakrabirawa Regiment, in 1962. Over the next three years, criticism of the United States increasingly became a focal point of mass demonstrations and rallies, many of them organized by the PKI. Participants called, among other things, for the expulsion of US ambassador Howard Jones and his successor, Marshall Green; the removal of US military bases in the region; and an end to US intervention in Vietnam. Anger was also directed against US allies, most notably Great Britain, whose embassy was ransacked by angry crowds in September 1963, but also India due to the 1965 conflict with Pakistan over Kashmir.

In January 1965, angered by the admission of Malaysia to the United Nations, Sukarno announced that he was pulling Indonesia out of the world body. Two months later, he placed the operation of foreign oil companies in Indonesia under government supervision. He then pressed for the establishment of a Conference of Newly Emerging Forces as a rival to the United Nations. But Sukarno's hopes for Asian-African unity against imperialism were dashed when

Figure 23. On July 26, 1965, the new US ambassador, Marshall Green, presented his credentials to President Sukarno, and that afternoon Communist youths marched to the ambassador's residence to denounce his appointment. (Associated Press)

Figure 24. US ambassador Marshall Green in Jakarta, ca. August 1965. (Beryl Bernay)

the Algiers Conference, scheduled for June 1965, was canceled.

July and August saw, in quick succession, an angry demonstration outside Ambassador Green's official residence and attacks on the US consulates in Medan and Surabaya. Against this backdrop, US officials became convinced that Indonesia was on a headlong slide to the left. In July, CIA director William Raborn advised the president that "Indonesia is well embarked on a course that will make it a communist nation in the reasonably near future, unless the trend is reversed."[7] A month later, Under Secretary of State George Ball and National Security Adviser McGeorge Bundy agreed that there should be a meeting "to alert the President to the seriousness of the situation in which the Communists may take over Indonesia," a development that Ball said "would be the biggest thing since the fall of China."[8]

Indonesian Independence Day celebrations on August 17, 1965, provided another opportunity for US embassy officials to fret about Sukarno's hostility. An embassy telegram reported, "The posters focused unmistakably on the principal target of Indonesian propaganda—the United States. American capital received chief attention in this display, accompanied by big letters spelling out in English 'To hell with American aid!' The British were linked with us in one particularly prominent banner bearing the NEFO [Newly Emerging Forces] device: 'Chase the British and the Americans out of Southeast Asia!'"[9]

## 8. Western Concern and Scheming

For at least a decade before October 1965, the United States and other Western powers worked assiduously to undermine Sukarno and the PKI. Their actions, overt and covert, accentuated political conflicts inside Indonesia and helped to create the conditions for the army's seizure of power and the mass violence that followed.

Figure 25. A demonstration at the British embassy in Jakarta resulted in significant damage, September 1963. (Associated Press)

Alarmed by the PKI's rapid rise and convinced that Sukarno was easing its path to power, the United States set out to weaken or destroy both. In 1957–58, the CIA provided direct financial assistance and flew bombing missions in support of anti-Sukarno rebellions in Sumatra and Sulawesi. The plan backfired when a CIA pilot, Allan Pope, was shot down and taken prisoner by Indonesian forces. Following the Pope fiasco, the United States adopted a new strategy. Viewing the Indonesian Army as the most reliable anti-Communist force and the institution most likely to support Western interests, the United States stepped up military training and assistance.

Western concern over Indonesia escalated dramatically after 1963, when Sukarno began his campaign of Confrontation with Malaysia. For a time, the British were a central focus of Sukarno's public denunciations, which led in turn to mass demonstrations and to the attack on the British embassy in September 1963. Yet while the United Kingdom was keen to stop Sukarno and the PKI, it was less eager than the Americans to seek an alliance with the army, whose troops it was fighting in Borneo. Eventually, however, British officials saw the

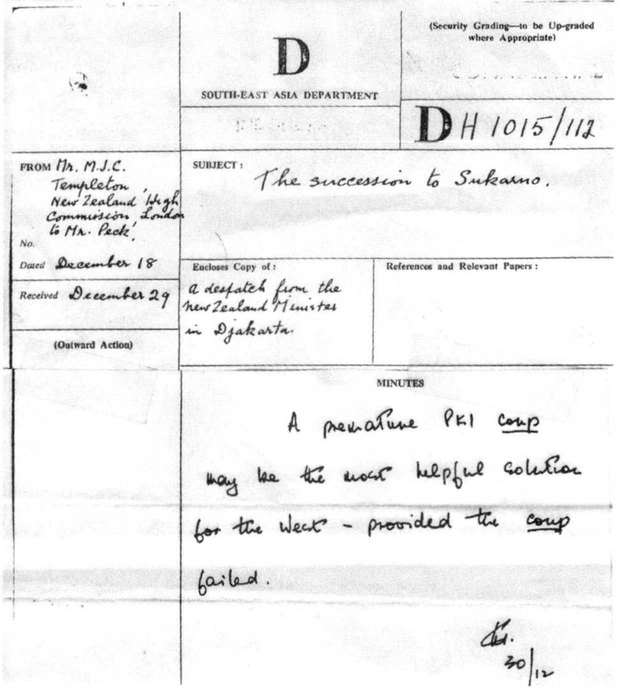

D

SOUTH-EAST ASIA DEPARTMENT

(Security Grading—to be Up-graded where Appropriate)

DH 1015/112

FROM Mr. M.J.C. Templeton, New Zealand High Commission, London to Mr. Peck.

No.

Dated December 18

Received December 29

(Outward Action)

SUBJECT: The succession to Sukarno.

Encloses Copy of: a despatch from the New Zealand Minister in Djakarta.

References and Relevant Papers:

MINUTES

A premature PKI coup may be the most helpful solution for the West – provided the coup failed.

30/12

Figure 26. British Foreign Office document suggesting “a premature PKI coup” as a possible solution to the political situation in Indonesia, December 1964. (UK National Archive)

possibility of working together with the army to eliminate Sukarno and the PKI—and end Confrontation.

By late 1964, British and US officials had become convinced that Indonesia was going to “fall” to Communism in the near future. Declassified US government documents from this time discuss a range of covert actions designed to prevent that outcome, including propaganda, psychological warfare, the secret disbursement of cash to reliably anti-Communist figures, and military action. British documents reveal that the United Kingdom and its Commonwealth allies contemplated provoking a premature left-wing coup that would provide an ideal pretext for a military intervention—in other words, more or less exactly what happened in October 1965. As a British Foreign Office document from December 1964 noted, “A premature PKI coup may be the most helpful solution for the West—provided the coup failed.”[10]

This was the context in which the infamous “Gilchrist Letter” appeared in early 1965. The letter referred ominously to a plan that was to be carried out in cooperation with “our local army friends.”[11] Already distrustful of the British, Sukarno and his supporters saw the letter as clear evidence of a plot to overthrow him—a claim vehemently denied by Britain and its allies. At about the same time, Sukarno raised the alarm about the existence of a shadowy “Council of Generals,” which he claimed was a group of CIA-backed generals aiming to stage a coup. While there is some doubt about the authenticity of the Gilchrist Letter, it is beyond dispute that US and British officials, and high-ranking Indonesian Army officers, were scheming to get rid of Sukarno and the PKI at this time.

## 9. Economic Decline and Raging Inflation

The rising political tensions of the early 1960s were aggravated by a rapidly deteriorating economic situation. The Indonesian economy experienced modest growth between 1950 and 1957, but between 1958 and 1965 annual growth fell to 1.7 percent, lagging behind population growth. The nationalization of Dutch-owned enterprises in December 1957 resulted in a sharp decline in exports. Two years later, Sukarno’s government adopted an eight-year national development plan that simultaneously favored greater self-reliance and promised more rapid growth. Matters were exacerbated by the huge military buildup beginning in 1962 in the context of the struggle to regain West Irian and continued the following year with the declaration of Confrontation. Meanwhile, Indonesia experienced low rainfall in 1961, a severe drought and massive volcanic eruption in 1963 (which resulted in a 10 percent decrease in the rice crop), and a strong El Niño event in 1965.

The Indonesian government responded to the economic decline of the early 1960s by printing money. The money supply doubled in 1962 and 1963 and increased by a further 156 percent in 1964 and by 280 percent in 1965. The result was hyperinflation, which led the price of rice and other essential commodities to rise quickly while wages and salaries remained stagnant. The rapid decline in the value of the rupiah also put imported goods beyond the reach of all but a small handful of wealthy or well-connected people. Apart from making life difficult for wage earners, these

Figure 27. As part of the campaign against poverty, hunger, and illiteracy, a government official known as "Singing Soeprapto" led peasants through fields in Java, 1962. (United Press International)

Figure 28. Women selling rice in a market in Jakarta, 1965.

Figure 29. A pedicab driver and a beggar in front of a banner showing Indonesia breaking the chains of imperialism, held by clownish capitalists. (John Bulmer and Harry Redl/*Illustrated London News*)

Figure 30. Scene on the outskirts of Jakarta, likely August 1965. (Beryl Bernay)

conditions fueled corruption among government and military officials and politicians and contributed to a growing sense of unease. Inflation was also disastrous for the private banking sector, with the last foreign bank closing in 1964. Black marketeering proliferated.

Against this backdrop, PKI campaigns against corruption, and in favor of price controls, collective bargaining rights, and wage increases, were popular with large sectors of the population, notably teachers, civil servants, wage earners, and even some soldiers. The PKI's popularity also grew in rural areas during these years, as the party shifted its attention to peasants. This change of focus came about in part because army control over nationalized Dutch industries and army-sponsored unions stymied advances among leftist industrial labor. It also stemmed from the increasingly dire circumstances in rural Java that drove many to join the BTI.

Politics increasingly dictated economic policy. In an address to the parliament in April 1965, Sukarno called for Indonesia to "stand on its own feet" (berdiri atas kaki sendiri), the abbreviation of which—"Berdikari"—became a new mantra. In August, the parliament passed a resolution pulling the country out of the World Bank and the International Monetary Fund. The economic situation was particularly dire in Central and East Java and fueled growing political tensions. Ruth McVey, who traveled through Java in mid-1965, wrote, "By early 1965, tensions were extremely high; travelling in rural Java at the time one could almost feel them physically in villages where the growing struggle for resources had condensed into class and religious hatred. Outbreaks of violence became frequent, and increasingly involved political groups and military units. There was an apocalyptic air: gurus taught of cataclysmic change, boy preachers appeared, and the vocabulary of politics, official and unofficial, was more and more given to words of violence."[12]

## 10. The Army in Politics

The Indonesian Armed Forces were born out of the Japanese occupation (1942–45) and the subsequent revolutionary struggle for independence (1945–49). These experiences imprinted critical legacies as well as contradictions, especially on the army. Organizationally, the mixture of units and officers from the Dutch colonial army, various Japanese-raised forces, and grassroots mobilization, together with the experience of the revolution, produced antihierarchical impulses that undermined the establishment of centralized command. Ideologically, internal uprisings left army leaders hostile to both the Communists, who had staged an uprising against national leaders at Madiun in 1948, and the Islamic military units and parties that rose in rebellion in 1949, demanding the new republic be based on Islam.

When Indonesia achieved independence in 1949, many officers as well as troops believed that the army had spearheaded the revolution, while the nation's civilian leaders had quarreled, engaged in fruitless negotiation, and shamefully allowed themselves to be captured. As a result, army leaders were suspicious of the idea of civilian supremacy over the military and were convinced they had a right, indeed an obligation, to play a role in national politics. That view deepened in the early 1950s as a succession of short-lived civilian governments appeared incapable of fulfilling the promise of independence.

The army was organizationally and politically the dominant service branch, with an estimated three hundred

Figure 31. General Achmad Yani, army chief of staff, 1964. (John Bulmer/Camera)

thousand troops and a territorial structure that mirrored the civilian administration. But central authority remained weak, and dissident regional military commanders played a central role in the outbreak of rebellions in Sumatra and Sulawesi in 1957–58. Paradoxically, these rebellions were an enormous boon for the army. The declaration of martial law in March 1957 allowed the army high command in Jakarta to establish far greater central control and set in motion a complete revamp of its territorial structure. When Sukarno nationalized Dutch economic assets in late 1957, many were turned over to the army, giving it new resources, a foothold from which to establish its own labor unions, and a strong stake in the new economic arrangements. And in 1959, army leaders welcomed the start of Guided Democracy, in the expectation that it would halt the PKI's rapid electoral advances.

The result of all of these dramatic changes was that Sukarno emerged as

Figure 32. Troops of the Army Paracommando Regiment (RPKAD) participate in a parade in Jakarta on January 5, 1965, as part of Sukarno's campaign opposing foreign military bases in Southeast Asia.

the fulcrum in an uneasy but relatively stable balance of power between the army, on the right, and the PKI, on the left. Within the armed forces, service branch rivalries intensified in the early 1960s. The army had developed deep ties to the United States, where many officers were sent for training. They included General Yani, who studied at Fort Leavenworth in 1955, became army chief of staff in 1963, and was among the six generals killed on October 1, 1965. Meanwhile, the air force and navy were the beneficiaries of Soviet hardware and training, and so they were inclined to support Sukarno's leftward drift and lacked outward hostility toward the PKI.

The senior officer corps within the army was generally pro-Western, but the army itself was far from homogenous. In fact, it was a microcosm of the nation. There were divisions between officers who identified with Jakarta and those whose careers had been made in the regions. Among the enlisted men there was a wide variety of political affiliation, including strong sympathies for the PKI and other leftist parties.

## 11. Militarization of "Volunteers"

Sukarno's policy of Confrontation to oppose the formation of Malaysia was accompanied by the recruitment of tens of thousands of "volunteers," who were given uniforms, put through basic military drills, and at times taught to handle weapons. In addition to domestic mobilization, more than a thousand volunteers from Sarawak, a part of Malaysia on the island of Borneo, were brought to West Java and prepared to infiltrate back into Malaysian territory. The recruitment

Figure 33. Female volunteers with guns marching in Jakarta, January 1965. Members of the PKI-affiliated Indonesian Women's Movement (Gerwani) were among those who volunteered to serve.

Figure 34. Members of the League of Upholders of Indonesian Freedom (IPKI) marching, probably in North Sumatra, mid-1965. (United Press International)

Figure 35. Members of the NU women's organization Muslimat training in Jakarta, July 1965. (*Sejarah Muslimat Nahdlatul Ulama*)

of paramilitary forces intensified in early 1965, following Sukarno's call for Indonesia to pull out of the United Nations.

For the PKI, Sukarno's foreign policy opened new opportunities on the domestic front. In January 1965, PKI leaders called for workers and peasants to be trained and armed. The army pushed back against the idea, fearing that it would strengthen the Communists and perhaps even pave the way for a PKI seizure of power. Nevertheless,

Figure 36. Police volunteers marching in Jakarta, August 1965. (Beryl Bernay)

Figure 37. Uniformed women on parade for Independence Day in Jakarta, August 17, 1965. (Rory Dell/ Camera)

General Yani repeatedly stated that the policy was up to Sukarno, as supreme commander of the armed forces. In some regions, military commanders did take up the idea. In North Sumatra, for example, Major General Mokoginta began training workers and peasants associated with the League of Upholders of Indonesian Freedom (Ikatan Pendukung Kemerdekaan Indonesia, or IPKI) but not those from leftist organizations.

Women figured prominently in this new militarization. Their recruitment was in part intended to demonstrate that the entire Indonesian population was behind Sukarno's policy of Confrontation, and in part because women marching in uniform added to the numbers and spectacle at official ceremonies and military parades.

In addition to volunteers recruited and trained as auxiliaries to the armed forces, militarization also extended to the political parties. NU's paramilitary wings, Ansor and the Ansor Multipurpose Front (Barisan Ansor Serbaguna, or Banser), conducted physical training and practiced marching, as did the PNI's Pemuda Marhaenis, the PKI's Pemuda Rakyat, and the IPKI's Pemuda Pancasila.

In April 1965, while hosting a visit by Chinese premier Chou En Lai, North Korean premier Kim Il Sung, and Vietnamese prime minister Pham Van Dong, Sukarno announced that he was prepared to lend men and arms to peoples struggling for independence. Three days later, five thousand volunteers, accompanied by a band, marched through Jakarta to the North Vietnamese embassy and presented themselves to the ambassador, declaring that they were willing to help expel the American aggressors.

## 12. Revolution and the Atom Bomb

With the declaration of Guided Democracy in 1959, Sukarno introduced a new slogan: the Three Principles of the Revolution (Tiga Kerangka Revolusi). They were a unitary and democratic republic, a just and prosperous society, and international friendship and an end to colonialism and imperialism. Sukarno repeated this slogan over the years to come, becoming increasingly adamant that workers and peasants were key to achieving these goals. In early 1965, he declared, "We, indeed, do not yet have an atomic bomb but who dares say that we are under-developed in political consciousness, concepts, ideas and ideology."[13]

The pursuit of unity and justice at home was intimately related to Sukarno's vision of Indonesia's position in the international realm. In January 1965, Sukarno laid the cornerstone for a nuclear reactor in West Java, and over the next few months, he and members of his government made increasingly frequent statements about Indonesia's nuclear ambitions. "If necessary," Sukarno declared, "we seize power with arms. If necessary, we seize power with airplanes, and if necessary, as I said last night, we will seize power with an atomic bomb."[14] While there was little scientific substance to Indonesia's nuclear program, the United States and other Western governments were deeply concerned that Sukarno might

Figure 38. Uniformed volunteers oppose the formation of Malaysia during a ceremony at which President Sukarno laid the cornerstone for a nuclear reactor in Serpong, West Java, January 21, 1965. The banner declares opposition to the neocolonial formation of Malaysia in accordance with the Three Principles of the Revolution. (United Press International)

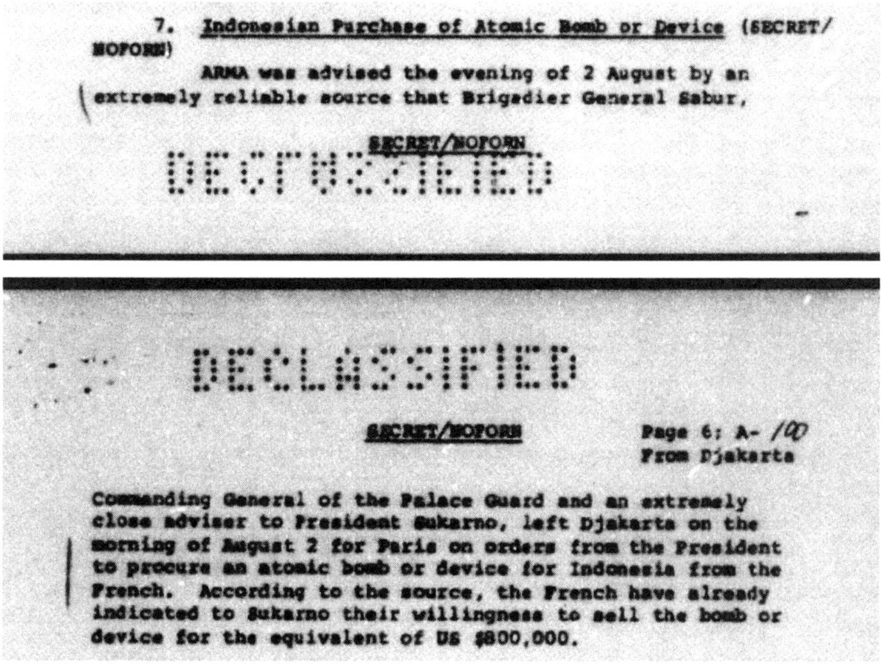

7. Indonesian Purchase of Atomic Bomb or Device (SECRET/NOFORN)

ARMA was advised the evening of 2 August by an extremely reliable source that Brigadier General Sabur,

SECRET/NOFORN

DECLASSIFIED

DECLASSIFIED

SECRET/NOFORN

Page 6; A- 100
From Djakarta

Commanding General of the Palace Guard and an extremely close adviser to President Sukarno, left Djakarta on the morning of August 2 for Paris on orders from the President to procure an atomic bomb or device for Indonesia from the French. According to the source, the French have already indicated to Sukarno their willingness to sell the bomb or device for the equivalent of US $800,000.

Figure 39. Telegram from the US embassy in Jakarta to the State Department, August 9, 1965, expressing concern about Indonesia's intention to purchase an atomic bomb from France. (National Archives and Records Administration)

obtain a nuclear device from another state. In August 1965, the US embassy reported anxiously that a close confidant of the president—the commander of the Presidential Guard, Brigadier General Sabur—had gone to Paris to purchase a nuclear device.

Yet, for Sukarno, the lure of technology was always subordinate to the revolutionary potential of the masses, first unleashed in the struggle for independence. In his 1965 Independence Day address, he roared, "We are going to defend this freedom to the death, to the death, and if necessary—as I have said before—we are going to defend it with atom bombs! But do not forget that the strength of the People are also atom bombs, in fact even more powerful than real atom bombs!"[15]

## 13. Political Spectacle and Mass Mobilization

Sukarno's Guided Democracy had the unintended consequence of pushing party politics into overdrive, with the parties and their affiliated mass organizations competing to recruit members and mobilize mass actions. That trend accelerated after 1963 as Sukarno embarked on Confrontation with Malaysia and as both his foreign and domestic policies began to hew increasingly to the left. The PKI and its affiliates were the chief beneficiaries of this shift, and they were especially adept at mass mobilization, but other parties and institutions, including the army, also joined the fray. By 1965, mass mobilization in the form of demonstrations, parades, and mass rallies had reached fever pitch, with parties and organizations of every political persuasion mouthing revolutionary slogans as they competed for Sukarno's favor. Intense political competition also played out in the mass media, especially the dozens of national and regional newspapers, as different organizations sought to create or control them in order to trumpet their positions and rally supporters.

In August 1964, an alliance of anti-Communist parties formed the Body to Support Sukarnoism (Badan Pendukung Sukarnosime, or BPS), with support from forty newspapers. BPS was an umbrella organization headed by Minister of Trade Adam Malik, a founder of the "national Communist" party Murba, which opposed the PKI and proposed the adoption of a one-party system as a way to head off PKI advances. Sukarno quickly came to view BPS as distorting his own thinking and as a covert attack on the PKI. In December 1964, Sukarno banned BPS and shut down several newspapers that had vocally promoted it; the following month he ordered a "freeze" on Murba as well. While the ban on BPS benefited the PKI, it also turned out to be a boon for the army, which secured control over two of the major newspapers. Indonesian News (*Berita Indonesia*) was relaunched as War News (*Berita Yudha*), and Freedom (*Merdeka*) as Armed Forces Daily (*Harian Angkatan Bersendjata*).

Through early 1965, Sukarno adopted an increasingly defiant posture. At the Special Session of the Provisional People's Consultative Assembly (Majelis Permusyawaratan Rakyat Sementara, or MPRS) in April, he announced that

Figure 40. Crowd gathered in Bali to see Sukarno and Cambodian head of state Prince Norodom Sihanouk, August 1965. (Beryl Bernay)

Indonesia would soon enter a new phase of the revolution:

> This year sees the end of our twentieth year of independence, and the twentieth year of the Republic. . . . With our Republic as the sharpest weapon to carry out our revolution, we have concentrated our efforts over the last twenty years on consummating the first stage of our revolution, i.e. the national democratic stage. Considering that there are clear indications from the present situation—and considering what we have already achieved—this stage is already almost finished. During this stage of our revolution, we crushed Nekolim [neocolonialism and imperialism] and feudalism, in order to create our own democratic national life. Now we step to the following stage. The revolution is beginning to enter the stage of Indonesian socialism.[16]

In the following months, Sukarno and his allies embarked on a frenetic campaign of major celebrations involving monumental banners and bunting, oration, and marching. On May 1, he addressed a huge crowd in Jakarta in celebration of May Day. Adorning the stadium was a massive banner in socialist-realist style depicting a fist smashing capitalists and bureaucrats and declaring, "Workers of the World, Unite." Later the same month, he joined Aidit before an even larger crowd celebrating the forty-fifth anniversary of the PKI. And in a celebration of the anniversary of the PNI in July, he again suggested that Indonesia was set to embark on a new socialist phase of its revolution.

Figure 41. Sukarno enjoying a laugh with young supporters, ca. September 1965. (Beryl Bernay)

Figure 42. Sukarno speaking on May Day 1965. The slogan at the top reads, "Workers of the World." During his address, Sukarno compared the United States' role in Vietnam to Hitler's involvement in the Spanish Civil War. (Bettman-Corbis Collection/Getty)

These events provided opportunities for pomp and militancy and for Sukarno to demonstrate his authority through the mobilization of large and enthusiastic crowds.

## 14. Politics in the Streets

After the imposition of Guided Democracy in 1959, politics increasingly played out in the streets. Parties of all political stripes and their mass organizations sought to demonstrate their power, and win the president's ear, through the mobilization of ever-larger crowds at mass rallies, parades, and demonstrations. In this way, millions of men and women from all walks of life—including students, peasants, workers, artists, writers, and teachers—became directly involved in party politics and were caught up in the bitter conflicts that ensued.

Although virtually all parties adopted the language and symbols of the revolution favored by Sukarno, the differences among opposing groups were clear. On the left, demonstrators from various mass organizations, such as Pemuda Rakyat, Gerwani, and the Unified Movement of Indonesian University Students (Consentrasi Gerakan Mahasiswa Indonesia, or CGMI), demanded the "retooling" of anti-Communist officials, the

Figure 43. Festive atmosphere at a PKI rally in Yogyakarta. (Moelyono)

Figure 44. Students in Jakarta protest US policy with a giant effigy of Uncle Sam holding a "savage" atomic bomb, February 1965.

Figure 45. Wall in North Sulawesi, with graffiti backing Sukarno's opposition to India and support for Pakistan. (Beryl Bernay)

Figure 46. As part of Indonesian Independence Day celebrations, police and soldiers oversee the burning of American Information Service publications, including Tarzan comics and racy romance novels. (ANP)

banning of rival organizations, and the ouster of US ambassadors. On the right, members of NU, Ansor, the Islamic University Students' Association (Himpunan Mahasiswa Islam, or HMI), and other organizations insinuated that Sukarno and the PKI had become puppets of China, warned that the revolution was drifting off course, and denounced the PKI and its mass organizations for their alleged atheism.

An early example of the new style of politics came in September 1963, when thousands of angry demonstrators attacked the British embassy in Jakarta, in protest of British support for the newly formed state of Malaysia. Press photographs from the time show

Figure 47. Young Communists march to demand that Sukarno ban the eighty-thousand-strong Islamic University Students' Association (HMI) in Jakarta, September 9, 1965. Their sign protests "capitalist-bureaucrats." (Keystone)

Figure 48. Members of HMI stage a counterprotest against the PKI's calls for a ban on their organization, Jakarta, September 13, 1965. The poster reads, "Eliminate HMI over my dead body." (National Library of Indonesia)

young men destroying embassy property and torching the ambassador's official car. By 1965, mass demonstrations and rallies had become increasingly frequent and volatile, as members of rival organizations, some of them very young, protested openly in the streets.

These protests sometimes led to open clashes between opposing groups. Despite claims that such confrontations were provoked by the Left, both sides showed a willingness to resort to violence. A report from the US consulate in Surabaya describes a confrontation between rival organizations in August

1965 in which the threat of violence appeared to come mainly from Muslim groups:

> The Moslems staged a demonstration . . . on August 10 in which they threatened violence if their demands were not met. When on August 14, just before the national holiday celebration, the PKI-PNI staged their own demonstration . . . a Moslem group quickly appeared on the scene armed with knives and sickles. Only the presence of Army troops between the two groups prevented the outbreak of serious disorders. The demonstrated willingness of the Moslems to defend their interests by resort to violence and the presence of a well-organized group ready to carry out their threats apparently led the East Java Chief of Police to comment in a public police ceremony on August 26 that the situation in East Java is "grave."[17]

Still, even in 1965 the politics of the street were not always violent. Many events had a festive air and took the form of picnics and parades in which marching drum bands, dancers, popular singers, and decorated floats played a prominent role. Such events offered a welcome respite from the stresses of everyday life, especially as the economy deteriorated. They also attracted many young people to the ranks of one or another party or organization, expanding those groups' followings.

## 15. Foreign Journalists in Jakarta

There were few Western journalists based in Jakarta in the early 1960s, but a number of foreign correspondents visited intermittently to report on political developments. Visiting journalists often stayed at Hotel Indonesia and gathered at the Jakarta Foreign Correspondents' Club, which was cofounded by Frank Palmos, a young, Indonesian-speaking Australian journalist, and the AFP correspondent Frank de Jong. But Sukarno's growing hostility to the United States resulted in some journalists having difficulty obtaining visas, as well as an outright ban on *Time* magazine.

*Newsweek*'s Hong Kong bureau chief, Robert McCabe, was jailed for twenty-nine hours and then expelled during a visit in April 1964. Yet the magazine's Tokyo correspondent, Bernard Krisher, was warmly welcomed by Sukarno on two visits later that year. In May 1965, Neil Sheehan of the *New York Times* interviewed PKI leaders Aidit and Lukman in Jakarta and spent a week in Bali assessing the political situation, and especially the rise of the PKI over the previous ten years. He shared his detailed notes on PKI leaders and organizing with officials at the US embassy.

Female journalists were especially prominent. Beryl Bernay, a young American, arrived in Jakarta in August 1965 as a stringer for ABC News. As she later wrote, "I knew all of Sukarno's wives and was the first foreign journalist to know the Japanese wife, Dewi, his favorite at the time. Our 'friendship' gained me increased access to Sukarno on social as well as official occasions."

Figure 49. The model and author Cindy Adams poses with members of Sukarno's palace guard, the Tjakrabirawa Regiment. (Cindy Adams, *Sukarno, My Friend*)

Figure 50. The American journalist Beryl Bernay interviewing Sukarno at the presidential palace, September 1965. (Beryl Bernay)

This culminated in an interview with Sukarno on film (subsequently aired on ABC News), followed by an invitation to dine that evening with Sukarno and Dewi. Also in September, the American freelance journalist Carol Goldstein, who had interviewed Sukarno and other key figures during her first visit to Indonesia in 1963, arrived in Jakarta and was on hand to take some of the most memorable photographs of events in the city on October 1 and over the following two weeks.

The most unusual—and controversial—foreign correspondent in Jakarta in early 1965 was Cindy Adams, a model turned journalist from New York City. In 1961, her husband, the comedian Joey Adams, had been appointed by President Kennedy to serve as a cultural ambassador to Southeast Asia, and during a visit to Jakarta the Adamses met Sukarno. Sukarno was evidently taken with Ms. Adams, so he asked her to return to Jakarta in early 1965 to collaborate on his autobiography. The two became close, and Sukarno threw a going-away party for her in April 1965, complete with an electric band (despite Sukarno's publicly professed disapproval of rock and roll).

# II. Crisis in Jakarta

Figure 52. Cartoon in the PKI newspaper *Harian Rakjat*, October 2, 1965. The caption reads, "Lieutenant Colonel Untung, a Tjakrabirawa battalion commander, rescues President Sukarno from a coup by the Generals' Council." (*Harian Rakjat*)

## 16. The September 30th Movement

In the predawn hours of October 1, 1965, teams of soldiers set out from the outskirts of Jakarta to two elite neighborhoods in the center of the city to arrest seven senior army officers. Their mission was planned by a group that called itself the September 30th Movement, led by Lieutenant Colonel Untung, a battalion commander of the Tjakrabirawa Regiment (the presidential guard). In the course of the operation, three of the targeted generals were killed, including army commander Lieutenant General Yani, while three others were taken alive. A seventh, the minister of defense, General Nasution, managed to escape, but in the chaos his five-year-old daughter was fatally wounded and his adjutant was detained. The soldiers then drove to Halim Air Base just south of the city, where the surviving captives were killed and the bodies of all seven victims (six generals and the adjutant) were dumped down a well in an old rubber grove known as Lubang Buaya (Crocodile Hole).

While these events were unfolding, another group of soldiers—perhaps one thousand in all—took up positions on Jakarta's Merdeka Square, where key government offices and telecommunications installations were located. At 7:15 a.m., the national radio station broadcast the first of several announcements by the movement. It declared that "a military move" had taken place within the army with the help of troops from other service branches. This move, it said, was designed to prevent a planned "counterrevolutionary coup" by a self-styled "Council of Generals . . . a subversive movement sponsored by the CIA." The announcement also expressed disgust at the corrupt and immoral lifestyles of

*far left*
Figure 53. Lieutenant Colonel Untung of the Tjakrabirawa Regiment, leader of the September 30th Movement. (Associated Press)

*left*
Figure 54. Colonel Abdul Latief of the Jakarta Regional Military Command. (Tribunnews)

the generals and dismay at their lack of concern for the well-being of rank-and-file soldiers. A further announcement that afternoon declared that Sukarno's cabinet had been "decommissioned" and that a "Revolutionary Council" had been set up to take over state functions.[1] Military actions in support of the movement, including the arrest and killing of some senior army officers, also took place in Central Java.

These events marked a critical turning point in Indonesian history, providing the army, under the leadership of Major General Suharto, with a pretext for the systematic destruction of the PKI and its allies, a sustained attack on Sukarno, and the eventual seizure of power. But even today, more than half a century later, there is controversy about certain aspects of the movement, especially in regard to the possible role played by the PKI, Sukarno, and Suharto.

Among the most important questions in dispute has been the role of the PKI. From the outset, the army and its allies insisted that the party masterminded the September 30th Movement and that its actions were an attempt to seize state power. To buttress its claims, the army circulated false allegations that the generals were tortured and mutilated with razor blades while PKI women sang and danced naked around them. These inflammatory claims fueled public fury against the PKI and formed the basis for the massive campaign of violence against the party and its affiliates that followed. And yet the available evidence suggests that, far from being a PKI attempt to seize power, the movement was more or less what its leaders claimed it to be: a move by disgruntled middle-ranking army officers, angered by the lascivious lifestyle and counter-revolutionary politics of their own commanders and convinced that those generals were working with the CIA to stage a coup d'état. While it is likely that Aidit was privy to the plan—both he and his close associate, a shadowy figure named Sjam Kamaruzaman, were at Halim Air Base on October 1—there is no credible evidence that Aidit himself was

Figure 55. Brigadier General Supardjo and his wife, Triswati. (Kumpulan Kisah dan Sejarah)

Figure 56. Sjam Kamaruzaman. (National Library of Indonesia)

the movement's mastermind, or that the PKI leadership was aware of the plot.

A further source of controversy has been the suggestion that Sukarno was involved in the plan to kidnap the generals or knew about it but did nothing to stop it. It was on the basis of those allegations that he was eventually forced from office. In support of the claim, critics have noted that on the morning of October 1, Sukarno made his way to Halim where the movement's leaders had gathered, that he remained silent for almost two days after the kidnapping and killing of the Generals, and that when he finally did speak, he failed to condemn their actions forcefully. All of these things are true, but they are only part of the story. Not mentioned in such accounts is the fact that it was standard procedure for the president to relocate to Halim in times of crisis, that a delegation from the movement had tried but failed to locate him at the palace early on the morning of October 1, and that when he reached Halim on his own initiative later that morning, he spoke with only one of the

movement's leaders, Brigadier General Supardjo. Moreover, it is now clear that when he learned that some or all of the generals had been killed, Sukarno not only refused to endorse the movement but urged Supardjo to call it off to avoid further bloodshed.

More intriguing and controversial are the indications that Suharto, who spearheaded the campaign against the movement and the PKI, knew about the plot in advance but allowed it to unfold. It is striking that despite his seniority and strong anti-Communist credentials, Suharto was not among those targeted by the movement, and the soldiers who occupied Merdeka Square on the morning of October 1 made no attempt to control the office of the Army Strategic Reserve Command (Komando Cadangan Strategis Angkatan Darat, or Kostrad), the powerful strategic army unit Suharto commanded. It is also notable that he had close personal and professional ties with some of the movement's principal leaders. These included Untung, who was a family friend and someone with whom Suharto had served during the national revolution and later in West Papua. Another movement leader, Colonel Latief, testified that he met Suharto late on the evening of September 30 to inform him of the planned operation, just hours before it was launched. Taken together, these facts suggest that the movement's leaders had reason to believe that Suharto would support their initiative. They were mistaken.

Figure 57. Suharto and his wife, Tien, enjoying a picnic with the leader of the September 30th Movement, Lieutenant Colonel Untung, likely in the early 1960s. This photograph confirms that the two men were close family friends, adding credibility to suggestions that Suharto had advance warning of Untung's plans. (Courtesy of Stanley Adi Prasetyo)

Figure 58. RPKAD convoy in Central Jakarta, October 1, 1965. (Beryl Bernay)

## 17. Suharto's Counter-movement

Within hours of the September 30th Movement's first radio announcement, other army units mobilized to crush it. The counter-movement was led by Major General Suharto, commander of Kostrad. By late afternoon, the troops under his command had regained control of central Jakarta, and by dawn the following day, October 2, the movement troops and leaders who had gathered at Halim Air Base had fled. The movement had been crushed less than twenty-four hours after it began.

At 5:30 a.m. on October 1, Suharto received information from neighbors about shootings and possible abductions at the homes of several generals. He immediately departed for Kostrad headquarters, located on the east side of Merdeka Square, arriving just before 7:00 a.m. Fifteen minutes later, Untung's first statement was broadcast over the radio. At this point, Suharto became aware that two of the crack battalions—the 454th and the 530th—brought to Jakarta under his own command to participate in the Armed Forces Day celebration on October 5 were actively supporting the September 30th Movement. From his own office overlooking Merdeka Square, he could see that these battalions were guarding the north side of the square, where the presidential palace and army headquarters were located, the west flank, where the national radio station and Ministry of Defense were based, and the south side, where the telecommunications building was situated.

Although the aims of the movement and the course of events were still far from certain, Suharto decided to take command of the army and respond to

Figure 59. Troops loyal to Suharto use armored vehicles to block the Hotel Indonesia roundabout in central Jakarta, October 1, 1965.

the presumed threat. In this, he received immediate and full support from the two most powerful officers with direct command over troops in Jakarta: the Jakarta military commander, Brigadier General Umar Wirahadikusumah, and the commander of the Army Para-commando Regiment (Resimen Para Komando Angkatan Darat, or RPKAD), Colonel Sarwo Edhie. Umar ordered tank battalions into the streets, while Edhie summoned several of his companies to deploy to Kostrad headquarters. With military superiority assured, at 9:00 a.m. Suharto sent emissaries to demand that battalions 454 (from Central Java) and 530 (from East Java) surrender. If they did not obey his order by 6:00 p.m., he threatened, loyal troops would be sent to attack their positions. By late afternoon, the 530th Battalion had complied with his order, while the 454th had fled to Halim Air Base. Quick action by Sarwo Edhie's paratroopers secured the radio and telecommunications buildings.

Figure 60. Soldiers and a civilian on a bicycle in Jakarta, October 1, 1965.

Figure 61. Troops guard positions near Merdeka Square in central Jakarta, October 1, 1965. (TopFoto)

Figure 62. General Nasution (at microphone), who narrowly escaped capture on the morning of October 1, giving a press conference later that day. (Beryl Bernay)

Meanwhile, there was a flurry of activity at Halim. After extended discussions, at 1:30 p.m. Sukarno signed an order appointing Major General Pranoto Reksosamudra to replace the murdered Yani as army commander. An emissary was sent to Kostrad headquarters to summon Pranoto to see the president, but Suharto would not allow Pranoto to go, on the grounds that the army could not risk losing another general. Suharto was disobeying orders from the commander in chief.

Suharto and his allies moved quickly to consolidate their advantage that evening. Umar declared a curfew and ordered the closure of most media outlets, with the exception of the newspapers. Units of Edhie's paratroopers were deployed to the vicinity of Halim. Suharto then sent couriers to instruct Sukarno to leave Halim to avoid becoming a casualty in the upcoming assault. In the face of these moves, Sukarno decided to go by car to Bogor, two hours' drive south of the capital. Soon after, Suharto broadcast a prerecorded announcement over the radio: "Dear listeners, it is clear that the actions [of the September 30th Movement] were counterrevolutionary and that it must be destroyed down to the very roots. We have no doubt that with the full assistance of the progressive and revolutionary population, the

Figure 63. Major General Suharto with Jakarta regional military commander Brigadier General Umar Wirahadikusumah (far right). (National Library of Indonesia)

counterrevolutionary September 30th Movement will be crushed to bits."[2] The following morning, the leaders and remaining troops of the September 30th Movement abandoned Halim, some returning to the city and others fleeing by road, train, or plane. The movement was over.

On the morning of October 3, seeking to reassert his authority, Sukarno made a broadcast over Radio Republic Indonesia calling on the population to remain calm but to maintain "vigilance" and "preparedness." He added, "The leadership of the army is directly in my hands, and I have temporarily appointed Maj. Gen. Pranoto Reksosamudra . . . to carry out the daily tasks of the army. I have designated Maj. Gen. Suharto, Commander of the Strategic Command, to restore security and order in accordance with the policy I have just outlined."[3]

## 18. Generals' Exhumation and Funeral

Sukarno's October 3 plea for calm was quickly drowned out by events on the ground and by a concerted propaganda offensive orchestrated by the army. These developments marked a decisive shift in the political balance against the PKI and the president and signaled the onset of a campaign of violence and mass incarceration.

On the morning of October 4, the bodies of the slain generals were discovered in the old well at Lubang Buaya, and later that day they were exhumed by a navy diving team. Suharto and other military officers were on hand to witness the exhumation, and the event was documented by army photographers and film crews. The grisly photographs and film footage were later published in the army-controlled media—and distributed to the foreign press—alongside

Figure 64. Trucks carrying the generals' coffins entering Kalibata National Heroes Cemetery, Jakarta, October 5, 1965. (*Paris Match/Marie Claire*)

Figure 65. RPKAD soldiers carrying the generals' coffins to their gravesites, October 5, 1965. (National Library of Indonesia)

Figure 66. An official showed this photo of the generals' exhumation to the American photojournalist Beryl Bernay and allowed her to document it. (Beryl Bernay)

Figure 67. Major General Suharto with Brigadier General Sabur, commander of the Tjakrabirawa Regiment (second from right with sunglasses and beret), October 5, 1965. (Associated Press)

Suharto's remarks pointing the finger of blame at the PKI and fabricated stories that the generals had been mutilated by Gerwani members. These official images and fabrications were crucial in igniting popular anger against the Left.

Equally important was the massive military funeral held for the generals the following day, October 5. Starting from Merdeka Square, the procession of trucks, tanks, and thousands of heavily armed soldiers wound through the streets of Jakarta to the Kalibata National Heroes Cemetery, where the generals were buried. US ambassador Green, who was among the foreign dignitaries in attendance, described the scene in a telegram to Washington later that day: "Generals' funeral procession passed embassy corner at 1045 hours along streets crowded with thousands of silent people and guarded by armored vehicles and troops. Funeral cortege preceded by armored cars and 30 truckloads of army para-commandos with automatic weapons and fixed bayonets. Seven coffins shrouded with Indonesian flag affixed to frames welded on armored trucks contained remains. . . . Funeral cortege is most impressive display of army might as well as reverence for its slain leaders."[4]

This display of "army might" and "reverence for its slain leaders" was amply recorded by official army photographers and by the foreign and local press, and it was widely distributed through the media in the days thereafter. These images also became an essential visual foundation for the official glorification and memorialization of the generals as "national heroes."

## 19. Western Responses and Collusion

Western powers, including their ambassadors in Jakarta, expressed confusion about who had done what on the morning of October 1, but they were enthusiastic about the potential the events had for an Indonesian political reversal. Many diplomats, however, noted the need for caution so as to prevent Sukarno from linking the army's response to Western imperialism.

At midnight on October 4–5, Ambassador Green sent a telegram to the US secretary of state, titled "Guidance on Treatment of Situation Jakarta," which was to be shared with the Voice of America and with other embassies:

Figure 68. Swedish cartoon showing China's tentacles around Sukarno, October 2, 1965. The caption, in Swedish, reads, "For a long time, the American attitude toward Sukarno was 'understanding'—but it has recently become much more critical, as Sukarno has adopted a violently anti-American stance and moved closer to China." (Bill Mauldin/*Chicago Sun-Times*)

Figure 69. US ambassador Marshall Green and military attaché Colonel Willis Ethel attending the generals' funeral, October 5, 1965. (Carol Goldstein)

Figure 70. Letter from British ambassador Andrew Gilchrist to UK Foreign Office, October 5, 1965. (UK National Archive)

"Real villain [is] Peking-oriented PKI and its adherents, cause of tragedy [is the] poison of hate they have pumped into this country. Not only stress PKI silence, but work in, based on factual info, PKI involvement [in the] aborted Sept 30 coup attempt."[5] With regard to the images of the murdered generals, Green also commented that "references to similar brutalities by PKI at Madiun in 1948 may be usefully insinuated."

The American interpretation of events came fully into public view on October 10 when the *Washington Post* published an editorial by former ambassador to Indonesia Howard Jones with the title "Indonesian Coup Was a Red Bobble."[6] But US officials were concerned that the army leadership would not seize the opportunity to crush the PKI. US secretary of state Dean Rusk made his views clear in a telegram to the US embassy in Jakarta: "If [the] Army's willingness to follow through against the PKI is in any way contingent upon or subject to influence by US, we do not wish [to] miss opportunity for US action."[7]

1011/65

CONFIDENTIAL

BRITISH EMBASSY,

DJAKARTA.

5 October, 1965.

Dear Ted,

I have never concealed from you my belief that a little shooting in Indonesia would be an essential preliminary to effective change in Indonesia; but it makes me sad to think that they have begun with the wrong people.

2. Without feeling any great admiration for Yani as a political figure, I nevertheless got on well with him personally. Two years ago when I was in difficulties over the women and children in Balikpapan and no one would dare to help me, I went to Yani. The interview was correct and brief, and ended by Yani saying he would arrange things as I wanted. "Would you like to have it in writing?" "Not necessary - not when I am dealing with an officer and a gentleman." This pleased him, and thereafter we would generally hobnob briefly in a corner at official receptions, exchanging cynical remarks with considerable mutual satisfaction; he was also a reliable channel when I wanted to put in a word of warning about dangerous aspects of konfrontasi and so on. He was said to be corrupt, but that was (I think) only because of his silly, stupid, greedy wife.

3. As for Parman, I regarded him as very agreeable indeed for an Indonesian. He knew his job thoroughly but never went beyond it into any degree of personal hostility or discourtesy.

4. I shall miss them both and regret that they should have met such dirty deaths. I think I used the words cruel and ruthless in drawing a pen-picture of Aidit for you, the day after I first met him, and you can see I was not far wrong.

5. I enclose a copy for my friend the Colonel in the Ministry of Defence, who knew Parman well.

Yours ever,
Andrew

(A. G. Gilchrist)

US officials knew little about Suharto. To redress this gap, a US embassy cable provided biographical information, concluding, "Suharto has been described as a first-rate soldier and is noted for his smart appearance as well as military ability. He displayed courage, skill and determination during the days following the October 1 assassination of the Army's top commanders, when he collected his Strategic Command raiders and moved swiftly to retake key points in Djakarta with a minimum of fighting. His anti-Communist credentials leave nothing to be desired. He has a good reputation as incorruptible and lives modestly."[8]

## 20. Army Propaganda and the Press

The army moved quickly to exercise control over the country's media outlets and used them effectively to spread inflammatory propaganda against the PKI and its affiliates. On the evening of October 1, the army commander of the Jakarta region declared a "state of war" and ordered a ban on all newspapers except for the armed forces' own *Harian Angkatan Bersendjata* and *Berita Yudha*. Oddly, the next day the PKI newspaper *Harian Rakjat* was allowed to publish its morning edition, which included an editorial supporting the September 30th Movement. One possible explanation for this anomaly is that the army had a hand in orchestrating the editorial and allowing publication in order to incriminate the PKI.

Within a few days, a number of newspapers were allowed to resume publishing, though under close army supervision and often by reprinting news provided by the Army Information Center (Pusat Penerangan Angkatan Darat). Army ideologues seized control of the narrative by manipulating the name of the September 30th Movement. The military newspapers first abbreviated the name Untung had used, "Gerakan 30 September," to "G.30.S." Then, adjusting the word order to "Gerakan September 30," on October 8, the press introduced the inflammatory portmanteau

Figure 71. Young men reading the army daily *Berita Yudha* in Jakarta, October 10, 1965. (ANP)

Kita Tidak Mau Dimakan Dus Kita Melawan !(Bung Karno)

# ANGKATAN BERSENDJATA

BATJAAN PRADJURIT, VETERAN HANSIP, PURNAWIRAWAN, SUKARELAWAN DAN RAKJAT PEDJOANG PROGRESIF REVOLUSIONER

SABTU, 9 OKTOBER 1965 — 13 DJUMADIL ACHIR 1385 H.

GANTUNG AIDIT DAN KONTJONJA

## Setengah Djuta Massa Aksi Dari 46 Orpol/Ormas Tuntut Pembubaran P. K. I.

Berdiri Dibelakang Bung Karno Dgn. Tekad Menumpas Kontra-revolusi "Gestapu"

— EDITORIAL —

KALIBATA, 5 Oktober 65.

Figure 72. Front page of the armed forces daily, *Angkatan Bersendjata*, October 9, 1965. The headline reads, "Half a Million Demonstrators from 46 Mass/Political Organizations Demand PKI Banning." The photographs above the headline show the destruction of PKI facilities by demonstrators and a banner that reads, "Hang Aidit and His Henchmen." The editorial (left) names the PKI and its affiliates as the "puppet-masters" of the September 30th Movement and uses the provocative term "Gestapu" to describe the movement.

Figure 73. Cartoon in armed forces daily showing a man, representing "the people" and the military, eradicating the September 30th Movement "down to the roots." The roots in the figure spell out "PKI." (*Angkatan Bersendjata*)

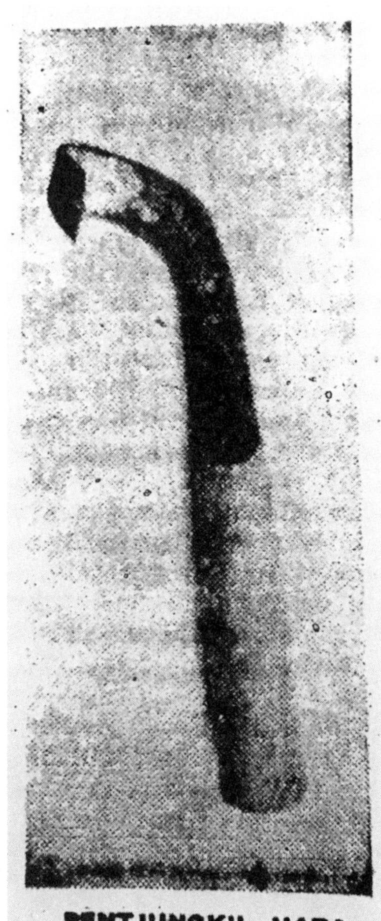


Figure 74. A rubber tapping tool allegedly used as an "eye gouger" by Gerwani members on the morning of October 1, published in an army newspaper, October 13, 1965. (*Berita Yudha*)

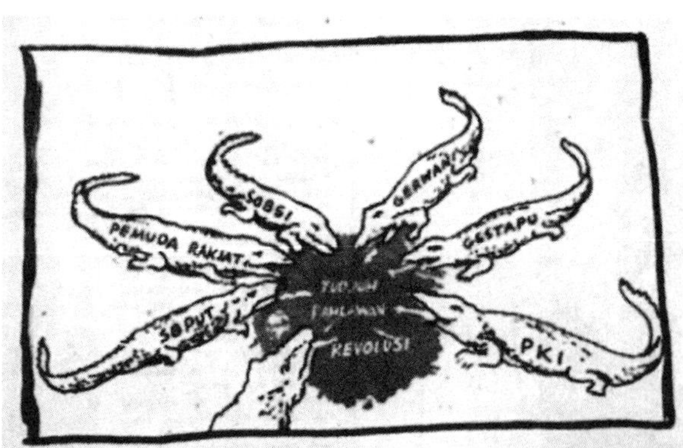


*left, top to bottom*

Figure 75. Man displaying three picks like those allegedly used to mutilate the generals on October 1, 1965. The autopsy of the generals' bodies, which was never released to the public, reveals that no such mutilation took place. (*Paris Match/Marie Claire*)

Figure 76. Political cartoon in the armed forces daily, October 8, 1965, spelling out "G30S," the army's abbreviation for the September 30th Movement. (*Angkatan Bersendjata*)

Figure 77. Cartoon depicting seven crocodiles, representing the September 30th Movement, the PKI, and its affiliates devouring the generals on October 1, 1965. First published in the daily *Duta Masjarakat* on October 20, 1965, this color version was published in the Indonesian University Students' Action Front newspaper in 1966. (Beryl Bernay)

"Gestapu," equating Untung's movement with Nazi Germany's secret state police. Finally, the newspaper publishers created the compound "G.30.S/PKI," thereby directly incriminating the PKI.

With the exhumation of the generals' corpses on October 4, the army added the salacious story that members of Gerwani had performed naked dances and engaged in an orgy and then cut the generals' genitals with razors and gouged out their eyes. Following the army's direction, newspapers across the country also printed false accounts alleging that PKI members had stockpiled "eye gougers" to be used against their captives, that they had prepared scores of wells into which they intended to throw their enemies, and that Colonel Katamso and his family had been chopped up into small pieces by PKI assailants in Central Java.

Army propaganda received a boost from the new newspapers established by its own officers. Brigadier General Ahmad Sukendro, a prominent anti-Communist who had once participated in an army exchange at the University of Pittsburgh, oversaw the formation of a sensationalist new paper called *Fire* (*Api*) in early October. Brigadier General Sugandhi, the director general of the armed forces staff, who oversaw the armed forces newspaper, started the English-language *Daily Mail*, which took a particularly pro-American line. As the US embassy reported in mid-October, "Among signs of new life that appears to be resurgent in population previously numbed or hypnotized by PKI propaganda is avid newspaper reading. As expressed to Emb[assy] off[icer] by number of Indonesian friends, now there is something really to read in papers. Housewife remarked gaily, 'I'm spending half my budget on buying newspapers.' Price starts high when papers just off press and cheapens as news succeeded by later developments. Even betjak (pedicab) boys and small shopkeepers are reading and sharing papers. Last night just prior to curfew time, copies of new Sukendro backed evening paper *Api* selling like hotcakes."[9]

## 21. Graffiti as Propaganda

Party banners, giant government billboards, stenciled handbills, and painted graffiti were central to the hothouse politics under Guided Democracy. In the days after October 1, 1965, new graffiti appeared on walls and streets across Jakarta, often covering over existing PKI banners and slogans. But the balance of forces was still uncertain. In Jakarta, the anti-PKI graffiti appeared first in the center of the city and the more affluent neighborhoods, while PKI strongholds, such as the port area and Glodok (Jakarta's Chinatown), had little or none.

The new graffiti both echoed and provided fodder for the propaganda emanating from the armed forces' daily newspapers. Particularly prominent were slogans linking the September 30th Movement to the PKI, calls to crush the PKI, and graffiti connecting the alleged treachery of the PKI at Madiun in 1948 with the traitorous murder of the generals. While most of the graffiti was in Indonesian, some was in English, suggesting that it was aimed at least in part at an international audience.

Figure 78. Graffiti on the left equates PKI chairman Aidit with Muso, the PKI leader accused of leading an uprising in 1948, and below it the word "Traitor." (National Library of Indonesia)

*right, top to bottom*

Figure 79. "Will we allow our generals to be killed by PKI terrorism?" (Carol Goldstein/Keystone)

Figure 80. Graffiti on a fence in late 1965 reads, "Aidit is the brains behind September 30th [Movement]" and "Madiun II," implying that the September 30th Movement was a sequel to the 1948 Communist uprising. (Keystone)

Figure 81. Graffiti in front of a tire store on Hayam Wuruk Street, Jakarta. Beneath "PKI go to hell," it reads, "Aidit is a whoremonger causing trouble in Sadar Alley." Sadar Alley, a block behind the location in the photograph, was infamous for its sex workers. The implication is that Aidit and the PKI were nothing more than johns causing a ruckus in a brothel. (Beryl Bernay)

## 22. Anti-Communist "Action Commands"

With encouragement from the army high command, in early October leaders of twenty-seven "nationalist" and "religious" groups established an Action Command to Crush the September 30th Movement (the full Indonesian name was abbreviated KAP-Gestapu). This new organization was established to unite a wide range of groups that, despite their common opposition to the PKI, had little or no experience of collaboration. The leadership included key figures from the Muslim party NU, the Muslim mass organization Muhammadiyah, the Catholic Party (Partai Katolik), the Catholic Youth (Pemuda Katolik), and the army-backed League of Upholders of Indonesian Freedom (IPKI).

Soon, "action commands" of various kinds began to appear across the country. Among the earliest and most active of these was the Indonesian University Students' Action Front (Kesatuan Aksi Mahasiswa Indonesia, or KAMI), set up in late October. Although it was ostensibly an independent group, KAMI was encouraged by and worked closely with army authorities. Moreover, despite their clean middle-class appearance, its members were stridently, and sometimes violently, anti-Communist. As a political insider told the researcher Ruth McVey in 1966, "The students were fanatical right-wingers, used by the Army and [leading NU figure] Subchan. One could never be sure whom they would 'arrest' and what would happen if they did. They were not a democratic but a fascistic phenomenon."[10]

*above left*
Figure 82. Demonstrators at the mass rally in Taman Suropati, Jakarta, October 8, 1965. The placard in front, with blood dripping from the letters, reads, "Hang the PKI and those who sell out the country."

*above right*
Figure 83. The Islamic University Students' Association and other demonstrators with a poster reading, "Gerwani is immoral." (Beryl Bernay)

Figure 84. Members of the Indonesian Women's Action Front, one of the anti-Communist action commands set up soon after October 1, 1965. (Beryl Bernay)

In effect, KAP-Gestapu and the other action commands formed a central part of the campaign to eradicate the Left. In close collaboration with the army, they made declarations and organized rallies and demonstrations against the PKI and its affiliated organizations. Increasingly, they also committed acts of violence, including the burning and looting of PKI offices and homes and eventually attacks on real and alleged PKI members.

## 23. Attacks on PKI Offices

One of the first rallies organized by the anti-Communist action commands took place on the afternoon of October 4 in a park in North Jakarta. The demonstrators, numbering a few hundred people, then marched south through the city's Chinatown to the headquarters of the Army Strategic Reserve Command (Kostrad). The demonstrators presented a "request to the president" with four demands:

Figure 85. Anti-PKI demonstration by Muslim and Catholic youth groups. In addition to placards calling for the PKI to be dissolved, other banners read, "Catholic Youth," "Strengthen Religion," "Canisius Junior and Senior High School," and "Catholic Struggle." (Beryl Bernay)

Figure 86. PKI headquarters in Jakarta burned by an anti-Communist mob, October 8, 1965. The banner reads, “Death sentence for the kidnappers of the generals.” (Bettman-Corbis Collection/Getty)

Figure 87. Scene of explosion near PKI headquarters, Jakarta, ca. October 8, 1965. (Michel Le Tac/*Paris Match*/*Marie Claire*)

Figure 88. Soldier in front of PKI Jakarta branch sign, October 1965. (Agence France Press)

1. Ban or dissolve all parties and mass organizations directing, supporting, or sympathizing with [the] Sept 30 Movement which, according to authorities, include . . . the PKI and its mass organizations.
2. Ban newspapers and periodicals which directly or indirectly aided the Sept 30 September Movement such as *People's Daily* [*Harian Rakjat*]. . . .
3. Nationalize assets of counter-revolutionary organizations and figures.
4. Purge cabinet and state organs such as [the] National Front, Antara [news agency], Youth Front, [the] Indonesian Journalist Association and student organizations of counter-revolutionary elements.[11]

A larger rally took place the following day, October 5. Organized by the Youth

Figure 89. Soldier guarding scene of attack on PKI office, Jakarta, October 13, 1965. (United Press International)

Figure 90. Man painting "PKI" on a fence. (Beryl Bernay)

Anti-counterrevolution Action Command (Komando Aksi Pemuda Anti Kontra Revolusi), it echoed the more aggressive violent language that had been introduced by Suharto and others the previous day, ending with a call for all those involved in or sympathetic to the September 30th Movement to be "liquidated." According to an army account, the rally organizers "denounced in the strongest possible terms the villainous and barbaric actions of the September 30th Movement and the Revolutionary Council; condemned in the strongest possible terms the elements and groups who masterminded the September 30th Movement; and called for the liquidation of those actors."[12]

Three days later, on October 8, another mass rally was held in Suropati Park, in Central Jakarta. It was attended by an estimated half a million people from a wide range of political parties and more than forty mass organizations. Their leaders expressed condolences for the murdered generals and demanded that President Sukarno disband the PKI and uphold the state ideology, Pancasila.

Several thousand members of NU's youth wing (Ansor) and other groups set out on a thirty-minute march to the PKI headquarters in the Kramat neighborhood of Jakarta. There, watched by a large crowd, they set fire to the main PKI building, quickly reducing it to a smoldering heap of rubble, as demonstrators shouted "Kill Aidit!" and "Dissolve the PKI!" Meanwhile, other protesters ransacked a nearby building that contained PKI propaganda materials and equipment. To the roars of the crowd, they hurled hammer-and-sickle flags, leaflets, posters, typewriters, and duplicating machines onto the street. A telegram from the US embassy noted without comment that throughout the attack, "three fire engines stood by unused. Troops had cordoned off streets leading to communist headquarters but made no attempt to interfere."[13]

Figure 91. Sukarno at the presidential palace announcing the appointment of Major General Suharto as commander of the Operations Command for the Restoration of Security and Order (Kopkamtib), October 10, 1965. (Keystone)

## 24. The Operations Command for the Restoration of Security and Order

At a meeting with armed forces top brass on October 3, Sukarno appointed General Pranoto as caretaker for the armed forces and designated Suharto to oversee the "restoration of security and order." This decision, including the wording, shaped subsequent behind-the-scenes jostling.

A week later, on October 10, Sukarno held a press conference at which he glumly announced the appointment of Suharto to head a new Operations Command for the Restoration of Security and Order (Komando Operasi Pemulihan Keamanan dan Ketertiban, or Kopkamtib). The new command, and Suharto's appointment as its head, was later formalized in a series of presidential decisions dated November 1, November 12, and December 6.

In fact, Kopkamtib was not a new entity with its own staff structure and troops. Rather, the appointment provided Suharto with authority beyond the scope of his position as commander of Kostrad, effectively allowing him to circumvent the normal chain of command within the army and to draw on (and discipline) personnel in the army's vast territorial structure. On the evening of his appointment, Suharto issued an instruction to "cleanse" the army of all elements "directly or indirectly involved in" or "sympathetic to" the September 30th Movement.[14] The vague wording created extraordinary discretionary powers.

## 25. Mass Arrests, Interrogation, and Torture

The mass arrest of those suspected of involvement in the September 30th Movement began almost immediately after the movement's collapse on the evening of October 1. Among the first to be detained were soldiers and officers of the military units that had backed the movement. Army authorities also targeted members of the PKI-affiliated youth organization, Pemuda Rakyat, and its women's organization, Gerwani, both of which Suharto had named as culprits in his remarks at Lubang Buaya on October 4. The formation of Kopkamtib on October 10 signaled the start of an even

Figure 92. Members of the PKI-affiliated People's Youth (Pemuda Rakyat), under guard in an army truck, Jakarta, October 1965. (Bettman-Corbis Collection/Getty)

Figure 93. Detainees being transported under heavy military guard in Jakarta, October 10, 1965. Their uniforms suggest they may have belonged to one of the military units that supported the September 30th Movement. (Getty)

Figure 94. A Pemuda Rakyat member jumps from the back of a truck to enter a detention facility, Jakarta, October 30, 1965.

more widespread campaign of mass detention and interrogation.

Arrests were typically carried out by army and police units with assistance from members of anti-Communist political parties and mass organizations such as Ansor, Banser, Pemuda Katolik, Pemuda Marhaenis, and Pemuda Pancasila. Reports from across the country celebrated the close cooperation between "the people" and the armed forces in arresting and "exterminating" supporters of the September 30th Movement. Apart from high-ranking PKI leaders, some of whom subsequently were executed in custody, those detained included farmers, plantation workers, day laborers, teachers, civil servants, artists, and students.

Detainees were initially taken for interrogation at army and police installations, where they were classified according to their alleged degree of involvement in the September 30th Movement. Category A detainees were those alleged to have been "directly involved" in the movement, either because they took part in its planning and execution or because they knew of the plan but did nothing to stop it. Category B prisoners were those deemed to have been "indirectly involved" in the movement. In practice, this category was used for leading leftist figures for whom there was no evidence of actual involvement. As the attorney general explained, "Then there are the Category B prisoners. We know for certain they are traitors . . . but there is not enough evidence to bring them to court." Finally, Category C was for those "who may reasonably be assumed to have been directly or indirectly involved."[15] This category covered hundreds of thousands of ordinary members of the PKI and its mass organizations who had no knowledge of the movement and had committed no crime.

Detainees were routinely subjected to harsh treatment and torture. Common forms of torture included burning with cigarettes, electrocution, sexual assault or rape, and beating with lengths of wood, iron bars, and even the sharp, serrated tails of stingray fish. Information obtained under torture was used to track down still more suspects, while confessions were used in the army's propaganda offensive and in subsequent political show trials.

## 26. Untung Captured

During the night of October 1–2, as it became clear that Suharto was gaining the upper hand against the September 30th Movement in Jakarta, PKI chairman Aidit and Air Force Commander Omar Dhani flew from Jakarta to Yogyakarta. The army elite viewed their flight as proof of their complicity in the movement and made it a top priority to arrest the alleged ringleaders. Among the first to be captured were Colonel Latief of the Jakarta garrison and Lieutenant Colonel Untung.

On October 12, the military daily *Berita Yudha* ran photographs of Latief, who had been arrested three days earlier, and Untung, who (it reported incorrectly) was still being sought. In fact, Untung had been arrested on October 11. He had traveled from Cikampek, a key junction to the east of Jakarta, to Tegal, on the north coast of Central Java, when the bus on which he was traveling was stopped at a checkpoint and he was arrested.

Army accounts of the arrest were contradictory, with some claiming it was made by paracommandos and others asserting that members of the civil defense force were the heroes. The army also tried to disguise the fact that Untung had been beaten during his arrest. To account for his obvious black eye, one military publication concocted a story that while trying to escape, Untung had run into a telephone pole. Untung was also beaten while under interrogation,

Figure 95. Lieutenant Colonel Untung after his arrest, ca. October 12, 1965. The caption accompanying the photograph in a military history book explains that Untung, wearing a white shirt and black fez-style cap, has a black eye from running into a telephone pole. (*Sejarah Pengabdian Corps Polisi Militer Angkatan Darat, 1945–1978*)

appearing in an official photo with a badly swollen right hand. His coerced confession was used by the army as evidence that the September 30th Movement was masterminded by the PKI and as a means to pressure Sukarno into condemning and outlawing the party.

## 27. Attacks on PKI Property

The massive anti-Communist rally on October 8 was followed by attacks on the homes of PKI leaders in Jakarta. The attackers smashed windows and furniture, threw decorations and kitchenware into the street, and rummaged through books and papers. At Aidit's house, they claimed to have found "luxury goods" and 1 billion rupiah.[16] In the home of the PKI Politburo member Njoto, they

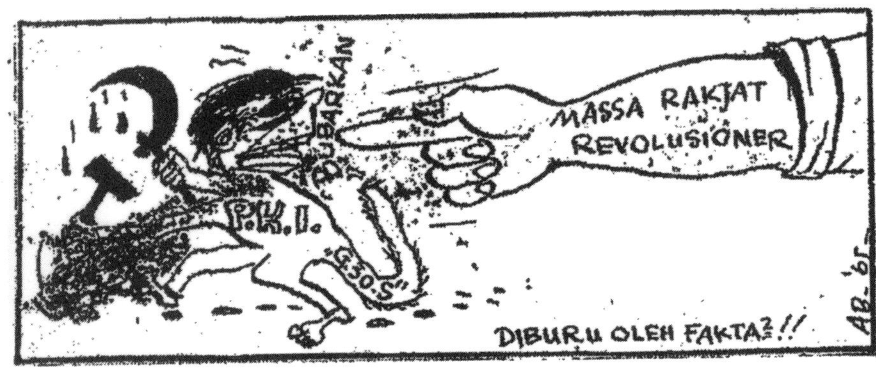


Figure 96. "Chased by the facts." Army cartoon depicting the revolutionary masses demanding that the PKI, whose long tail was the September 30th Movement, be banned. (*Angkatan Bersendjata*)

Figure 97. Demonstrators with banner reading, "Hang Aidit and his cronies, the puppet master of the September 30th Movement." (National Library of Indonesia)

Figure 98. Ransacked home of PKI Politburo member Njoto. A painting of fishing boats, a can of white oats, and documents are scattered on the ground. The graffiti at the top left reads, "Property of the armed forces." (Carol Goldstein/Keystone)

Figure 99. Man painting "Hang Njoto" while armed soldiers look on, October 1965. (Beryl Bernay)

Figure 100. Destroyed house in the Manggarai neighborhood of Jakarta, next door to the PKI-affiliated People's Cultural Institute (LEKRA) performance hall, October 13, 1965. (National Library of Indonesia)

claimed to have found the bloodstained uniform of General Nasution's personal aide, Captain Pierre Tendean, who was mistaken for the general and killed on the morning of October 1.

Journalists arrived to photograph the scenes of these attacks, including newly scrawled graffiti declaring that the properties now belonged to the armed forces. The military newspapers reported on these actions, declaring that the evidence recovered by youth groups proved the connection between the PKI and the September 30th Movement.

Over the next week, anti-Communist youths laid siege to additional properties belonging to the PKI and its affiliates. The headquarters of Gerwani, located close to PKI headquarters, was ransacked on October 11. Two days later, the top training school for PKI cadres, the Aliarcham Institute, located on the same street where Sukarno had declared independence in 1945, was attacked and looted. An exhibition hall near Manggarai Station, where the People's Cultural Institute (Lembaga Kebudayaan Rakyat, or LEKRA) had often held performances and exhibitions, was also ransacked.

Reported in the press, these actions in Jakarta set an example that was quickly copied by anti-Communist groups in many provincial capitals and district seats across Indonesia. Attacks on property were a prelude to direct violence against the bewildered members of the PKI and other leftist organizations.

## 28. Looting

The anti-Communist mobs in Jakarta and other cities were not simply out to press for the destruction of the PKI; they were also searching for incriminating evidence and intent on seizing trophies. A US embassy telegram on October 11 reported, "Headquarters of PKI youth arm Pemuda Rakjat, Communist labor

Figure 101. Attack on leftist bookstore in Jakarta, October 14, 1965. (Carol Goldstein/Keystone)

Figure 102. Men removing portraits of Dutch governors general from a colonial building, December 1949. (Henri Cartier-Bresson)

Figure 103. Looters with portraits of Sukarno, Jakarta, October 14, 1965. (Carol Goldstein/Keystone)

federation SOBSI, SOBSI civil servants affiliate SEPDA and PKI branch office in Djakarta suburb overrun by demonstrators October 10. Furniture smashed, windows broken, documents seized, cars overturned and interior of SOBSI and SEPDA buildings appeared to Emb[assy] Off[icer] to have been burned. On morning of October 11 Emb[assy] Off[icer] witnessed burning of main PKI bookstore which also houses PKI parliamentary representation's offices."[17] The journalist Carol Goldstein was present at the attack on the PKI bookstore, where she photographed youths hurling stones, and at a government office where youths posed with portraits they had seized of Sukarno. This image is eerily reminiscent of Henri Cartier-Bresson's photographs of men removing three hundred portraits of Dutch governors general from the governor's office in Jakarta the day before Indonesian independence was achieved in December 1949. In both cases, capturing portraits symbolized the capture of state power.

Similar reports came in from other

cities in Indonesia. The US consulate in Medan reported, “Moderate youth groups are systematically raiding, burning and wrecking communist head-quarters, bookstores, newspapers and homes [of] top party officials. Number of communists reportedly wounded and some killed in attacks.”[18]

## 29. Attack on Res Publica University

The army's propaganda was a multi-pronged effort. Alongside the central claim that the PKI had masterminded the September 30th Movement, army-controlled media promoted a complementary theory, never proven, about the involvement of China. This account began with reports that China had shipped one hundred thousand small arms to aid the PKI's seizure of power. Chinese treachery, in turn, was used to implicate the Indonesian Chinese community and especially its peak association, the Deliberative Association for Indonesian Citizenship (Badan Permusyawaratan Kewargane-garaan Indonesia, or Baperki), which had established Res Publica University campuses in Jakarta, Medan, Semarang, and Yogyakarta and increasingly backed Sukarno and his anti-imperialist agenda.

On October 15, anti-Communist demonstrators attacked Res Publica University in Jakarta. The following day, Indonesian troops and demonstrators entered and ransacked the office of the

Figure 104. Attack on Res Publica University, Jakarta, October 15, 1965.

Figure 105. An ethnic Chinese man protects himself from armed youths near Res Publica University, October 15, 1965. (Bettman-Corbis Collection/Getty)

Figure 106. Graffiti in Jakarta, mid-October 1965, attacking the PKI and accusing the ethnic Chinese Deliberative Association for Indonesian Citizenship (Baperki) of financing the party. (Beryl Bernay)

Chinese commercial consul. The Chinese Hsinhua news agency and Radio Peking protested these attacks, but their protests served only to stoke anti-Chinese sentiment. Soon KAP-Gestapu leaders and national newspapers demanded that Indonesia sever diplomatic relations with China.

## 30. Suharto Appointed Army Chief of Staff

Suharto's appointment on October 10 to head the newly established Kopkamtib was only the first part of the behind-the-scenes struggle between himself and President Sukarno. Pressing his case, the following day Suharto allegedly sent a taped confession by Colonel Latief to the president that implicated Sukarno in the September 30th Movement. There is little evidence that Sukarno was in fact involved, and less still that Latief had made such a confession. What is clear is that Suharto was doing everything in his power to force the president's hand.

As a result of this maneuvering, in a hastily assembled press conference on the evening of October 14, the president

Figure 107. President Sukarno announcing the appointment of Suharto as army chief of staff, October 14, 1965. (Keystone)

announced that he was appointing Suharto to command the army. The photojournalist Beryl Bernay, who had gotten to know the president quite well and attended the press conference, told the embassy that "this announcement was like taking medicine for Sukarno. She said he was unable to disguise the fact that he was angry about it." Subandrio, she commented, looked "scared."[19]

Two days later, on October 16, Sukarno formally installed Suharto as army chief of staff. In the chaotic two-week period after Untung's doomed movement, Suharto had not only crushed the conspirators and encouraged virulent calls for retaliation against the PKI but had also wrested sweeping authority from Sukarno through the establishment of Kopkamtib and had secured command of the army.

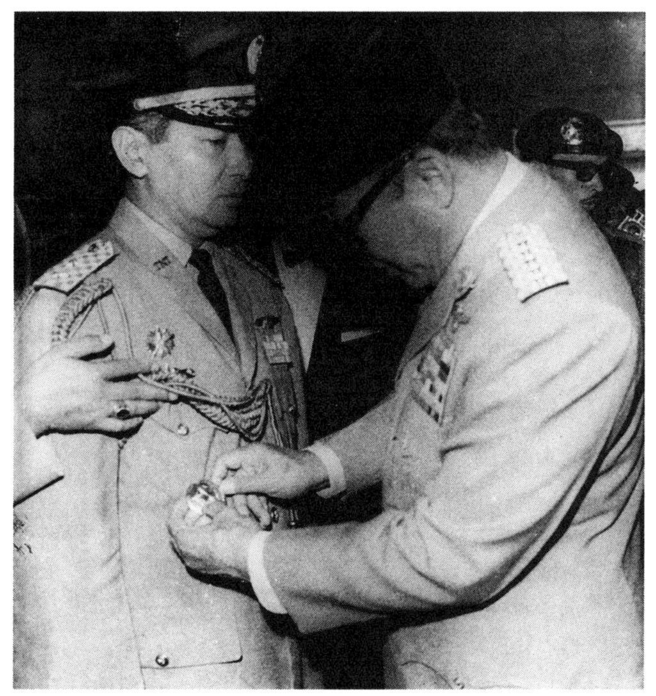

Figure 108. President Sukarno installs Major General Suharto as army chief of staff, October 16, 1965. (National Library of Indonesia)

# III. Onslaught

## 31. Army Paracommandos to Central Java

Jakarta was the primary focus of the September 30th Movement, but co-conspirators also took action in Central Java on the morning of October 1. Middle-ranking officers in the provincial capital, Semarang, staged a local coup, seizing army headquarters, while colleagues acted against subregional commanders in the cities of Yogyakarta and Purwokerto. Over the next three days, Diponegoro (Central Java) regional military commander Brigadier General Suryosumpeno rallied loyalist troops and reestablished control, but the pro–September 30th Movement leaders eluded capture and remained on the loose.

Figure 110. Colonel Sarwo Edhie, commander of the RPKAD. (Beryl Bernay)

The situation in Central Java was complicated by several factors. The PKI was the dominant party in the province, with millions of supporters in the leftist unions and the Indonesian Peasants' Front (BTI). Of equal concern to Suharto and army leaders, on the morning of October 2, PKI chairman Aidit had fled Jakarta on an air force plane and flown to the city of Yogyakarta. Finally, army leadership worried about its own strength in the province. For more than a year, the army had expressed concern that its ability to counter the PKI was compromised because many of the best units in Central Java were posted in Sumatra and Kalimantan to serve in the Confrontation campaign against Malaysia. Moreover, the loyalties of the remaining battalions were divided, with some estimates suggesting that up to one-third of all troops were pro-PKI.

With these considerations in mind, one day after being installed as the new army chief of staff, Suharto ordered RPKAD commander Colonel Sarwo Edhie to spearhead the army's efforts against the September 30th Movement mutineers and the PKI in Central Java. To this end, Edhie sent three companies of his own men, a cavalry company, and a military police company overland from Jakarta to Semarang. On October 19, Edhie joined his forces in the city of Semarang, where he oversaw a show of force that

Figure 111. Soldiers conducting a house-to-house search in Surakarta, October 1965. (Sutarto/Antara)

included attacks on property in the city's Chinatown and mass detentions. He then ordered the troops to move southward through Magelang to Yogyakarta and finally on to the city of Surakarta, which was the epicenter of PKI strength.

Citing an army source, the US embassy reported that when the RPKAD convoy was approaching the city of Surakarta on October 22, it was "blocked in village at outskirts by nine 'witches' from PKI women's affiliate Gerwani, who insulted them and refused to let them pass. After asking them quietly to give way, and firing into air, para-commandos were 'forced by their intransigence to terminate breathing of these nine Gerwani witches.'"[1]

## 32. Military Operations in Surakarta

RPKAD troops entered the city of Surakarta unopposed on October 22, but the situation there and in the surrounding region was highly uncertain. Over the previous weeks, wild reports and rumors (some perhaps started by the military itself) circulated that the PKI and its affiliates were preparing for guerrilla warfare by felling trees to block roads, and even that the PKI had carried out killings of its enemies. The reality was that most people—Communists and non-Communists alike—knew little about what had actually happened in Jakarta and had no idea why the RPKAD

had been sent to Central Java or what their orders were.

After arriving in Surakarta, RPKAD troops stormed through the city streets and narrow alleyways searching for Communists. Their top priority was to find and detain the city's mayor, Utomo Ramelan, who was a PKI supporter and head of the Surakarta branch of the National Front. On October 1, Ramelan reportedly issued a statement supporting the September 30th Movement, and the following day he met with Aidit, who had fled by plane to Yogyakarta and allegedly continued on to Surakarta. On the afternoon of October 22, Ramelan was arrested and his office secured; it was subsequently used as a detention center. RPKAD troops also seized pro-PKI signs and flyers and, as was the case in Jakarta, Semarang, and other cities, instigated the looting of Chinese-owned shops in the city center.

Edhie established his operational headquarters at the RPKAD Battalion III

Figures 112 and 113. Men in Surakarta reading a poster calling for people to support the September 30th Movement, and soldiers removing the same poster. That the photographer was present to capture both scenes suggests that the event was staged by the army for propaganda purposes. (Sutarto/Antara)

Figure 114. A man setting fire to a giant PKI logo and a sign from the Djajengan neighborhood branch of Pemuda Rakyat in Surakarta. In the background, a soldier stands in front of a crowd of dutifully attentive women and children. (Sutarto/Antara)

base in Kartasura, ten kilometers west of Surakarta at the strategic junction of roads leading north to the provincial capital of Semarang and southwest to the city of Yogyakarta. To facilitate RPKAD operations, on October 26 Governor Suryosumpeno declared a "state of war" in the provinces of Central Java and Yogyakarta. Edhie, in turn, announced the creation of a new Surakarta Joint Security Staff, effectively usurping the normal chain of command from the Diponegoro regional commander. He estimated that before October 1, 75 percent of the population in the Surakarta-Yogyakarta region was pro-Communist. Through a combination of mobilizing militias from the "nationalist" and "religious" groups, intensive propaganda, and direct military operations, he aimed to tip the scales in the other direction. Mass killings were to be the primary instrument for that reversal.

In mid-November, Suharto made an unannounced visit to Central Java to meet with Edhie and assess the situation. Shortly after Suharto's visit, Edhie flew to Jakarta to provide a further update, presumably with the ongoing search for Aidit high on the agenda. A day later, US ambassador Green reported in a diplomatic telegram that "General Suharto has ordered military commander[s] in East and Central Java to shoot without further investigation PKI members not involved in [the] September 30 Movement and to hold for interrogation those involved."[2] This was by no means a new policy; it was an acknowledgment of what the RPKAD and its allies had been doing since the day of Edhie's arrival.

Figure 115. Local security officials speak to a youth militia group in Grobogan, Central Java, while army personnel look on. (National Library of Indonesia)

## 33. Mobilizing Militias

Civilian militias, trained and led by the army, played a crucial role in the campaign to crush the PKI. The militias comprised two basic groups: local units of the national civil defense network (Pertahanan Sipil, or Hansip) and a variety of youth organizations affiliated with the anti-Communist political parties.

Hansip units had been formed in virtually every village in the country before 1965, and they had received basic military training in the context of the Crush Malaysia campaign. In theory, they were a ready source of manpower for the army after October 1. The catch was that some were not reliably anti-Communist. To address that problem, the army began by purging their ranks of "September 30 elements" before arming and mobilizing the "cleansed" units. In early November, for example, the Hansip staff headquarters in Boyolali, Klaten, and Cilacap Regencies—all PKI strongholds in Central Java—were placed under the direct control of local military commanders. In North Sumatra, twenty thousand members of the province's Hansip network were "cleansed" and then armed.

Equally important to the campaign of violence were the anti-Communist youth groups. The largest and best-known of these were the PNI's Pemuda Marhaenis (also known as Tameng Marhaenis), NU's Ansor and Banser, the Catholic Party's Pemuda Katolik, and IPKI's Pemuda Pancasila. In addition to these groups, which had existed before 1965, some anti-Communist militia units were formed with the army's blessing immediately after the alleged coup. In Aceh, for example, the Pancasila Defenders' Front (Front Pembela Pancasila) and the People's Defenders (Pembela Rakyat) were set up in the first two weeks of October.

Figure 116. A drum band made up of members of Ansor, an NU-affiliated militia group, puts on a display of force in Java. (Idayu collection)

With tens of thousands of members residing in neighborhoods and villages across the country, and with a history of bitter conflict with the PKI and its affiliates, these groups were easily mobilized into a vast anti-Communist auxiliary force.

The army's use of civilians in this way was no secret. As Colonel Edhie told a local journalist at the time, "We decided to encourage the anti-communist civilians to help with the job. In Solo [Surakarta] we gathered together the youth, the nationalist groups, the religious organizations. We gave them two or three days' training and sent them out to kill communists."[3] The deadly consequences

Figure 117. Members of a local militia on the slopes of Mount Merapi, Central Java, late 1965. Members carry sharpened bamboo poles, daggers, spears, and axes. (Bettman-Corbis Collection/Getty)

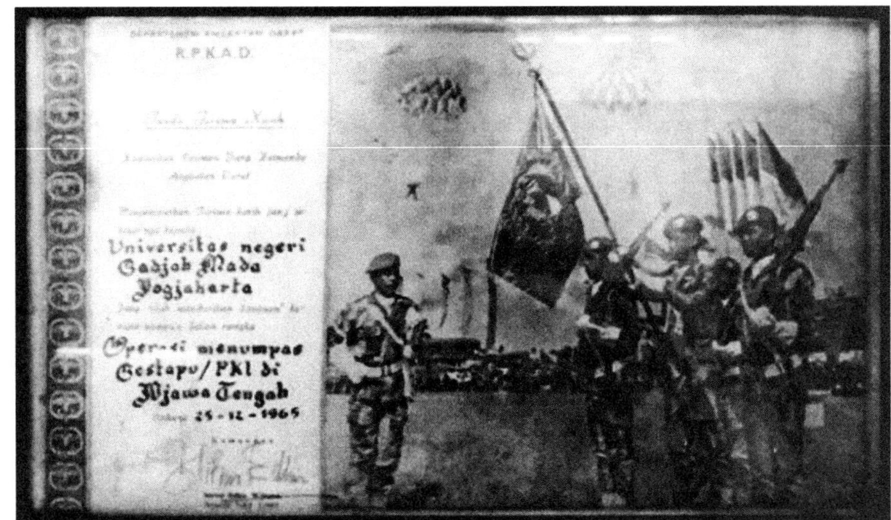


Figure 118. Certificate presented by the RPKAD to Gajah Mada University, Yogyakarta, for its support of the campaign against the PKI. (Abdul Wahid)

of the army's strategy were soon apparent. In November, Ambassador Green reported that "from 50 to 100 PKI are being killed every night in East and Central Java by civilian anti-Communist groups with blessing of the army."[4] Similar reports came from North Sumatra, Aceh, Bali, and elsewhere.

SLEMAN

SURAT TANDA TERIMA KASIH

Bupati Kepala Daerah Kabupaten Sleman atas nama PEPEKUPER Kabupaten Sleman mengutjapkan TERIMA KASIH kepada :

Nama : Surosarsjono.

Alamat : Gamblong V. Kal. Sumberrahayu Kec. Moyudan.

Daftar No. : 0418.

atas keselaannja memberikan pindjaman modal berupa uang dengan djangka waktu satu tahun tanpa bunga kepada Pemerintah Daerah Kabupaten Sleman dalam usahanja mengkikis habis sisa-sisa G.30.S./P.K.I. di Daerah Kabupaten Sleman.

Dibuat di : SLEMAN
Pada tanggal : SEPTEMBER 1969

BUPATI
KEPALA DAERAH KABUPATEN
SLEMAN

(K.R.T. MOERDODININGRAT)

Figure 119. Certificate of appreciation from the district head of Sleman, Yogyakarta, to an individual who provided a loan to support the campaign against the PKI. (Wikimedia Commons)

Armed with sickles, knives, machetes, hatchets, sharpened bamboo poles, and firearms, the militias worked closely with the army in detaining, transporting, and killing alleged Communists. In virtually every case, the violence began shortly after a military officer, or other state officials, arrived in a village and exhorted the population to join in crushing the PKI. The army also provided vital logistical support for these operations, which were organized and systematic. Once they were set in motion, however, the killings took decidedly brutal forms. A former militia leader from North Sumatra described the ways in which he and his men killed detainees and the impunity with which they did it: "We shoved wood in their anuses until they died. . . . We crushed their necks with wood. We hung them. We strangled them with wire. We cut off their heads. We ran them over with our cars. We were allowed to do it. And the proof is, we murdered people and we were never punished."[5]

Figure 120. Villagers rounded up by the military sit in a field, watched by militia members. It was common for the military to separate male and female detainees. (National Library of Indonesia)

## 34. Mass Arrests and Killings in Central Java

Between mid-October and the end of 1965, the army and its militia allies mounted intensive operations to "annihilate" the PKI in Central Java, arresting and killing members of the PKI and its affiliates. By the end of December, tens of thousands of real and alleged Communists had been detained—the vast majority of them poor peasants—and an estimated 140,000 others had been killed. Typically, local militias led army forces to the villages and houses of known or suspected Communists. Those who resisted, men and women, were beaten or killed on the spot. If they were not killed outright, detainees were loaded onto trucks and transported to one of dozens of places of detention for interrogation and processing. The number of detainees grew so quickly that regular prisons and jails were soon overflowing, and detainees were held instead in military encampments, at schools and government offices, and in private buildings and warehouses seized by the army. Detention was often a prelude to execution. Detainees were routinely taken from prisons and jails to killing sites—their bodies disposed of in rivers, plantations, caves, irrigation ditches, or holes dug by the prisoners themselves.

Spearheaded by the RPKAD, these operations initially focused on areas of known PKI strength in the vicinity of Boyolali, Klaten, and Surakarta. Very few photographs survive from these operations, but those that do paint a chilling portrait. One, published in Singapore's *Straits Times* on November 16, 1965, shows scores, perhaps hundreds, of detainees seated in a field, surrounded by what appear to be militia members armed with bamboo spears. Another, published in the *Washington Post* on November 15, 1965, shows several detainees lying on the ground next to a large trench, guarded by army paracommandos and men in civilian clothing. A third photo, published in *The Hindu*, and very likely from the same time and place,

Figure 121. Official army photo of detainees in a teak forest, Central Java. (Kopkamtib, *Gerakan 30 September Partai Komunis Indonesia*)

Figure 122. Detainees in a ditch guarded by soldiers, Central Java, November 1965. (United Press International)

shows two dozen men squatting in a long trench while armed soldiers stand at the ready.

These photographs highlight an unusual aspect of the operations in Central Java—namely, that on occasion foreign journalists were permitted to observe and document them, up to a point. Among those who accompanied army troops in late October and early November were the *Los Angeles Times* correspondent Arthur Dommen, the Canadian Don North, the Australian Frank Palmos, and B. K. Tiwari of the *Indian Express*. The army's goal in inviting these journalists to witness its campaign was no doubt to ensure that they told the story from the army's perspective. That goal may explain why none of the photographs they published show corpses or acts of killing.

In early December, army operations pushed up the slopes of Mount Merapi, a massive cone-shaped volcano of almost ten thousand feet, where key PKI leaders were thought to have taken refuge. A handful of photographs held in the Indonesian National Library, probably

Figure 123. The same scene as figure 122, but with men lying face down next to the ditch. A slightly different version of this photo is printed in a military volume with a caption noting that the detainees were waiting to be interrogated. (*Lukisan pemberontakan PKI di Indonesia dan penumpasannya*)

taken by an army photographer, offer a partial glimpse of what happened during those operations. In one, a group of six men, barefoot and with hands clasped behind their necks, is marched away in single file, while a dozen children look on from the village gate. Leading the way is a stern-faced militiaman carrying a sharpened bamboo pole, and following are two soldiers. In another, a woman cowers in the shadow of three grim-faced soldiers. A third is a close-up of an older man—identified in the caption only as a "BTI leader"—his shirt soaked with

Figure 124. Detained villagers walking under guard, Mount Merapi, Central Java, late 1965. (National Library of Indonesia)

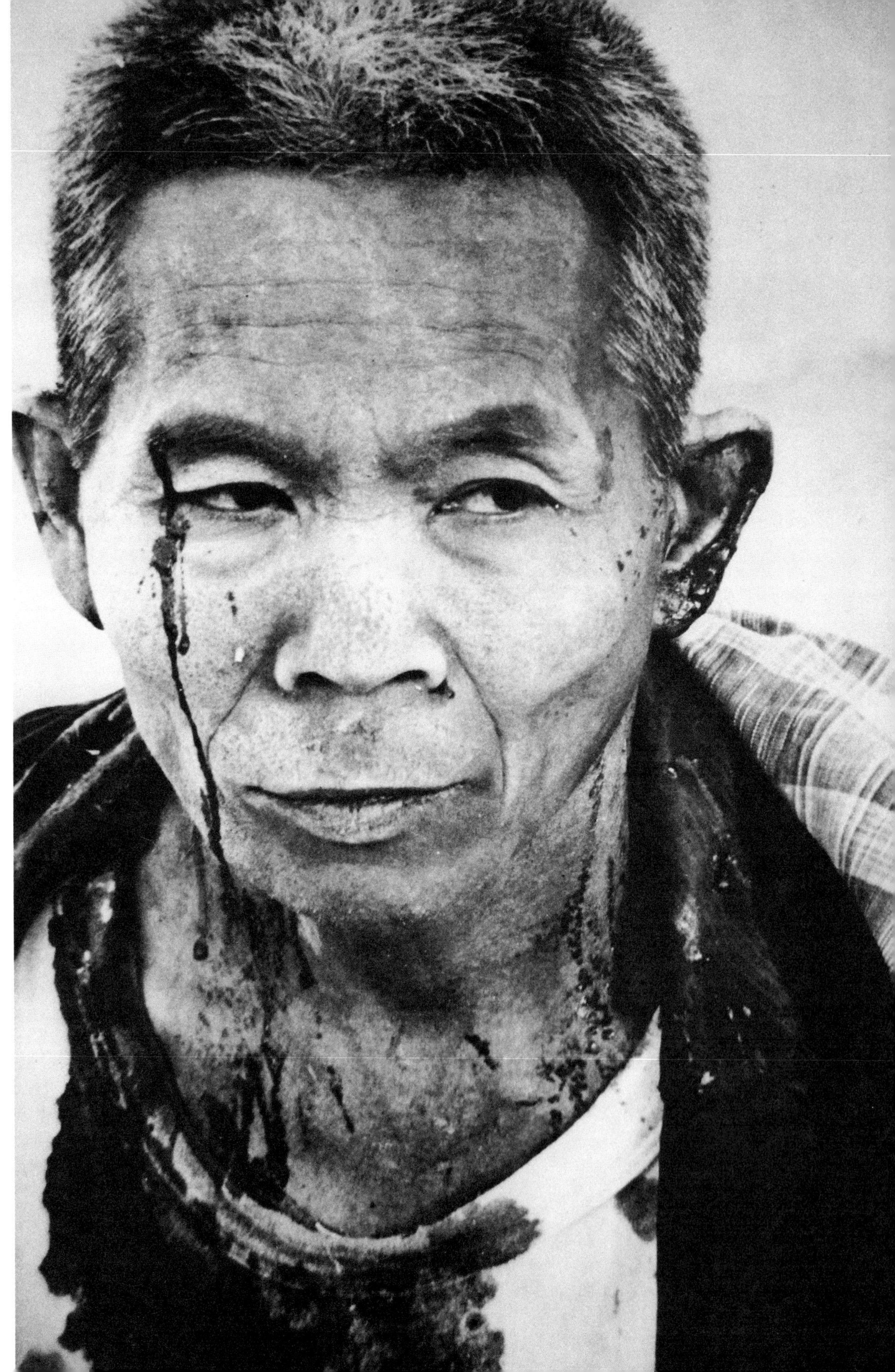

blood and with a wound above his right eye. Once again, no doubt because they were taken under army supervision, the photographs do not depict any corpses or acts of killing.

## 35. Photographers Moelyono and Djoko Pekik

Army authorities understood the value of photography as a tool in shaping public perceptions, and from the outset they used it strategically in their propaganda campaign against the PKI. One of the photographers who worked with the army in Central Java was Moelyono, a photojournalist with the Yogyakarta newspaper *Kedaulatan Rakjat*. Sometime in October 1965, Moelyono was invited to accompany the army as it began its campaign against the PKI. Riding with an army unit and donning a soldier's uniform, he documented the army's anti-Communist operations in the vicinity of Klaten, a reputed PKI stronghold not far from Yogyakarta.

In interviews with the anthropologist Karen Strassler many years later, Moelyono described the constraints under which he carried out this work. Military authorities determined what he could photograph and which images could later be published. He was told, for example, that he must not take photographs of someone being killed, or other "sadistic events." And while he was permitted to photograph corpses, he could not show their faces. One of his photographs from this time depicts the tangled corpses of two young boys, both alleged members of the Communist party affiliate Pemuda Rakyat whose killing Moelyono had witnessed. In the photo, the faces of the boys are not visible; as Moelyono later explained, they were deliberately arranged in that way before he took the photograph. It is also striking that, though they were shot, no blood is visible.[6]

Images of corpses were an exception, both in Moelyono's work and in virtually all official photos of the period.

Figure 126. Moelyono, a photojournalist who accompanied the army on its campaign against the PKI in Central Java. (Moelyono)

*opposite*
Figure 125. Bloodied member of the Indonesian Peasants' Front (BTI), Mount Merapi, Central Java, late 1965. (National Library of Indonesia)

Figure 127. Detainees with armed guards in Klaten, Central Java, late 1965. (Moelyono)

Much more common were photographs of hapless detainees, usually guarded by well-armed soldiers or police. Such images seem to have been deliberately staged to show that the authorities had firm, but calm, control of the situation. According to Moelyono, soldiers often struck a "pose" as he prepared to take such pictures.[7]

If some photographers, and their photos, were used by the army to create a reassuring, and essentially bloodless, portrait of the campaign to annihilate Communists, others fell victim to that campaign. One of those was a prominent young painter and photographer in the leftist People's Cultural Institute (LEKRA) named Djoko Pekik. A few weeks after the abortive September 30th Movement, Pekik fled to Yogyakarta, where he found work taking photographs for people in need of them for the newly required identity cards verifying "clean" backgrounds. Pekik was arrested in November 1965 and held without trial for seven years. The authorities confiscated all of his possessions, including a large collection of photographs he had taken documenting mass demonstrations in 1965. "The police took it all," he later recalled. "I was left with a pair of pants and one shirt, for seven years. Everything was taken, all my film and photos, and I had a lot of documentation. My photos of the demonstrations of that time are all lost."[8] By imprisoning leftist photographers and destroying their work, the authorities ensured that only those images whose production and dissemination they controlled would enter the public realm.

*opposite*
Figure 128. The corpses of two alleged Communists, Central Java, late 1965. Before Moelyono was allowed to take this picture, military personnel told him that the bodies had to be turned over so that their faces did not show. (Moelyono)

## 36. Aidit's Capture and Execution

In late November, PKI chairman Aidit was captured and killed just outside the city of Surakarta. Before his execution, he allegedly signed a lengthy written confession, admitting his and the PKI's leading role in the September 30th Movement and outlining his plans for an armed uprising. Despite the singular importance of these events, no reliable documentary evidence of them has been found. Still, available accounts—including one by Moelyono and another by the army itself—strongly suggest that Aidit's execution was ordered by the highest authorities, carried out by a high-ranking army officer, and subsequently covered up. Those accounts also tell us something about the curious history of the grainy photographs that are the only record of Aidit's capture and execution.

After flying from Jakarta to Central Java on October 2, Aidit reportedly moved from place to place for several weeks to avoid capture. Acting on orders from Suharto to "deal with" Aidit, Colonel Yasir Hadibroto (commander of the Kostrad Fourth Infantry Brigade) mounted an operation to capture him. On November 22, a task force commanded by Yasir discovered Aidit in a small house in Sambeng, on the outskirts of Surakarta. He had apparently been hiding in a room concealed from

Figure 129. Aidit in white with his army captors in Central Java, November 1965. (Soebekti, *Hari-hari terakhir Aidit*)

Figure 130. Aidit blindfolded just before execution. This was one of six photographs sent anonymously to the UK-based human rights organization TAPOL in 1979. The organization was founded and led by Carmel Budiardjo, who had been jailed for three years after 1965 and whose husband was imprisoned for more than ten years. (*TAPOL Bulletin*)

view by a tall cabinet. The moment of his arrest is captured in a photograph in which Aidit, dressed all in white, poses with his army captors.

By his own account, that photograph was taken by Moelyono. One source has suggested that the negative of the photo "disappeared" after being taken for processing by a military police major. Moelyono, however, insists that he developed the photograph himself and returned both the negative and the print to the army while keeping a copy for himself. A few months later, he gave that print to a Japanese journalist in exchange for a high-quality camera. The photograph was published in the major Japanese daily *Asahi Shimbun*. Moelyono's army superiors were not happy.

From the place of his capture in Sambeng, Aidit was taken to the residence of the mayor of Surakarta, a stately colonial home that had been commandeered by the RPKAD. There, he was forced to sign a confession written by one of his captors. He was photographed again, this time seated at a table, pen in hand. Another photograph shows a blindfolded Aidit being escorted by a soldier.

Shortly after these photographs were taken, Aidit was driven to a remote location northwest of the city, summarily executed, and dumped down an unused well. His executioner was none other than Yasir. An official army history published in 1982 described the execution as follows: "After the interrogation, and after Aidit had signed his confession, Col. Yasir Hadibroto took him out of the city by jeep. They turned off the main road at Boyolali and came to a dry well in the middle of a banana grove. There Aidit was shot dead. His body was thrown into the well and covered with banana tree trunks."[9]

Two days after Aidit's killing, Suharto flew to Central Java to receive a full report about the operation from Yasir. On his return to Jakarta, Suharto personally informed Sukarno, bearing a photograph as evidence that Aidit was indeed dead. Citing an internal army report and interviews with key officers, in early 1966 a Japanese journalist wrote, "Major General Suharto showed up at the Istana Merdeka [the president's residence] in Jakarta and handed over a photograph of Aidit's corpse to President Sukarno. Without a doubt, the president was deeply overwhelmed with emotion."[10]

Curiously, even after Suharto's visit, the army was not yet ready to make a public announcement that Aidit had been found and executed. On November 25, the military daily *Angkatan Bersendjata* ran reports that Aidit "would soon be captured."[11] Three days later, *Berita Yudha* reported that civilians had "taken out" Aidit.[12] These stories were clearly untrue. At a meeting with US embassy officials on November 26, General Nasution's wife confirmed that Aidit had already been killed. "Aidit is dead," she told them. "Our boys shot him in Central Java."[13] Why would the army try to obscure the capture and death of so central a figure as the PKI chairman? One possibility, suggested by a US embassy source at the time, is that it was deliberate misdirection intended to keep the news from Sukarno. Another possibility is that, by obscuring the circumstances of his death and the place of his burial, the army hoped to ensure that Aidit would not become a martyr.

Figure 131. "Progressive-revolutionary masses" "curse" the September 30th Movement. (*Api Pantjasila*)

## 37. Language and Violence

Anti-Communist propaganda in the aftermath of the alleged coup attempt used extremely violent language. In many instances, the rhetoric of Guided Democracy was turned inward—Crush Malaysia (Ganjang Malaysia) became Crush the PKI (Ganjang PKI), and safeguarding the revolution from the threat of imperialism became safeguarding the revolution against the threat of Communism.

Even while unleashing the wholesale slaughter of leftists, it would take time for the army to break from the language of the Left that had dominated national politics since the onset of Guided Democracy. For example, on October 27, 1965, Suharto handwrote a memo that highlights just how persistent that language was. In it, he declared that the continuing Indonesian Revolution was leftist, socialist, and anti-imperialist. Describing an attack on the Left to be part of a leftist "revolution" was nonsensical, of course, but it was an important element of the army's strategy for securing political power.

REVOLUSI INDONESIA

- REVOLUSI KIRI :
- REVOLUSI SOSIALISTIS
- REVOLUSI ANTI
  - IMPERIALIS.
  - KAPITALIS.
  - FEODALIS.
  - RASIALISME
- REVOLUSI SOSIALIS PANTJASILA = KIRI RELIGIUS.

Figure 132. Suharto memo of October 27, 1965, declaring that the Indonesian Revolution was and is leftist. (*Angkatan Bersendjata*)

### The Indonesian Revolution

- A leftist revolution
- A socialist revolution
- A revolution against
  - o Imperialists
  - o Capitalists
  - o Feudalists
  - o Racialism
- A Pancasila socialist revolution = Left religious

Harto [Soeharto]

Figure 133. Cartoon in an anti-Communist newspaper with the heading "Same Methods" depicting the Indonesian Socialist Youth (Pesindo) and the PKI as the perpetrators of the Madiun uprising in 1948 and the Pemuda Rakyat and the PKI as the perpetrators of "Gestapu" in 1965. (*Api*)

***Maunja Memang Begini!***

Figure 134. Army cartoon with the caption "This is what's wanted!" depicting those who undermine the economy, Gestapu/PKI, and subversives as rats being hung, December 26, 1965. (*Angkatan Bersendjata*)

## 38. Documentation and Propaganda

With the declaration of a state of war, Colonel Edhie and his RPKAD oversaw operations in every village in the thirty-five thousand square miles of Central Java and Yogyakarta. Photographers from the military-owned newspapers were embedded with troops as they conducted operations and mobilized village militias. Musicians, including nationally known singers, were brought in to entertain troops and enliven mass rallies.

Military operations received a further boost from journalists working for local newspapers in Surakarta, Yogyakarta, and Semarang. Army units identified prominent leftist figures, and journalists peddled sensational accounts. The major newspaper in Yogyakarta ran stories, often including mug shots, about a September 30th Movement "general" from the village of Prambanan who was caught in hiding, about the arrest of a "revolutionary council" in Kulonprogo District, and about a university student in Yogyakarta who was arrested with a hand-stenciled document for a plot, dating back to 1963, for two million Communist youths to seize political power.

Sensational newspaper stories and provocative images, like the cartoon depicting bloodthirsty Communists committing massacres in Central and East Java, further fueled the mobilization of the "religious" and "nationalist" mass organizations and attendance at mass rallies. Religious sanction contributed as well. For example, the leader of the NU women's organization Muslimat, Mahmudah Mawardi, declared that "those who have died resisting and wiping out the counterrevolutionary 'September 30th Movement' are martyrs who will go directly to heaven."[14]

Figure 135. Cartoon in an anti-Communist newspaper, with caption "Calm won't be restored until the 'Gestapu-PKI' devils have been eradicated." (*Api*)

There was always a tension between documentation and staging, bravado and propaganda. A handful of national and local photojournalists were allowed to travel with the military and photograph troops on patrol along narrow country lanes, resting in camp, and posing with their weapons. They took portraits of grim-faced militia members with machetes and smiling youths brandishing bamboo spears. And they documented captured weapons, detained peasants, and the occasional corpse. But there are virtually no images of real gore, and certainly no photographs of torturers or executioners or mass graves. Nowhere in the media was there an implication that tens of thousands of people had been massacred in Central Java by the end of December 1965.

Figure 136. Youth posing with a long knife and headband with the words "Allah is great," in Yogyakarta. The back of the photograph is stamped December 10, 1965, but it may have been taken by foreign journalists during a tour by the governor in mid-November. (United Press International)

Figure 137. Severed head displayed with a gun, ammunition, and documents, Central Java, late 1965. (Sutarto/Antara)

Figure 138. A detainee arrives at a military base, Jakarta, November 1, 1965. (National Library of Indonesia)

## 39. The "Cleansing" Campaign in Jakarta

While the anti-Communist violence spread across Central Java, a less visible but no less important campaign unfolded within key civilian institutions in Jakarta. Following the army's lead, government officials began a crusade to "cleanse" the civil service, the universities, and the media of anyone suspected of having leftist sympathies. In effect, this was the start of a massive purge of leftists from some of the most important institutions in the country. Apart from irreparably weakening those institutions, it set the stage for the arrest and killing of many thousands of civil servants, teachers, university professors, students, and others.

The "cleansing" campaign took place against the backdrop of an escalating power struggle between Sukarno and the army leadership. Mistrustful of the army's intentions, Sukarno openly questioned its account of the generals' deaths and refused to use the army's inflammatory term "Gestapu." Genuinely alarmed by the mounting violence against the PKI and determined to protect a vital political ally, he defended the party and appealed repeatedly for calm while he formulated a "political solution." But by the middle of October, it was clear that his authority was slipping and that the army and its allies were ignoring his pleas. Then, on the occasion of Suharto's appointment as army chief of staff on October 16, Sukarno described the events of October 1 as "a ripple in the ocean of the Revolution," a remark that angered the army command and further weakened his standing.[15]

Reflecting the political uncertainty of the early days after the alleged coup, the "cleansing" campaign started cautiously.

Figure 139. Pemuda Rakyat members under armed guard, ca. October 30, 1965.

Figure 140. Armed soldiers entering a high school in Jakarta, while students in uniform gather in the yard, late 1965. (Beryl Bernay)

Government ministries began by issuing public statements declaring their sadness at the deaths of the generals and echoing Sukarno's calls for calm and unity. By mid-October, however, such cautious pronouncements gave way to increasingly strident calls to "freeze" leftist organizations, to assist the military in "restoring order," and to "cleanse" personnel who might have been involved in the September 30th Movement. Ministries now urged employees to "prove" their "loyalty to the revolution" by helping to "cleanse" their workplaces of "play actors and counterrevolutionary traitors."[16] And on October 21, the cabinet presidium issued an instruction to all ministers with control of vital industries to suspend any personnel suspected of ties to the movement and to immediately fire "without honor" those who were definitely involved.

The campaign was pursued with special vigor by the ministers responsible for education. On October 12, the minister of higher education, Brigadier General Syarief Thajeb, issued an order closing fourteen universities known for their leftist affiliations. Among those was Res Publica University, which was attacked and burned by an anti-Communist mob the same day. A few days later, Thajeb instructed all university leaders to "cleanse" their institutions of "anyone involved in the September 30th Movement" and specifically warned Res Publica students that they would be arrested if they were found to have any connection to the movement. Meanwhile, the minister of education and culture, Artati Marzuki, called for all department heads to "assist in cleansing their departments" of personnel involved with the movement and to "report in writing any personnel who had not come to work since September 30."[17]

The purge was formalized by General Nasution in a November 12 order. A few days later, a presidential instruction titled "Cleansing Civilian Personnel of September 30th Movement Elements" was issued. The classification system spelled out in that instruction later became the basis for the formal classification of long-term political prisoners.

## 40. Attacks on the Ethnic Chinese and Chinese Embassy

While the army was overseeing a campaign of terror against the PKI and other leftists in Central and East Java, anti-Communist groups in Jakarta continued to make China a political target. For Suharto, attacking China was a way to discredit Sukarno. For KAP-Gestapu and the student organization KAMI, the Chinese embassy provided a convenient target for mass mobilization, not least because of long-standing anti-Chinese sentiment directed at Indonesia's own Chinese minority.

What was true in Jakarta was also true in other major cities. In North Sumatra, where outright violence had been kept to a minimum throughout the month of October, a mass rally of one hundred thousand people was held on November 2. The US consulate in Medan reported, "The demonstrators then marched on the Chinese Consulate where they attempted to present a statement to the Chinese Consul. The Consul refused to receive them, however, and the statement was given to an aide. The

Figure 141. Attack on Baperki's Res Publica University in Jakarta, November 13, 1965. (Bettman-Corbis Collection/Getty)

Consulate was under heavy military guard, including two armored cars, and the security forces were clearly determined to keep the crowd under control. Nevertheless, they permitted the delegation to tear down the Chicom [Chinese Communist] flag and the Chicom Consular shield. The Indonesian flag was run up in place of the Chicom flag."[18]

Anti-Chinese activities intensified a week later when word leaked that Sukarno intended to revoke the "state of war" in Jakarta. Jakarta military commander Brigadier General Umar Wirahadikusumah hurriedly issued a ban on the ethnic Chinese organization Baperki, and an order was given for the arrest of its leader, Siauw Giok Tjhan. Military authorities in several provinces followed suit by banning Baperki and by stage-managing ceremonies at which local branches burned organizational paraphernalia and declared their loyalty to the state ideology, Pancasila, the first point of which is belief in one God. Army newspapers accused Baperki of having funded the PKI and ran racist cartoons accusing the ethnic Chinese of causing economic hardship for non-Chinese Indonesians. In Surabaya, East Java, the newly appointed military mayor even issued an order for Chinese-owned stores to lower their prices by 30 percent.

A US embassy cable summarized the anti-Chinese campaign with a combination of crude Cold War stereotypes, sensitivity to the strategic aspects of ongoing political struggle, and concern about the fortunes of the ethnic Chinese population: "Linking of Chicom with

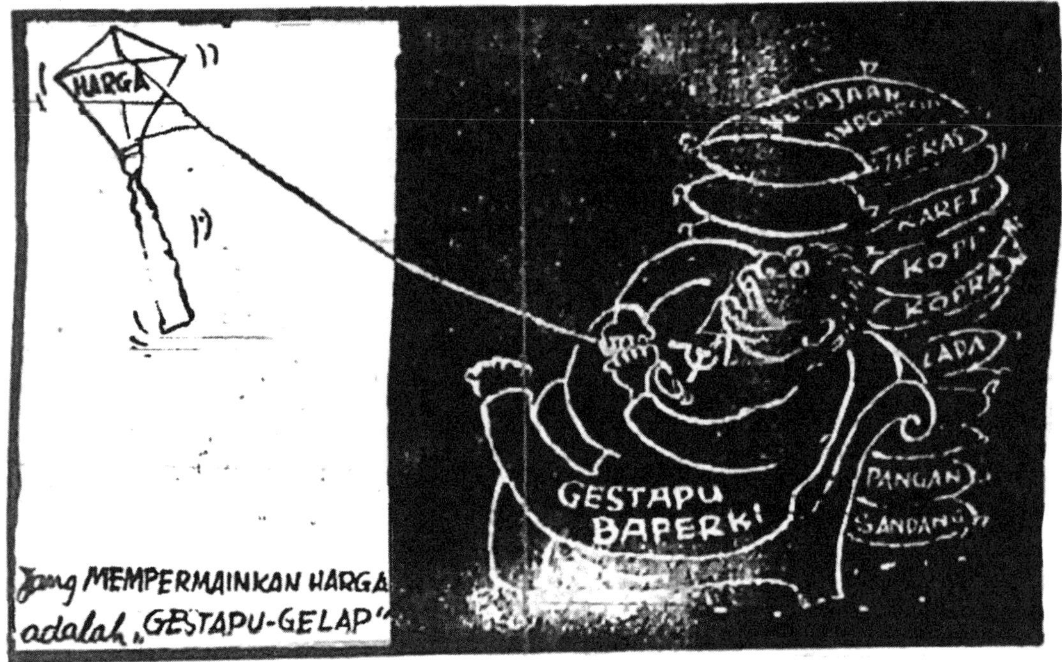


Figure 142. Cartoon published in an armed forces daily in December 1965 shows an obese Chinese businessman, identified as backing Baperki and the September 30th Movement, hoarding rice, coffee, and other commodities, causing prices to soar as high as a kite. The caption at left reads, "Price manipulators are the 'hidden Gestapu.'" (*Angkatan Bersendjata*)

PKI and September 30th Movement has blackened Chicom image for long time to come and emotional, heavy-handed Chicom treatment of events here both in their official protests and in Chicom propaganda support of Sept 30 Movement long after Sukarno and Subandrio had shifted to more subtle tactics, has greatly contributed to extent of Chicom debacle. Endemic Indo[nesian] hostility to local Chinese has also contributed, of course, particularly in view of ease with which Baperki could be linked to both Chicoms and PKI."[19]

## 41. Detention Centers in Jakarta

Army operations in Jakarta had started by focusing on the military units involved in the September 30th Movement and specific Communist groups that were alleged to have been involved on the morning of October 1. By mid-October, roundups had expanded to target anyone who belonged to a leftist organization. As a result, the available prisons were soon filled beyond capacity.

There was a disjuncture in the processes of arrest and detention, with little information provided when detainees were dropped off en masse. Prison authorities had to determine who the detainees were. Given limited facilities, they also needed to tally how many detainees they were holding. Officers from the Jakarta military command periodically provided figures that were reported in the press: in mid-October, the official figure was 1,334 prisoners; by mid-November this had risen to 2,200. In a conversation with US embassy officials a week later, the deputy foreign minister gave the far higher figure of 7,000 detainees in Jakarta.[20]

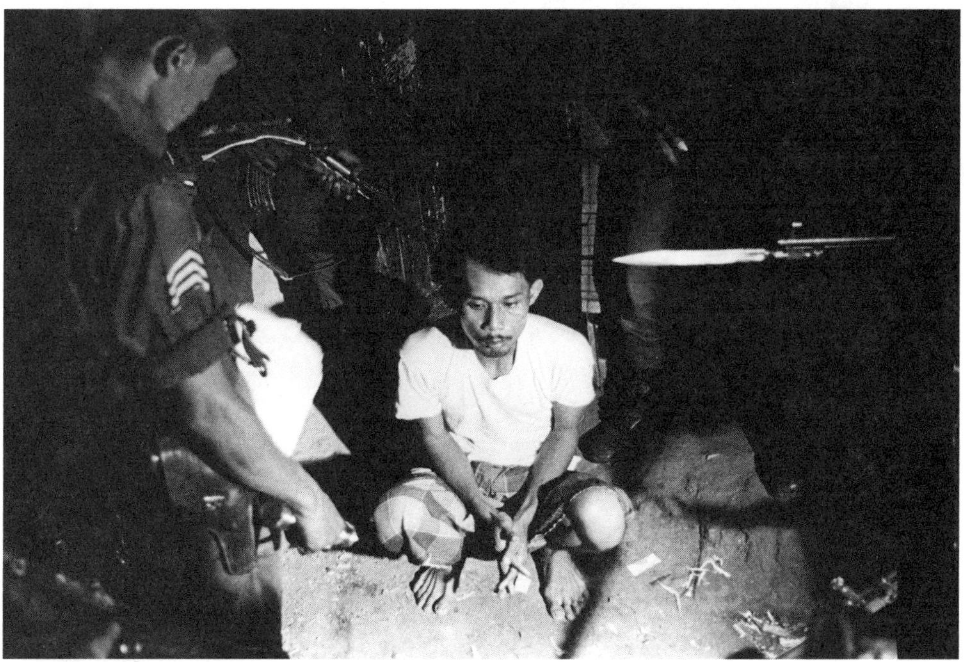

Figures 143, 144. A detainee on display in Salemba Prison, Jakarta, November 26, 1965. Online publications often claim the detainee was about to be executed. That may have been the case, but it obscures the fact that this was a photo opportunity set up for the Jakarta regional military commander, who was visiting with journalists. (Bettman-Corbis Collection/Getty, Rory Dell/Camera Press)

Figures 145, 146, 147. Prisoners in Tangerang Detention Center in Jakarta on the occasion of a visit by the Jakarta regional military commander, Brigadier General Umar Wirahadikusumah, late November 1965. (National Library of Indonesia)

Senior army officers periodically conducted formal inspections of the prisons, often inviting members of the press to accompany them. Print journalists and a television crew documented the inspection of captured troops and weapons, including pistols, machine guns, and a rocket launcher, at the Bekasi District Military Command, to the east of Jakarta. A television crew was also present during the interrogation of Lieutenant Colonel Untung and the PKI Politburo member Njono.

In late November, the army announced that Jakarta military commander Brigadier General Wirahadikusumah was to be transferred to serve as commander of the Army Strategic Reserve. Before leaving office, Wirahadikusumah visited a number of prisons together with a full entourage from the press corps. On November 26, at Salemba Prison, detainees were paraded before him and made to pose with hands held behind their heads while soldiers pointed machine guns and bayonets at them. While Wirahadikusumah had taken prompt action in support of Suharto's moves on October 1–2, 1965, he had not issued an outright ban on the PKI in the greater Jakarta area but only a lighter "freeze" on the party's activities. Remarkably, it was not until December 7, 1965, his last day as commander of Jakarta, that he formally banned the PKI.

## 42. Local PKI Branches Disband

The demands made by anti-Communist organizations and publicized in the military-controlled press fueled mass arrests and killings and caused widespread fear among the millions who were members of leftist organizations. In many provinces, authorities issued instructions temporarily freezing all PKI activities or banning the party altogether. Desperate to avoid arrest or worse, local branches of the PKI, its unions, and other affiliates held formal

Figure 148. Facing the West Java regional military commander, Major General Ibrahim Adjie, Communist Party members take an oath disbanding the local PKI branch in the historic Fatahillah Square, Jakarta, December 6, 1965. (National Library of Indonesia)

Figure 149. Cartoon showing the West Java provincial authority ordering the PKI to disband. Scheming out of sight below are two characters from Javanese shadow-puppet stories: Durno, a duplicitous character, and Sangkuni, a manipulative provocateur. Foreign Minister Subandrio was often referred to by his opponents as Durno, while Sangkuni represents Third Deputy Prime Minister Chaerul Saleh. (*Api*)

ceremonies, overseen by military personnel, at which they voluntarily "dissolved" themselves. These ceremonies often involved the burning of party attributes and organizational documents, declarations disavowing Communism, promises that members would report to the authorities at specified times, and pledges of allegiance to the Republic of Indonesia. Throughout the last months of 1965, the press carried numerous reports as well as paid advertisements about local PKI branches and affiliates that had disbanded.

Banning the PKI was one of the central demands made by the army and KAP-Gestapu, but many anti-Communists viewed these stage-managed local actions with suspicion. In West Java, anti-Communists fretted that dissolution ceremonies were in fact a form of protection, preventing the physical elimination of Communists. Elsewhere, concerns were expressed that the dissolution of the PKI was a political compromise that might allow Sukarno to retain his position.

## 43. Violence in the Outer Islands

Outside Java, there was much more variation in the timing of the mobilization against the PKI, the nature of anti-Communist alliances, and the intensity of the violence. These differences reflected the influence of political parties, the proclivities of regional military commanders, and the strength of provincial PKI branches.

During the first two weeks of October, calls for the destruction of the PKI in the major cities of Sumatra, Kalimantan, and Sulawesi were spearheaded by the youth groups and student organizations affiliated with the Islamic parties (especially supporters of the banned Masyumi), the PNI, and in Sumatra the army-backed IPKI. These early demonstrations often descended into looting of Chinese-owned stores in central business districts. In North Sumatra, demonstrators set fire to shops; in Balikpapan, East Kalimantan, a blaze engulfed 1,400 homes, though authorities were quick to place the blame on the PKI. While anti-Communist forces made their voices heard on the streets in the outer islands, the army-controlled press reported that Communists were taking flight. In North and West Sumatra, the papers claimed that Communists were fleeing to rural areas and preparing to take up arms. But with one major exception, anti-Communist mobilization in early October did not immediately result in mass arrests or killings.

These geographical differences depended to a great extent on the response of regional military commanders. In Medan, North Sumatra, Major General Mokoginta issued an instruction

Figure 150. Members of the leftist Manufacturing, Construction and Transport Union sit with hands behind their necks after capture by Indonesian Army troops, probably in Pontianak, West Kalimantan. (United Press International/ TopFoto)

Figure 151. Demonstrators in Makassar destroying the houses of PKI leaders, October 15, 1965. (*Lukisan pemberontakan PKI di Indonesia dan penumpasannya*)

on October 2 for all personnel under his command to obey only orders coming from Sukarno. Despite this order, the regional military commander of Aceh, who was Mokoginta's subordinate, unleashed mass killings that quickly resulted in the killing of at least six thousand alleged Communists. In North Sumatra, by contrast, Mokoginta ordered a freeze on PKI activity in mid-October, and it was not until early November, following a massive rally in the city center, that mass killings began there. In southern Sumatra, regional military commanders issued local bans on the PKI in Jambi, South Sumatra, and Lampung in mid-December, and only then did mass violence ensue.

In Kalimantan, despite early demonstrations in Pontianak and Banjarmasin calling for the destruction of the PKI, regional military commanders were more cautious. In West Kalimantan, Brigadier General Ryacudu even provided protection for the head of the provincial branch of the PKI and banned the party in early December only because of intense pressure from civilians. Bans followed in South Kalimantan on December 20 and Central Kalimantan on December 25. In Sulawesi, the first mass killings were in the town of Bone, with unspecified "violence" reported in Manado and other cities, all before regional military commanders had issued regional bans. Further east, violence against the PKI did not commence until early 1966. On the island of Flores in East Nusa Tenggara, where the military commander was reluctant to support the anti-Communist campaign, there were no killings until February 1966. Following his replacement by a Suharto loyalist that month, and with the enthusiastic backing of the local Catholic clergy and youth group, thousands were killed in a matter of weeks.

## 44. The RPKAD Arrives in Bali

As in Central Java, the RPKAD played a decisive role in Bali. Although there was some violence on the island in November, the onset of mass killings in Bali coincided with the arrival of RPKAD troops. Shortly after their arrival, RPKAD commander Colonel Edhie reportedly told a journalist that whereas in Java his troops had to encourage the population to kill the PKI, in Bali his troops had to restrain them. In fact, the RPKAD appears to have followed the same playbook in Bali that it used in Central Java, and the results were fundamentally the same—the mass killing of tens of thousands of people who had committed no crime.

The first RPKAD troops landed in Bali on December 7. The following day, they conducted a massive "show of force" in the capital city, Denpasar. Heavily armed soldiers in their distinctive red berets paraded through the city accompanied by armed vehicles and trucks. According to the PNI-affiliated daily *Suara Indonesia*, the display had the desired effect: "They don't even need to see the red beret [of the RPKAD]," it reported. "It is enough simply to hear the roar of a truck, and the hearts of the big-shot G-30-S types begin to beat wildly with fear."[21]

The RPKAD set about mobilizing and training militia groups to assist in the campaign to annihilate the PKI. The most important and feared of these militias was the Pemuda Marhaenis, also known as Tameng Marhaenis, a youth group affiliated with the right wing of the PNI. Dressed in black and sporting military-style berets and insignia, they roamed from house to house in groups of eight or ten, terrorizing, arresting, and killing alleged Communists. In the north and west of the island, bands of the NU-affiliated group Ansor were also active. Like the militias in Java, those in Bali operated alongside and under the command of the RPKAD and local army units, and they were permitted, indeed encouraged, to carry machetes, knives, and firearms. In the course of their joint "cleansing" operations, tens of thousands of real and alleged leftists were detained and later killed.

In the town of Negara in western Bali, some six thousand detainees were killed by troops in just three days. The executions were organized and systematic. According to eyewitnesses, dozens of army trucks loaded with detainees from surrounding villages formed a slow procession leading to a large warehouse. As each truck reached the warehouse, the detainees, their hands tied, were unloaded and taken inside, where they were shot by soldiers. The operation in Negara was no exception. Twenty years later, a woman who lived near an army detention camp in South Denpasar vividly recalled the endless roar of military truck engines, the unloading of scores of detainees, and the sound of automatic weapons fire.

Figure 152. RPKAD officer having his portrait taken in a photo studio in Bali, late 1965. The painted backdrop is of the Taman Ujung water palace in Karangasem in eastern Bali. (Wong Sangar)

Figure 153. Members of the Pemuda Marhaenis militia in Bali, late 1965. (National Library of Indonesia)

A US diplomatic cable reported on a meeting between a member of the embassy staff and a young RPKAD company commander, who had served in the eastern part of Bali: "As an example of what was going on in Bali, [the officer] related how his men had come across a burned out village with many already decomposed bodies lying among the ruins. The village elders told him that men in a neighboring village were the culprits. When [his] men arrived at the near-by village they were met with knives and rocks. His company had then wiped out the entire village."[22]

## 45. Mass Killings in Bali

In the years before the alleged coup, Bali had been the site of serious conflict over land, and by 1965 it had become a stronghold of the PKI and its farmers' organization, the BTI. On the other side were followers of the PNI, some supporters of the banned Indonesian Socialist Party (PSI), and, in the north and west of the island, a small number of NU members. Tensions had mounted in 1964 and 1965 as local PKI and BTI branches carried out unilateral land occupations (*aksi sepihak*) in their push to implement national land reform laws. In some areas, land was successfully redistributed to farmers belonging to the PKI and BTI, and it was in those areas that the postcoup violence was most intense. The official anti-Communist campaign provided a perfect opportunity for revenge and for the land to be taken back.

The killings were also set in motion by a major shift in the balance of political forces in Bali in late 1965. Before the alleged coup, the PKI and its affiliates had been on the rise and appeared to have the sympathy of the governor, Anak Agung Bagus Suteja, and the regional

Figure 154. Detainees under guard in Bali, late 1965. (National Library of Indonesia)

Figure 155. Militia member with a machete in Bali, late 1965. (National Library of Indonesia)

Figure 156. Woman with child, Bali, late 1965. (National Library of Indonesia)

military commander, Brigadier General Sjafiuddin, both of whom were staunch Sukarnoists. PKI members and sympathizers also occupied key positions in the provincial and district-level government apparatus. For a time, these figures were able to resist or soft-pedal Suharto's orders to annihilate the PKI. But by mid-November, Governor Suteja had effectively been stripped of his authority and the army had begun to shift its allegiance from Sukarno to Suharto, opening the door for anti-Communist figures to take the lead.

Equally important in stimulating the killing was the inflammatory rhetoric employed by Bali's anti-Communist political and religious leaders. Following the example set in Java, they claimed to have found evidence of PKI plans to stage a coup in Bali and to assassinate prominent anti-Communist figures. They also told their followers that the PKI was intent on destroying their religion, and that to kill PKI members was a religious obligation that would be legally acceptable. In an address in October 1965, the leading political figure Ida Bagus Oka told his audience, "There can be no doubt that the enemies of our revolution are also the cruelest enemies of religion and must be eliminated and destroyed down to the roots."[23]

The killings that ensued followed two basic patterns. In some cases, suspects were rounded up and taken by truck to a remote location—a field or forest, near a river or beach, an empty building or a warehouse—before being executed by soldiers. In other cases, army commanders deputized villagers and local militias to carry out the executions in their own or neighboring villages. In this way, thousands of Balinese became implicated in the execution of their neighbors, friends, and even close relatives.

Although the vast majority of those targeted were men, women were not spared. In particular, members of Gerwani were detained and subjected to harsh interrogation, in the course of which some allegedly confessed to heinous acts. One woman admitted that Gerwani members had planned to seduce army officers in order to obtain weapons for the PKI, and then murder and castrate them, as the army falsely claimed Gerwani members had done to the six generals on October 1. The local paper dutifully reported the alleged confession: "It is clear from these revelations how base and depraved PKI plans were. After scraping as much profit as possible from their shameless sexual activities, Gerwani members were supposed to murder and cut off the genitals of their victims."[24] Such stories further heightened animosity toward the PKI and laid the groundwork for massive violence.

By mid-1966, an estimated eighty thousand alleged leftists, or roughly 5 percent of the island's population, had been killed. Contrary to popular wisdom and official claims, the killing was not the result of a spontaneous outpouring of religious fervor or a cultural predisposition to "running amok." It was the product of relatively recent social and political conflicts and the deliberate efforts by military and political authorities to inflame those conflicts and destroy the PKI.

# IV. The Fact-Finding Commission

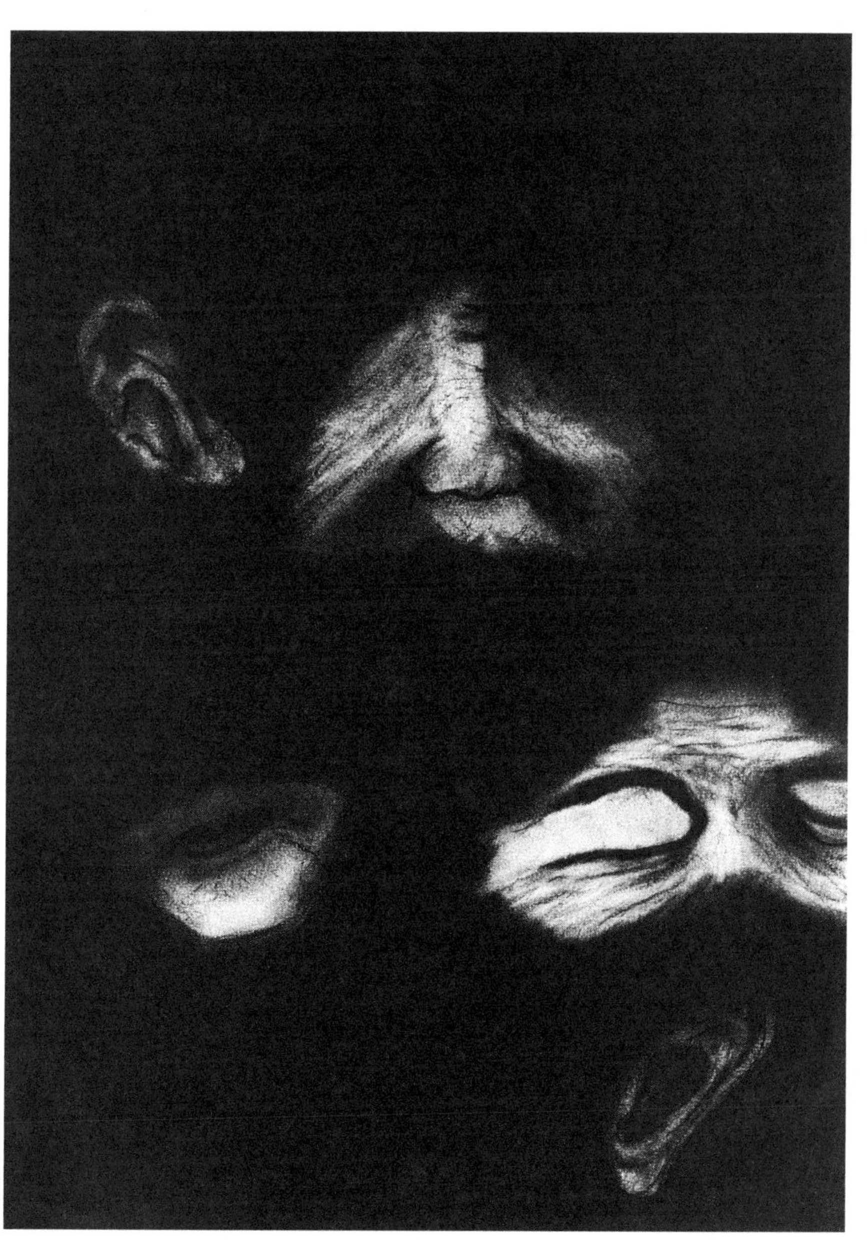

## 46. Sukarno's Fact-Finding Commission

Defying the army's demand that he ban the PKI, and perhaps taking advantage of a lull created by the start of the Muslim fasting month and the approach of Christmas, at a meeting of the Supreme Operations Command (Komando Operasi Tertinggi, or KOTI) on December 23, Sukarno made a surprise announcement that he was appointing a Fact-Finding Commission to investigate the post–October 1 violence. The president

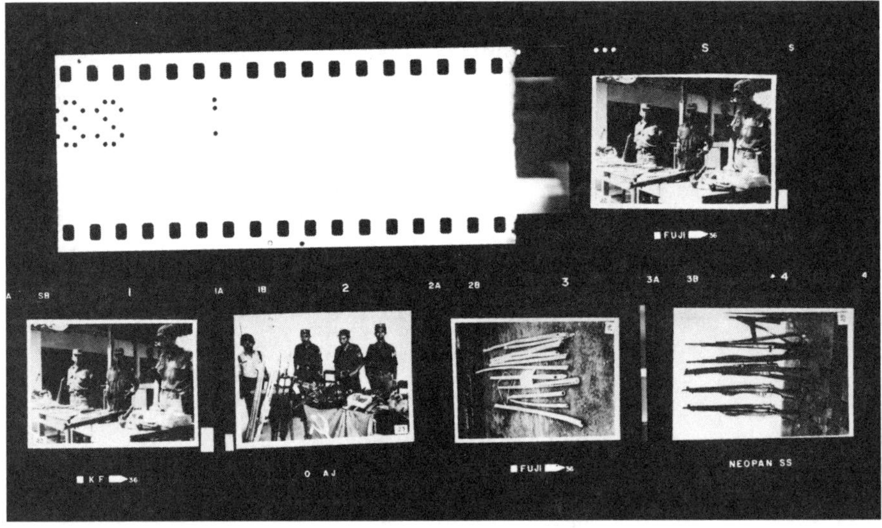

Figures 158, 159. Thumbnail contact sheets from the Fact-Finding Commission investigation in Central Java. (National Library of Indonesia)

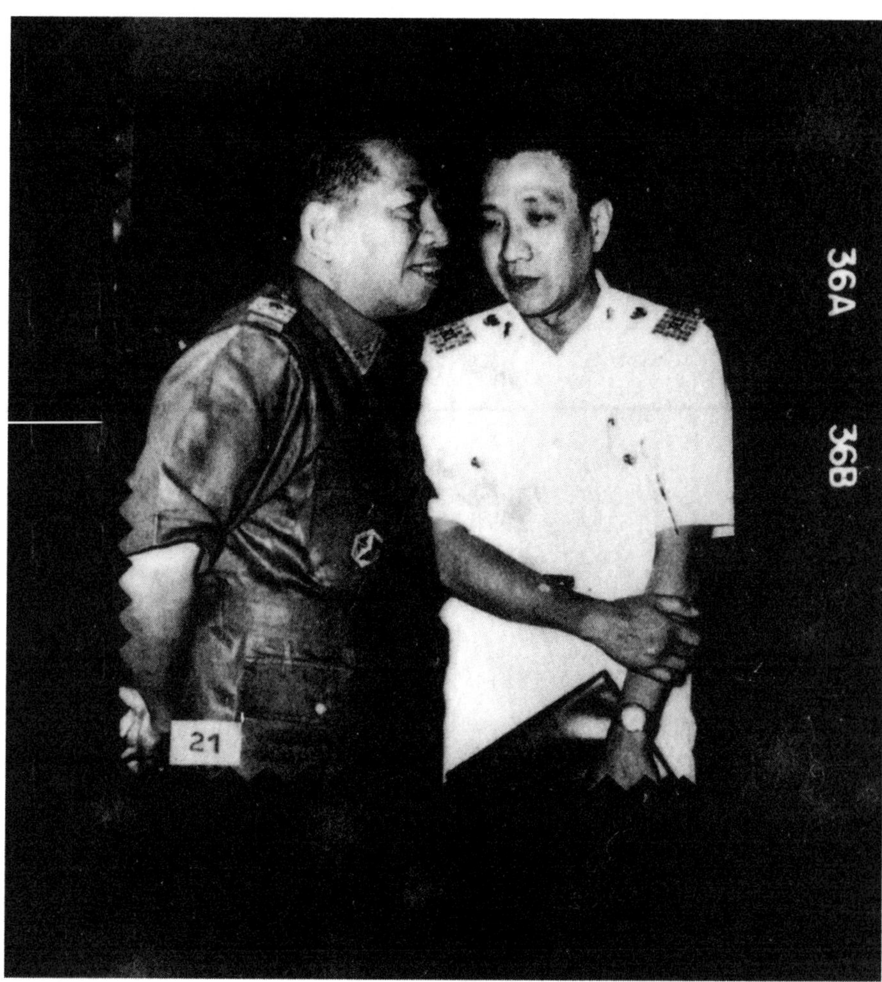


Figure 160. Commissioner Oei Tjoe Tat (in white) and a military officer, Central Java. (National Library of Indonesia)

instructed the commission to "gather facts and data about the deteriorating situation in North Sumatra, Central Java, East Java, and Bali as a result of the epilogue to the counterrevolutionary G.30.S. event, including the number of victims, causes, etc., that would be of use in bringing an end to and resolving the dire situation."[1]

The commission was given a mere eleven days—from December 27, 1965, until January 6, 1966—to carry out its investigation. The nine-member commission, headed by Minister of the Interior Major General Soemarno Sosroatmodjo, included the national police chief, the minister of information, the minister of agrarian affairs, a minister of state, a member of the Supreme Operations Command, and representatives from the Christian Party, the NU, and the PNI.

With few members and so little time in which to carry out their mandate, the commissioners split into smaller teams for brief visits to each of the four designated provinces. From arrival until departure, however, these teams were operating as the "guests" of provincial military authorities, who determined where the commissioners could travel, whom they could meet, and what was said. The commissioners visited several

Figure 161. Military personnel display evidence seized from alleged Communists in Central Java. (National Library of Indonesia)

detention centers. They examined a range of "evidence," including semi-automatic weapons, bamboo spears, documents, and PKI banners. The commissioners also held formal hearings to obtain testimony from witnesses.

A day after the commission began its work, US ambassador Marshall Green informed the State Department in Washington, DC, that "establishment of this commission has greatly angered Suharto who [is] still smarting over Sukarno welshing on his promise to ban PKI. Military is now in mood to take forceful measures against Sukarno." Green's source, however, told him that the army would probably not make a major move until late January, when the commission was expected to submit its report, adding that the report would likely "whitewash PKI involvement."[2]

The final report, which was submitted to Sukarno on January 10, was a mere fourteen pages long. The commission estimated that a total of 78,000 people had been killed and that 106,000 people were being detained in the four provinces. About a year later, the journalist John Hughes had a conversation with one of the commissioners (likely Oei Tjoe Tat) and asked if the commissioner believed that the figure of 78,000 killed was accurate. "He laughed merrily," Hughes wrote. "'Oh dear me, no,' he said, 'that was nowhere near the right figure.' 'My own view,' he replied unblinkingly, 'is that about ten times as many as that were killed.' Taken aback, I asked him to spell that out again. Was he really saying that although the commission had reported 78,000 people killed, he himself believed the figure to be 780,000? 'Yes, that's right,' he assured me. 'You mustn't forget that when we talked to officials and village headmen after the coup, they were trying to downgrade the figures of people they'd killed.'"[3]

A set of photographs taken by the commission team tasked with the investigation in Central Java has survived in the National Library of Indonesia. The collection provides a grim window into the condition of detainees and the investigative techniques that were used.

## 47. From Palace to Prison in Surakarta

Once the RPKAD entered the city of Surakarta in October 1965, thousands of people who belonged to the PKI and other leftist organizations were rounded up and detained. The army exercised ultimate authority over the makeshift detention sites but often tasked civil defense units as well as members of various anti-Communist organizations with guard duty. By December, however, the army made efforts to consolidate the detention process—not simply to improve security but also to facilitate the work of the new regional investigative and prosecutorial teams authorized by Kopkamtib.

One of the largest new detention sites visited by the Fact-Finding Commission was in Sasono Mulyo, the residence of the crown prince of Surakarta, located adjacent to the royal palace. The ruler, Pakubuwono XII, had received an honorary military rank during the revolution and in the late 1950s had joined the army officer corps and moved to Jakarta, leaving a relative in charge of palace affairs. In early November 1965, he visited Surakarta for three days, meeting with Sarwo Edhie and the Central Java military commander to learn about circumstances in the "operations area." Three weeks later, the first detainees were brought to his sprawling palace.

Sasono Mulyo was a male-only facility. Barbed wire was hung to cordon off the prisoners, and temporary walls made of woven bamboo were erected. Meals initially consisted of rice twice a day, but over time the rice was changed to less desirable grains such as boiled bulgur or even rice husks, with few or no vegetables. These limited provisions forced detainees to rely on food brought by relatives, deliveries that were not always regular and involved the risk that family members might also be questioned.

Figure 162. Detainees in Sasono Mulyo, residence of the crown prince of Surakarta, December 1965. (National Library of Indonesia)

Figure 163. Military personnel question Sasono Mulyo detainees behind barbed wire on which laundry has been hung. (National Library of Indonesia)

Figure 164. Detainees listening to briefing from a military officer at Sasono Mulyo. (National Library of Indonesia)

Figure 165. Detainees at Sasono Mulyo respond to questioning by military personnel.

Army officers appointed to the regional investigative team oversaw the collection of data and interrogation of the detainees. The most important questions concerned the individuals' membership in leftist organizations, knowledge of the September 30th Movement, and identification of PKI leaders and their whereabouts. The aim was to classify the detainees in accordance with Kopkamtib instructions: Category A for those with direct involvement in or knowledge of the September 30th Movement; Category B for those who showed through "action, word, or deed" support for the movement; and Category C for those who were suspected of being involved in or sympathetic to the movement. Following classification, some detainees were released, while others were held for more than a year. In March 1967, 185 inmates at Sasono Mulyo were taken by train to Cilacap and then by boat to the notorious Nusa Kambangan Prison, off the south coast of Java.

## 48. Gerwani Members in Detention in Surakarta

During their brief visit to Surakarta, the Fact-Finding Commission team inspected a detention facility for women, most of them members of Gerwani. Official photographs of that visit show a military officer, possibly a member of the team, speaking with small groups of women. Those images, taken under military supervision, do not fully capture the realities of arrest and incarceration for the women detained in Surakarta and elsewhere. Thousands of women, including girls as young as fourteen, were initially rounded up and subjected to interrogation and sexual abuse. Hundreds were eventually transferred to prisons and camps where they were detained without charge or trial for many years.

For some, the ordeal began with what seemed a simple request by police or civil authorities to come to the office of the subdistrict head to "attend a

Figure 166. A military officer interrogating members of Gerwani in the Surakarta city hall detention center. The women avert their gaze. (National Library of Indonesia)

Figure 167. A sign at the Surakarta detention center holding alleged Gerwani members reads, "Detainees are not allowed to bathe outside the camp, nor get water from outside." (National Library of Indonesia)

Figure 168. Pointing back over her shoulder, a young woman answers a military officer's question, December 1965. (National Library of Indonesia)

meeting" or to "answer a few questions." For others, it began with a knock at the door in the middle of the night, or arrest in broad daylight by unidentified armed men or soldiers. In almost every case, the women were then loaded onto trucks together with men and taken to various places of detention, including neighborhood police stations, the city hall, military police headquarters, and army barracks. Eventually men and women were separated and held in different rooms or facilities.

In later accounts, many women detainees vividly remembered the moment of their arrest and the anguish of being forcibly separated from their children. One Gerwani member from Surakarta, arrested in early October just days after giving birth, recalled, "Then they threw me into the back of a truck. I didn't know what had happened to my baby who was only two days old. . . . I screamed and shouted, begging to be able to bring my child with me. But they all ignored me. In fact, one of the soldiers answered my screams by grabbing my hair and jerking my head around hard. 'Quiet!' he shouted. 'Women like you killed our Generals!'"[4]

Like the men, women detainees were interrogated about their knowledge of the September 30th Movement, their membership in leftist organizations, and the whereabouts of other members. Also like the men, women were punched, kicked, and beaten with sticks in the course of their interrogation. And like the men, some women were removed from their places of detention at night and summarily executed. A woman detained at Surakarta's city hall recalled, "One night four of my women friends were removed from our cell and didn't return. I found out from a guard who was a decent man. He said, 'Sorry, ma'am, but the four women are not coming back. They were taken away and, as people say, they were played,' that was the term they used back then. 'Wait,' I asked, 'what does "played" mean?' And he said it means 'killed.'"[5]

In Surakarta and elsewhere, detained women also experienced sexual violence. Some were made to strip naked, ostensibly so that interrogators could check whether they had a tattoo that Gerwani members were purported to have on their thighs. Others were forced to perform sexual acts on their captors or were raped. Most were also verbally abused by their captors—accused of being whores and killers, guilty of the depraved acts of which Gerwani members had been falsely accused by the army.

## 49. Detainees and an Exhumation in Klaten

The army-controlled press had run a barrage of articles during the second and third weeks of October claiming that the PKI was turning Central Java, and especially the city of Surakarta and the surrounding districts of Klaten and Boyolali, into a "pilot project" or "base area" for guerrilla warfare. After the arrival of the RPKAD on October 18, there were further reports that members of the PKI's affiliates had massacred their political opponents in various locations and had begun to organize armed resistance. The main newspaper in Yogyakarta, *Kedaulatan Rakjat*, published sensational stories about the September 30th Movement "generals,"

Figure 169. Djojudo (tall, thin man on left), from Klaten in Central Java, who the military claimed was a "general" of the September 30th Movement. (*Kedaulatan Rakjat*)

with accompanying photographs of rail-thin older men, dressed in sarongs, staring blankly at the camera.

In mid-November, the governor of Central Java, Marine Brigadier General Mochtar, conducted an inspection tour of the province. Several foreign journalists were allowed to join the governor's entourage, including the *Los Angeles Times* correspondent Arthur Dommen and the Australian journalist Frank Palmos. In the village of Djambu Kidul, in Klaten District, the governor oversaw the exhumation of six graves in the village cemetery, containing a total of eighteen corpses. The group was also shown twenty-six more holes that the PKI was alleged to have dug in preparation for

Figure 170. Detainees assembled in a village in Klaten, Central Java, most likely for presentation before the visiting members of the Fact-Finding Commission. (National Library of Indonesia)

Figure 171. Detainees in a village square in Klaten, Central Java. Several of the men are wearing black hats called kopiah or peci, derived from the Ottoman fez, which is a sign of being a devout Muslim. (National Library of Indonesia)

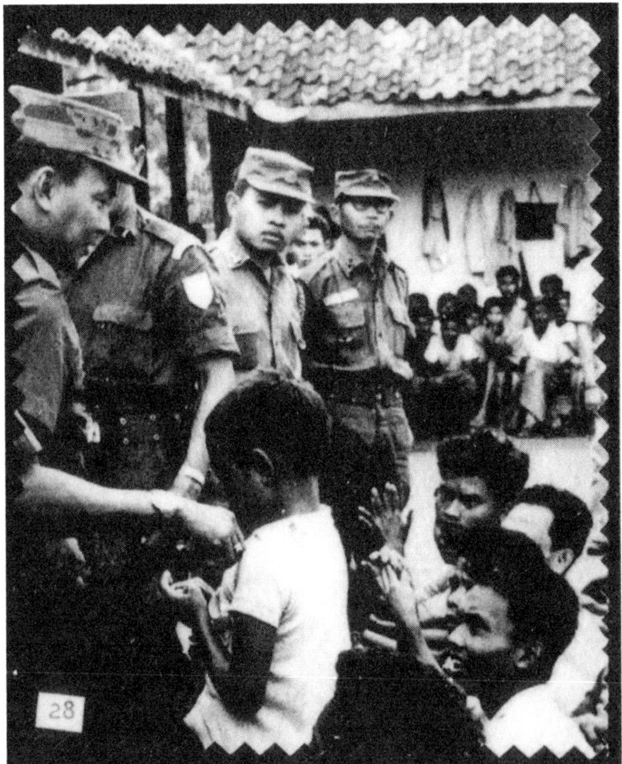


Figure 172. A boy kissing the hand of a military officer, a traditional act of submission to elders or those of high status. (National Library of Indonesia)

additional victims. A local newspaper published grainy photographs taken by its photojournalist showing villagers exhuming the graves under the watchful eye of soldiers. The caption explained that the exhumation was done so that the victims could be given a proper burial.

In late December, members of the Fact-Finding Commission visited Central Java for several days to gather information. In addition to meetings and a visit to the main prison in Yogyakarta, the commissioners toured Klaten, where they were received by local officials, military units, and leaders of mass organizations, and were shown detainees. The commissioners were also taken to the village of Djambu Kidul, where the eighteen alleged victims of the PKI had been exhumed and reburied in early November. Inexplicably, the notes accompanying a set of photographs taken during the visit state that one photograph is of the exhumation of a single mass grave

Figure 173. Members of the Fact-Finding Commission, accompanied by local military personnel, witness the exhumation of bodies near Klaten, December 1965. The stench from the rotting corpses forced the commissioners to cover their noses. (National Library of Indonesia)

Figure 174. The remains of the deceased were placed in coffins for reburial. (National Library of Indonesia)

containing eighteen victims in Djambu Kidul and that another is of their reburial in individual wooden coffins. But if the alleged victims had already been exhumed and reburied in early November, why did the commissioners feel it was necessary to do so again, and why was the description of six separate graves altered to claim that the corpses had been buried in a single mass grave?

The likely answer is that the exhumation and reburial were staged to emphasize the official story of PKI "terror" and to distract from evidence of widespread anti-Communist violence. In a similar vein, a local newspaper reported that the purpose of the commission's visit was to gather information on the September 30th Movement, failing to mention that the commission was also tasked with assessing post–October 1 detention and killings of leftists.

# V. The Struggle for Power

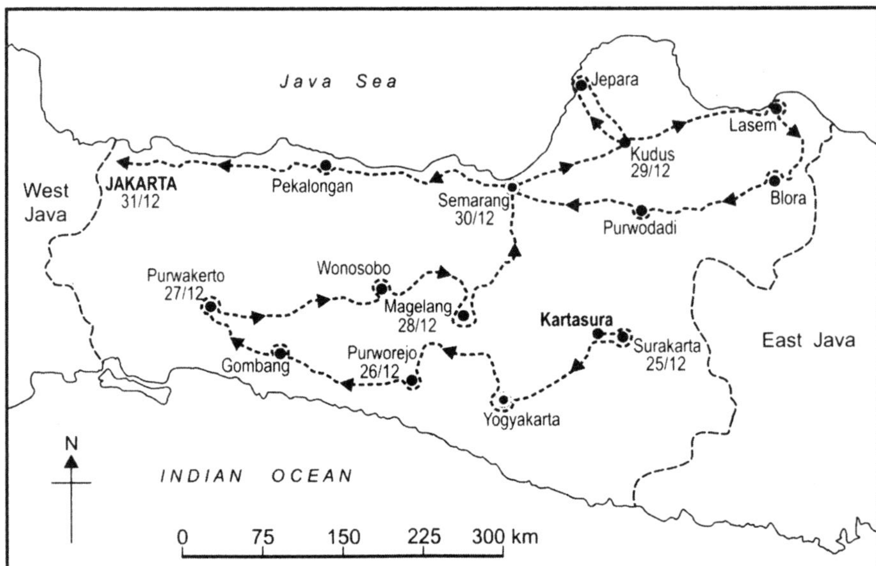


Figure 176. Map of RPKAD victory tour through Central Java before the return to Jakarta, late December 1965.

## 50. Show of Force in Jakarta

In December 1965, two months after Jakarta-based RPKAD troops had been dispatched to Central Java, the army announced that, their mission completed, they would be returning to their home base. Before leaving, however, five RPKAD battalions along with cavalry units staged a one-week tour of the province. The convoy of sixty-five vehicles traveled from Colonel Sarwo Edhie's temporary headquarters in Kartasura through Yogyakarta to Purwokerto, doubling back along the mountain road through Wonosobo to Magelang, home of the military academy, to the provincial capital of Semarang, through the northeastern cities of Kudus, Blora, and Purwodadi, and then back along the coastal road through Pekalongan and Tegal. In each town and city, crowds assembled for the spectacle, some to greet heroes, others out of fear, and children for the novelty and excitement. The convoy reached Jakarta on December 31.

On the morning of January 4, 1966, Edhie assembled the two RPKAD battalions that had served in Central Java and units that had remained in the capital in Senayan, Central Jakarta, for a show of force. Edhie rode atop a jeep, holding his baton aloft in celebration. Suharto addressed the troops, whom he praised for their "sterling success" in Central Java, and he noted that RPKAD troops, in addition to restricting the September 30th Movement's room for maneuver, had helped the population understand the situation and debunked "false propaganda."

Despite the army's muscular posturing, a report prepared by the US embassy the following day warned, "Political situation even more obscure than usual as result of recent acceleration of behind-the-scenes maneuvering and further confusion over reported

Figure 177. Colonel Sarwo Edhie, commander of the RPKAD, overseeing the show of force on January 4, 1966. (National Library of Indonesia)

Figure 178. Soldiers and armored vehicles on display, Central Jakarta, January 4, 1966. (National Library of Indonesia)

Sukarno trip abroad. Return of crack Army para-commando troops from provincial areas also raised questions concerning direction of political movement."[1]

## 51. The "Three Demands of the People"

By mid-December 1965, the army high command's primary concern had shifted from the PKI to Sukarno and control over the state apparatus. With the start of the Muslim fasting month on December 24 and Christmas the following day, anti-Communist demonstrations in Jakarta and other major cities subsided temporarily. As a result, bickering emerged among anti-Communist forces. There were sectoral suspicions between the "religious" and "nationalist" factions as well as strategic disputes between leaders who focused their demands solely on the PKI and others who insisted that Sukarno be overthrown.

Under army guidance, on January 10, 1966, the two largest action fronts—representing Islamic university students and Islamic high school students, respectively—held a mass rally at the national legislature to present what they called the Three Demands of the People (Tri Tuntutan Rakyat, or Tritura). The demands were dissolution of the PKI and its affiliates, appointment of a new cabinet, and reduction of food prices. The students called themselves the Generation of '66, setting up a divide

Figure 179. Anti-Communist demonstrators in Bogor, West Java, January 1966. (Getty)

between themselves and the Generation of '45 that had come of age during the struggle for independence. Suharto sent a written message supporting the students' cause: "I regard these actions as manifestations of social control. I know that the demonstrations have proceeded in an orderly and highly disciplined way. . . . Students in fact stand in the midst of the people, are aware of the people's difficulties and understand the wishes of the people, from whence we came, by whom we were brought up and for whom we struggle."[2] A few days later, apparently acting on instructions from the army, gasoline stations in Jakarta lowered their prices from 1,000 to 250 rupiah per liter, with follow-on reductions in bus fares.

Sukarno pushed back against the army's maneuvers. At a cabinet meeting in the presidential palace in Bogor on January 15, he delivered a fiery speech calling for his supporters to "gather your forces, form your fronts, defend Sukarno."[3] The following day, Foreign Minister Subandrio made a radio address calling for the establishment of a Sukarno Front. The aim was to mobilize a counter-movement that could challenge the action fronts in the streets. This move, in turn, prompted KAP-Gestapu leader Subchan to call for the largest demonstration yet, urging university students from Bogor and Bandung to march all the way to Jakarta.

## 52. Commanders' Statement of Loyalty

While mass student demonstrations were putting increased pressure on Sukarno and his ministers, the army had additional cards to play. On January 16, in his capacity as coordinating minister for defense and security and army commander, Suharto handwrote a statement declaring that he and the commanders of the navy and air force remained loyal to President Sukarno. The statement read as follows:

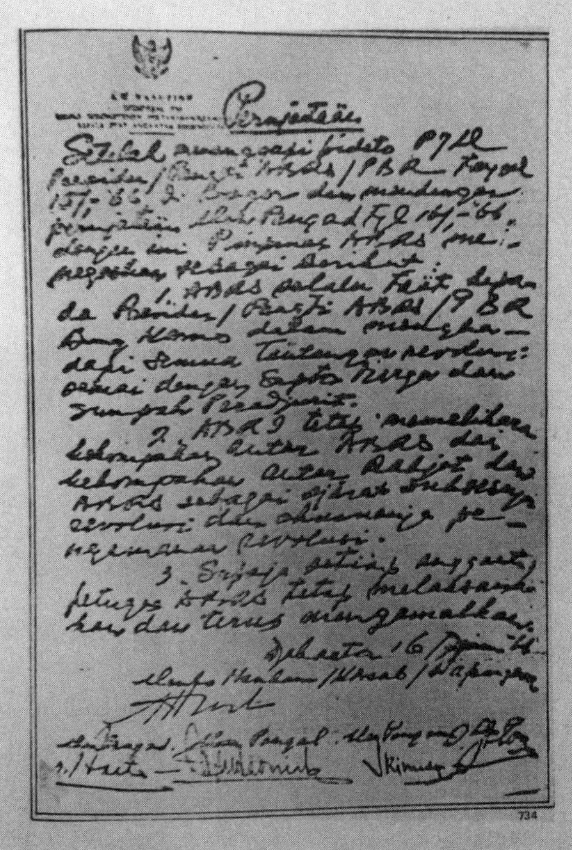

Figure 180. Official statement penned by Suharto declaring the loyalty of the Indonesian Armed Forces to Sukarno. (National Library of Indonesia)

In accordance with the speech by His Excellency the President, High Commander of the Armed Forces and Great Leader of the Revolution, on January 15, 1966, and after hearing the statement made by Minister and Army Commander [Major General Suharto] on January 16, 1966, the leaders of the Armed Forces of Indonesia declare the following:

1. The Indonesian Armed Forces will always be loyal to President, High Commander, and Great Leader of the Revolution Sukarno in facing all challenges to the revolution in accordance with the Seven-Point Pledge and the Soldier's Oath.
2. The Armed Forces of the Republic of Indonesia continue to uphold the unity within the military and unity between the people and the military as a condition for the success and security of the Revolution.
3. All members of the Armed Forces are to implement and carry this out with devotion.

Djakarta, January 16, '66
Coordinating Minister for Defense and Security and the Army Commander
Harto

Even officials at the US embassy in Jakarta, who expressed enthusiasm about the army's ongoing attack on the political Left, acknowledged that the commanders' statement of loyalty was in fact duplicitous: "By mid-week it had become apparent that the Army's reaction was tactical and that its resolve to alter the balance of power in Indonesia was to be maintained under the facade of public allegiance to Sukarno's wishes. Several reliable sources reported that Nasution and Suharto had ordered party and student leaders to continue demonstrations in an effort to bring down the Cabinet and particularly Subandrio, but to ease off on slogans and demands directed against or personally offensive to Sukarno."[4]

## 53. Extraordinary Military Tribunals

On December 10, 1965, in a sign of the army's ability to dictate policy outcomes, the Supreme Operations Command (KOTI) issued a decree authorizing Suharto to appoint members of an Extraordinary Military Tribunal (Mahkamah Militer Luar Biasa, or Mahmillub) to try the alleged masterminds of the September 30th Movement. The aim was not just to pursue legal action against those deemed responsible but to provide a legal facade for the ongoing repression and to bring to light evidence that would tarnish Sukarno's image.

A mere ten days after the announcement—and long before a decision was made about who would be tried—the senior judge told a US embassy official that he had "already decided that [the] sentence for convicted participants in

Figure 181. PKI Politburo member Njono being led into court, February 14, 1966. He was sentenced to death later that month. (United Press International/TopFoto)

Figure 183. Cartoon showing "defenders of the PKI" trying to level the scales, depicted as a hammer and sickle, while Njono and Untung flail on the other side. (*Trisakti*)

30 Sept Movement would be death."[5] The court convened in early February. The first person brought to trial was Njono, a member of the PKI Politburo who had been appointed chairman of the PKI's Jakarta branch in late 1964. An editorial in the army daily *Angkatan Bersendjata* commented,

> We have seen and observed a real communist in action when facing the Mahmillub. And, to be frank, we were quite impressed. The guts he possesses to revoke all that he has said during preliminary investigations! The judge has called him a "big liar," and would very much like to advise and remind Njono not to keep on telling lies, but, alas, the defendant has no religion whatsoever.
>
> The judge and all other members of Mahmillub know what kind of person sits before them: a thoroughly moulded communist! . . . To a real communist, reality rests only in doctrines of communism and institution of party. Hence, Njono's strong conviction that [the] PKI had nothing to do whatsoever with the Gestapu![6]

Predictably, the court found Njono guilty of subversion and armed rebellion and sentenced him to death. Next up was Untung, nominal leader of the September 30th Movement. Following a short trial, he was found guilty on similar charges and sentenced to death on March 7, 1966.

## 54. Sukarno Hangs On

Despite the failure of the Sukarno Front to gain traction in early January, Sukarno continued to push back against the army's maneuvers and the student attacks on his authority. One target was the foreign press corps. In late December, he ordered the expulsion of an Australian correspondent. He followed up in mid-January by instructing Foreign

*opposite*
Figure 182. Lieutenant Colonel Untung in court. On March 7, 1966, the panel of judges sentenced him to death. (Camera Press)

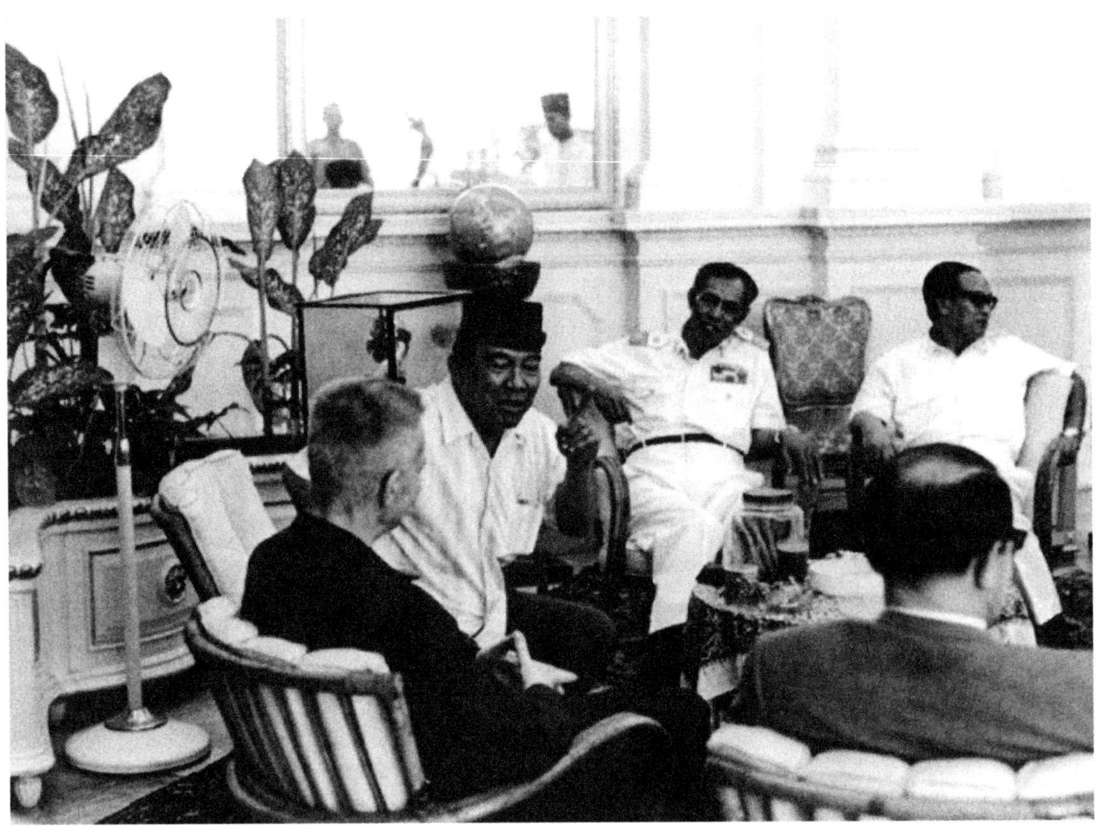

Figure 184. Sukarno speaking with guests, most likely diplomats from China, ca. March 1966. (*Paris Match/ Marie Claire*)

Minister Subandrio to expel the American journalists from the Associated Press and United Press International and a stringer working for the *New York Times*. Most of the other Western correspondents gathered to say goodbye prior to the departure of the Americans on January 19.

But it was not until mid-February that Sukarno attempted to reassert his authority over the state apparatus. He began by summoning to the palace student leaders who opposed KAMI and encouraging them to revive the Sukarno Front. Days later, in a fiery speech, he announced that he was reshuffling his cabinet—which would now be called the "improved" Dwikora Cabinet. The key change was that Nasution was dropped as minister of defense and security and the portfolio redefined as the Ministry of Defense. Nasution's removal represented a direct attack on the anti-Communist leadership of the army, while the redefinition of the ministry implied that the armed forces should no longer play a role in internal security. At the same time, Sukarno ordered that responsibility for PKI prisoners be moved from the army to Attorney General Sutardhio.

In seeking to reassert his authority, Sukarno was not completely alone. He continued to have the allegiance of some high-ranking officials, political party leaders, and elements of the military, as well as a strong popular following in parts of the country. Among officials, he could still count on the loyalty of Foreign Minister Subandrio, Third Deputy Prime

Minister Chaerul Saleh, and Minister of State Oei Tjoe Tat. Perhaps more important, because they were in a position to take direct political action, he had the support of some PNI and other party leaders who opposed the KAMI students or feared the rise of political Islam. The president also continued to command loyalty in some branches of the military, notably in the marines and the air force but also among some army officers. The commanders for West Java and Bali, for example, were both devoted Sukarnoists. Finally, in spite of everything that had happened since October, Sukarno remained a revered and popular figure in large parts of the country, especially in East Java and Bali.

The residual power of Sukarno and Sukarnoism was a significant constraint on the army's goal of removing the president and dictated how it went about doing so. A direct attack was out of the question, so indirect methods were used instead. The political trials, set in motion by the army in February 1966, were one part of that strategy. They provided a perfect opportunity to insinuate that Sukarno may have been involved in the events of October 1, and in that way to undermine his authority. The army also sought to weaken Sukarno by attacking his least popular officials. The most common target was Subandrio, who was subjected to vicious attacks in the media and in mass demonstrations, where he was called a "Dog of Peking," "Killer of the Generals," and similar names.

Finally, Sukarno's efforts to assert his authority were simply ignored or obstructed by the army leadership. A clear example came in early March, when the attorney general held a ceremony in Central Java to announce the release of PKI prisoners. The ceremony took place just a few weeks after the president had ordered that responsibility for PKI prisoners should be turned over from the army to the attorney general. Suharto attended the ceremony, not to take part in the handover but to ensure that it did not take place.

## 55. Attacks on Sukarnoism

The term "Sukarnoism" had gained prominence in August 1964 when, in the face of rumors about the president's kidney disorder and declining health, Chaerul Saleh established the Body to Support Sukarnoism (Badan Pendukung Sukarnoisme, or BPS). Despite the name, the real target of the BPS was the PKI, which Saleh and others believed was seeking to undermine the state ideology, Pancasila. By late 1964, with the squabble between BPS supporters and the PKI reaching fever pitch, Sukarno banned the BPS and a number of newspapers that had been its most vocal proponents. In doing so, he was clearly siding with the PKI.

In mid-January 1966, as the army's onslaught against the PKI and the president intensified, Sukarno and his allies attempted to reassert their authority. This effort was signaled by a fiery speech Sukarno delivered to the plenary cabinet session on January 15. Hours later, supporters plastered handbills throughout the city extolling the president. The following day, in a radio address, Subandrio called for the formation of a new Sukarno Front "to defend [the president] against his enemies."[7] The front drew heavily on support from the PNI,

*(top)* Figure 185. Army soldiers and marines guard the presidential palace, Jakarta, February 25, 1966. (United Press International)

*(bottom)* Figure 186. Marines attack anti-Communist demonstrators in Jakarta, February 25, 1966.

and especially its white-uniformed youth group. But after a few token rallies, little came of this initiative.

Meanwhile, the army intensified its attack on Sukarnoism. There were, in fact, two different expressions of this attack. On the one hand, the army and the student action fronts renewed their campaign against high-level officials who remained personally loyal to the president. The primary targets were Ministers Chaerul Saleh, Subandrio, and Oei Tjoe Tat, who had served on the Fact-Finding Commission, and West Java military commander Major General Adjie. By February 1966, these individuals had little or no room for maneuver but remained the most obvious symbols of Sukarno's continuing authority as president. On the other hand, the army employed the term "Sukarnoism" to identify and undermine organizations that still had the potential to take action in defense of the president. Within the security forces, the air force was viewed as containing leftist (including Communist) elements, and the marines remained overwhelmingly loyal to the president, even engaging in direct confrontations with the anti-Communist action fronts in Jakarta and Surabaya in February 1966.

## 56. The Death Toll

No one knows how many people were killed in Indonesia in 1965–66. Estimates range from the Fact-Finding Commission's very low interim number of 78,000, to a figure, attributed to a Kopkamtib research team, of more than one million, to a high total of three million, reportedly claimed by Edhie just before his death. Between these figures, many scholars have settled on a total death toll of 500,000, though less because of hard evidence and more because it serves to indicate the horrific scale of the violence.

Officials at foreign embassies in Jakarta periodically tried to assess the death toll, debated their respective estimates, and sought to manage media coverage. In January 1966, British and Australian diplomats estimated that some 400,000 had been killed. Meanwhile, after a three-week tour of the country in February, the Swedish ambassador, Harald Edelstam, reported to Stockholm that "the true number in Java is without doubt between 500,000 and 1 million people."[8] Edelstam shared his assessment with British ambassador Gilchrist, who reported it to London, noting, "The Ambassador and I had discussed the killings before he left, and

b. Djumlah angka korban dari pihak G.30.S.

Setelah kami mengadakan penelitian jang sesaksama mungkin, dapat diperkirakan djumlah angka dari para korban sbb:

| | | |
|---|---|---|
| 1. Bali | :........................ | 12. 500 orang. |
| 2. Djawa Timur | :........................ | 54. 000 orang. |
| 3. Djawa Tengah | :........................ | 10. 000 orang. |
| 4. Sumatera Utara | :........................ | 2. 000 orang. |
| | Djumlah | 78. 000 orang. |

Figure 187. Death toll as shown in the Fact-Finding Commission report. The total is incorrect. (*Laporan tentang Fact-Finding Commission KOTI*)

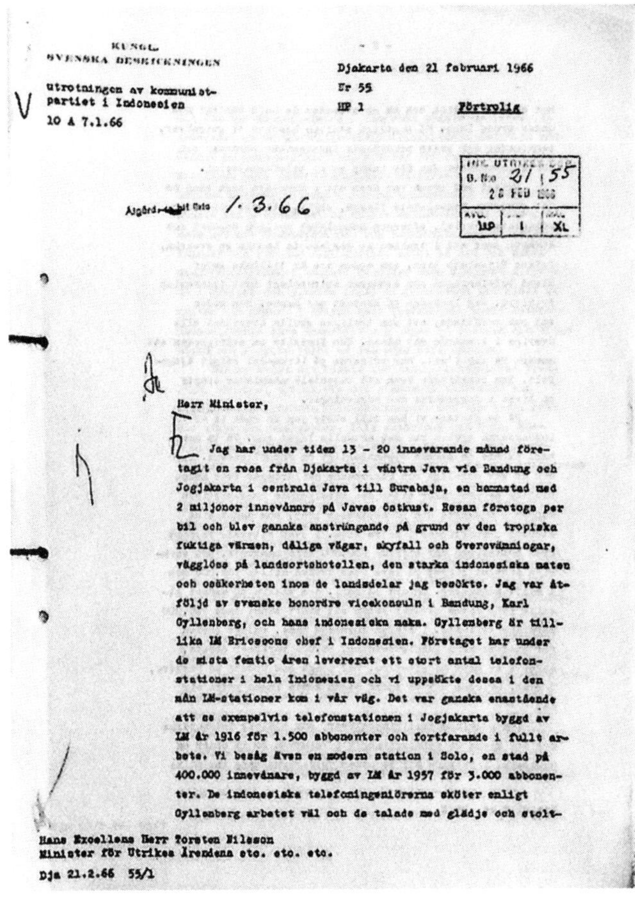

KUNGL.
SVENSKA BESKICKNINGEN

utrotningen av kommunistpartiet i Indonesien
10 A 7.1.66

Djakarta den 21 februari 1966
Nr 55
HP 1
**Förtrolig**

INK. UTRIKESDEP.
D. No 21/55
28 FEB 1966
HP | I | XL

Åtgärd–bilt Oslo 1.3.66

Herr Minister,

Jag har under tiden 13 – 20 innevarande månad företagit en resa från Djakarta i västra Java via Bandung och Jogjakarta i centrala Java till Surabaja, en hamnstad med 2 miljoner innevånare på Javas östkust. Resan företogs per bil och blev ganska ansträngande på grund av den tropiska fuktiga värmen, dåliga vägar, skyfall och översvämningar, vägglöss på landsortshotellen, den starka indonesiska maten och osäkerheten inom de landsdelar jag besökte. Jag var åtföljd av svenske honoräre vicekonsuln i Bandung, Karl Gyllenberg, och hans indonesiska maka. Gyllenberg är tillika LM Ericssons chef i Indonesien. Företaget har under de sista femtio åren levererat ett stort antal telefonstationer i hela Indonesien och vi uppsökte dessa i den mån LM-stationer kom i vår väg. Det var ganska enastående att se exempelvis telefonstationen i Jogjakarta byggd av LM år 1916 för 1.500 abbonenter och fortfarande i fullt arbete. Vi besåg även en modern station i Solo, en stad på 400.000 innevånare, byggd av LM år 1957 för 3.000 abbonenter. De indonesiska telefoningenjörerna sköter enligt Gyllenberg arbetet väl och de talade med glädje och stolt-

Hans Excellens Herr Torsten Nilsson
Minister för Utrikes Ärendena etc. etc. etc.

Dja 21.2.66 55/1

Figure 188. Swedish ambassador Harald Edelstam prepared a series of memoranda in 1966, in which he highlighted the scope of the violence. In this document from February 1966, he wrote, "The true number in Java is without doubt between 500,000 and 1 million people. In Bali alone, the beautiful island separated only by a narrow strait from the east coast of Java, 200,000 people have been slaughtered." (National Archives of Sweden)

he had found my suggested figure of 400,000 dead quite incredible. His inquiries have led him to consider it a very serious under-estimate."[9]

Gilchrist and his diplomatic colleagues had good reason to trust Edelstam's conclusions. Unlike most ambassadors, who never left Jakarta and relied almost entirely on official briefings, Edelstam had traveled extensively through Java, Bali, and Sumatra and based his estimates on information he had gathered from a range of unofficial sources. Nevertheless, in their public statements, Western officials sought to downplay the numbers. In April 1966, for example, the political affairs officer at the US embassy wrote,

> During a recent discussion of this subject with the reporting officer that was centered on the desirability of downplaying the extent of the carnage, [an embassy source, name deleted] said that 300,000 would be a conservative figure for the number of persons killed in Indonesia as an aftermath to the Gestapu. If the commonly cited figures for the provinces are to be believed, the total would reach one million persons. Unfortunately, it is impossible to weigh the countervailing effects of exaggeration (which is especially common in Indonesia) and the interest of many persons involved to cover up some of the crimes. The truth can never be known. Even the Indonesian Government probably has only a vague idea of the truth. We frankly do not know whether the real figure is closer to 100,000 or 1,000,000 but believe it wiser to err on the side of the lower estimates, especially when questioned by the press.[10]

US ambassador Green, who was involved in these discussions and was well aware of Edelstam's higher estimates, thought it would be best to cite a figure of 150,000 when speaking with the press. While he and other ambassadors could genuinely say that they had no way of knowing the true figure, this underestimate served to obscure the extent of the mass killings and provided crucial political cover for the emerging military regime.

Meanwhile, Indonesian officials offered wildly varying estimates of the numbers killed. In January 1966, for example, Indonesia's ambassador to

Canada told officials that as many as 500,000 had been killed. Likewise, in a briefing for Western military attachés in Jakarta that month, an Indonesian military officer cited the figure of half a million dead. And in September, a Suharto emissary told State Department officials in Washington that 1.2 million had been killed.

In short, while it is impossible to say exactly how many people were killed in 1965–66, the consensus figure of 500,000 is hardly a fantasy of wild-eyed government critics. On the contrary, it is consistent with most official claims and statements, and it is much lower than some. As such, it should be regarded as a conservative estimate, at least until there is reliable evidence to the contrary.

Figure 189. University of Indonesia students with a straw effigy of Foreign Minister Subandrio, Jakarta, March 2, 1966. The caption in *Time* magazine read, "Effigy of ex-Foreign Minister Subandrio—orientally yellow and Communistically necktied—is labeled 'Dog of Peking' by students." (Harry Redl/*Time*)

## 57. Students Push the Envelope

By early March 1966, a gap had emerged between the army leadership and the student movement in Jakarta. Student leaders had come to view Suharto and the army as overly respectful of Sukarno and unnecessarily cautious in their actions. For the army, by contrast, the students were pressing the boundaries the army had set, which risked triggering intra-armed-forces conflict and the possibility that Sukarno would precipitate conflict that could no longer be controlled. The American chargé d'affaires, Edward Masters, reported that even Brigadier General Sukendro, whose inflammatory newspaper *Api* had been closed in November 1965, believed that "the Army leadership had been shamed by the students' courage and may now 'become patriots instead of soldiers.'"[11]

For several months, the anti-Communist action fronts had directed their deepest scorn at Foreign Minister Subandrio. On March 2, 1966, students at the University of Indonesia invited foreign journalists into their "war room," where they showed off a giant effigy of Subandrio that the students intended to burn together with Subandrio's office that afternoon. As the convoy approached Merdeka Square, however, the students were turned away by military troops and were forced to return to the university, where they hung the effigy atop a crane with a sign reading "Dog of Peking."

Despite the fact that students still mocked the United States, US diplomats came to view the Generation of '66 as the great hope for regime change and a full reorientation of Indonesian domestic and foreign policy:

Figure 190. Demonstrators at the University of Indonesia, March 2, 1966. The effigy of Foreign Minister Subandrio can be seen in the background. (Bettman-Corbis Collection/Getty)

Figure 191. HMI protesters with an effigy of Uncle Sam and a banner with the words "the barbarity of imperialism," Jakarta, early March 1966. (*Paris Match/Marie Claire*)

Figure 192. Women running a "public kitchen" from the back of a military truck to feed demonstrators. (Beryl Bernay)

While the political antics of the long-time Indonesian leaders . . . are being followed closely, a fresh, new generation has pressed to the forefront demanding to be heard. The anti-establishment youth says that the people are asking for bread but are still being given stones. In the purposeful move of Indonesian youth toward something better than the chaos bequeathed by their parents lies the possibility of real progress for the country. Unhampered to a large degree by the old psychological bonds of complexes and superstitions, these young people are receptive to and hungry for new ideas, and determined to wrest from the tangle of these past few months a decent future for themselves and their country.[12]

Students in Jakarta and other cities seemed largely oblivious to the ongoing violence in rural areas, and especially in the outer islands. Like US embassy officials, they saw themselves as heroic actors in a struggle to end a corrupt authoritarian regime. In this view, they had the support of a wide swath of the middle-class urban population, including women who provided them with food, shelter, and clothing during months of demonstrations.

## 58. Suharto Seizes Power

On March 11, 1966, President Sukarno signed an order transferring executive authority to Lieutenant General Suharto. Best known by its Indonesian acronym, Supersemar, the "Order of March 11" (Surat Perintah Sebelas Maret) provided a crucial "legal" fig leaf for the army's

Figure 193. Suharto declaring the nationwide ban on the PKI, March 12, 1966. (Bettman-Corbis Collection/Getty)

seizure of power and signaled the beginning of the end for Sukarno and the political Left. On March 12, Suharto issued a decree formally dissolving the PKI. A week later, fifteen members of Sukarno's cabinet were arrested, all of them leftists.

The events of March 11 occurred against the backdrop of mounting protests and violence by anti-Communist groups. On March 8, demonstrators attacked and ransacked the Foreign Ministry, scrawling anti-Subandrio slogans on its walls, smashing furniture, and slashing the tires of official vehicles. The graffiti included drawings of Subandrio as a small Pekingese dog or hanging from a gallows, and slogans like "Murderer of the Generals" and "Headquarters of the Suffering of the People." The next day, the office of China's New China News Agency was attacked and several employees were injured, prompting a formal protest from Chinese authorities. On March 10, demonstrators overran the Chinese embassy and a house used by the Chinese commercial attaché, where they burned furniture and official documents. The same day, a large group descended on the presidential palace and had to be turned away by troops.

Angered and worried by these indications of growing opposition and strife, Sukarno gathered political party leaders at the palace on March 10 and convinced them to join him in condemning the student protesters. The president hoped for a similar outcome at a cabinet meeting on March 11, but his plans were interrupted in dramatic fashion. As the meeting proceeded, the commander of the Presidential Guard, Brigadier General Sabur, rushed in and handed Sukarno a note that said unidentified troops were advancing toward the palace. In fact, they were soldiers of Colonel Sarwo

Figure 194. Suharto (left) behind Sukarno after the transfer of executive authority, March 11, 1966. Foreign Minister Subandrio is in the center. (Beryl Bernay)

Edhie's regiment, the RPKAD, and their intentions were clearly hostile. Understanding the danger, Sukarno hurried to his waiting helicopter and flew to his summer residence in Bogor about forty miles away, accompanied by Subandrio and Saleh.

Later that afternoon, three senior army generals (Basuki Rachmat, Amir Machmud, and Mohammad Jusuf) arrived from Jakarta by car to confront the president. Before leaving Jakarta, they had been briefed by Suharto and, on that basis, had drafted an order for Sukarno to sign. By the end of their tense meeting, Sukarno had signed the document, which authorized Suharto "to take all necessary steps to guarantee security and calm and the stability of the running of the government and the course of the Revolution."[13]

Exactly what was said in that meeting is unknown, and the army insisted that Sukarno had signed the order willingly. But it is abundantly clear that he had been given an ultimatum of some kind by the army—perhaps he was told that his security could not be guaranteed unless he signed the document. In any case, by ordering paracommandos to surround the presidential palace and by sending three senior army generals to confront him in Bogor, Suharto had sent an unambiguous message that Sukarno's fate was in his hands. In the words of a US official, he had carried out a "courteous constitutional coup."[14]

## 59. Army Victory Celebration

At six o'clock on the morning of March 12, 1966, Radio Jakarta broadcast the text of Announcement One from the Crush Malaysia Command (Komando Ganjang Malaysia), signaling the transfer of effective authority from Sukarno to Suharto. Thirty minutes later, the army announced that it would hold a "show of force" starting that morning. Ambassador Green sent the following description to the State Department:

> Parade or "show of force" began about 1000 hours at sports stadium with units taking almost two hours to pass Hotel Indonesia. Military column moving from south to north was joined at hotel by numerous busses, trucks and private cars loaded to capacity with yelling students coming from their assembly point at University of Indonesia. Student vehicles merged and were interspersed thereafter with military column.

Figure 195. British-made Alvis Saladin FV601 armored vehicles parade past civilians in central Jakarta, March 12, 1966. (*Paris Match/Marie Claire*)

Figure 196. Column of French-made AMX-13 tanks, which Indonesia purchased in the early 1960s, in Jakarta, March 12, 1966. (*Paris Match/Marie Claire*)

Figure 197. Pro-military youths swarm an armored vehicle, March 12, 1966. (*Paris Match/Marie Claire*)

Figure 198. For the army, the March 12 event was both a celebration and a media opportunity. (United Press International)

Included in parade were full battalion of RPKAD (at both beginning and end of column), sizeable contingent from 328th (Kudjang) Battalion, close to 100 armored cars and tanks, several truckloads of Brawidjaja troops attached to Kostrad, two trucks of police mobile brigade, one truck of marines (KKO), approximately one battalion of regular Siliwangi infantry and ten trucks of artillery. Civilian contingents include some 19 trucks of uniformed Ansor (NU youth), one truck from Gasbindo labor union and enormous number of student vehicles. One truckload contained student wearing bloody shirt as symbol of student dead. Other students on foot or mounted on top of tanks. Large crowds lined parade route for miles. They were in festive mood, threw flowers and cheered troops and, in particular,

the students. Both students and troops shouted slogans such as “Hang Subandrio,” “Long Live KAMI,” “Long Live the Armed Forces” and “Ban (left-wing) PNI.” Students were especially exuberant, whooping and shouting over their well earned victory.[15]

This was more than a celebration. The army intentionally scheduled the military convoy to begin while Sukarno was holding a meeting with all regional military commanders, thereby serving as a blunt repudiation of his authority. It was also a carefully planned media opportunity, with both foreign and domestic journalists present to mark the army’s triumphant victory.

Figure 200. Civilians ride in a convoy of trucks through the Pasar Baru neighborhood of Jakarta, March 1966. A foreign journalist in the foreground is taking photographs. ((National Library of Indonesia)

*opposite*
Figure 199. Civilians riding an army tank, with young women sitting in front. While celebrating the defeat of the PKI and the army’s ascension to power, many urban youths knew little about the ferocity or scale of violence in rural areas. (*Paris Match/Marie Claire*)

# VI. Allegiances and Suspicions

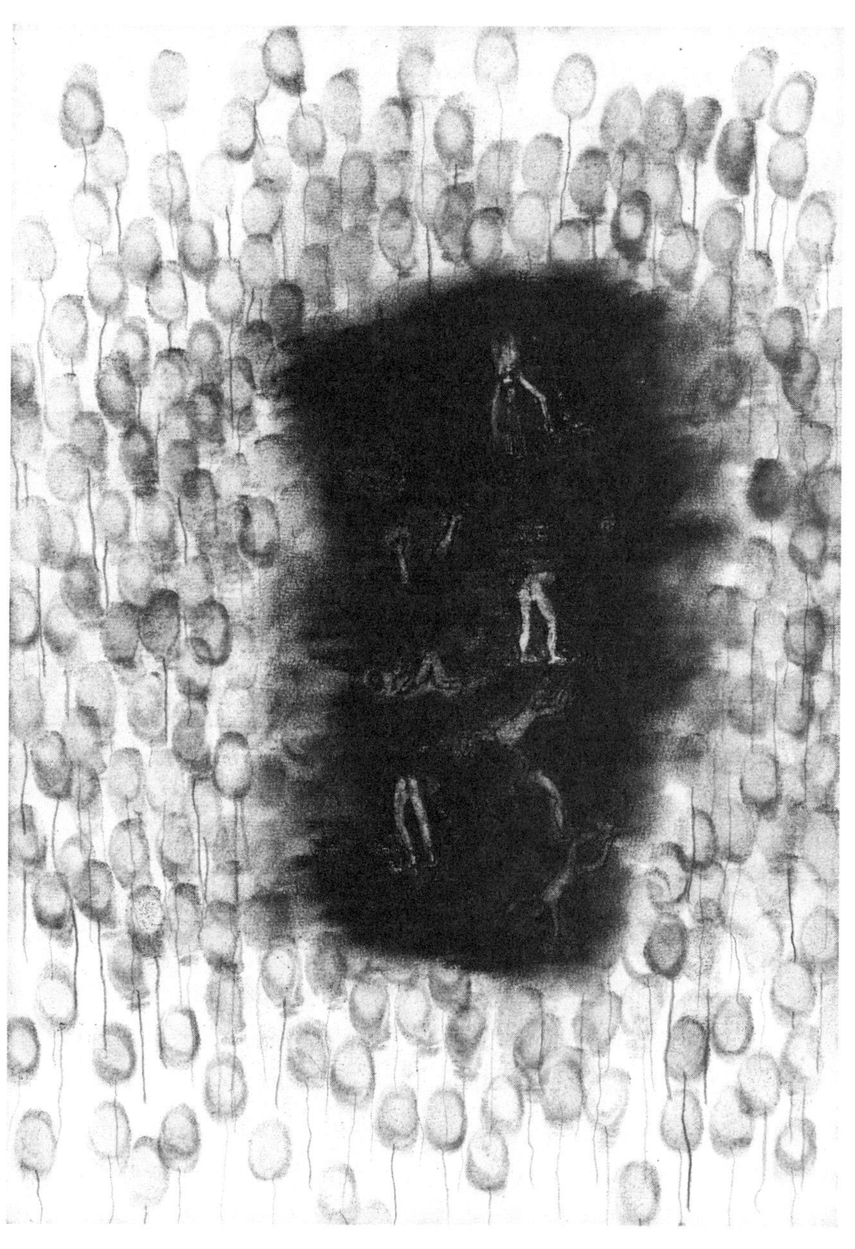

Figure 202. On a visit to the prestigious Bandung Institute of Technology in April 1966, General Nasution (right) met with Tjipto Sukardhana, commander of the student regiment. (National Archive of the Republic of Indonesia)

## 60. The Army-Student Alliance

Following the transfer of executive authority to Suharto on March 11, army leadership sought to harness student activism even more closely to its own aims. The army sanctioned the formation of student regiments at many elite state universities. On some campuses, paramilitary training was held, with students taught how to shoot rifles and operate machine guns. But the real emphasis was on uniforms and ceremonial inspections by regional army commanders. The student regiments helped to cement relations with the army and, perhaps of greater importance, served as a means of policing political activism on university campuses.

In Jakarta, the student action fronts—KAMI and the Indonesian Youth and Student Action Front (Kesatuan Aksi Pemuda Pelajar Indonesia, or KAPPI)—served as a vanguard in the army's ongoing struggle against Sukarno. While Suharto continued to move slowly against the president, student groups, often with army encouragement, staged demonstrations and hung banners throughout the city calling for the removal of members of the new cabinet and for lower consumer prices. Following cues from Suharto, students painted "Return to the 1945 constitution" and "Long live Suharto" around Jakarta. To consolidate the disparate student bodies and extend their reach throughout the education system, in early April the army sponsored a meeting in Yogyakarta at which a new national student union was established. The following month, KAMI and KAPPI cosponsored a four-day symposium titled "Rise of Generation of '66: Charting a New Course," with Vice President Mohammad Hatta and other high-profile figures delivering oblique attacks on Sukarno.

There was, however, also considerable regional variation in army-student relations. On a visit to Bandung in mid-April 1966, Nasution told KAMI leaders that only 10 to 20 percent of their

Figure 203. A soldier teaches university students how to operate a machine gun, Jakarta, March 23, 1966.

Figure 204. Soldier teaching a youth to shoot a gun. (Beryl Bernay)

demands had been met, and he encouraged a continuation of their actions.

In parts of Central and East Java, by contrast, there were frequent clashes between student groups demanding Sukarno's removal and those affiliated with the PNI. In Yogyakarta, days after the army-sponsored meeting, the formation of the local branch of the new student union led to physical clashes between rival student groups. Fighting between KAMI and PNI student groups was reported in Surakarta and Semarang. Tensions also stemmed from the political affiliation and sympathies of university rectors. In May, for example, the pro-PNI rector of Airlangga University in Surabaya called marines to campus to fend off aggressive KAMI students, who were backed by the locally based 507th Infantry Battalion.

Figure 205. The NU militant Subchan ZE, on his bed with books and a submachine gun, 1966. (Co Rentmeester/ LIFE Picture Collection)

## 61. The Role of Muslim Leaders

Muslim leaders, especially those associated with the NU, played a crucial role in the mass violence of 1965–66 and in the political maneuvering that accompanied it. Broadly speaking, they were staunch critics of the PKI and Sukarno and worked closely with the army after October 1. Within days, for example, members of the NU leadership called for the PKI to be banned, while the NU's paramilitary organizations, Ansor and Banser, became actively involved in army-coordinated mass arrests and killings. Meanwhile, many NU leaders and religious figures encouraged their followers to join in the violence.

While this account is broadly accurate, it obscures some important complexities. Far from being unified in its posture toward the PKI and Sukarno, NU leadership was deeply divided. On one side were the so-called "accommodationists" (including NU chairman Idham Chalid), who preferred to work with Sukarno and took a more moderate line on the PKI. On the other were the "militants" (notably the young firebrand Subchan), who were staunchly anti-Communist and critical of Sukarno and cultivated good relations with other anti-Communists, especially in the army.

Before October 1, 1965, the accommodationists had dominated the scene, but the events of October 1 changed the balance of power. Reluctant to act against the president, the accommodationists kept a low profile (Chalid reportedly even went into hiding for several days) and played only a marginal role in the party's decisions at that crucial juncture. By contrast, militant leaders immediately reached out to their contacts in the army, and with their approval began to mobilize opposition to the PKI. With army support, Subchan took the lead in setting up the anti-Communist action

Figure 206. General Nasution, wearing an Ansor cap, with Dr. Imam Chalid during NU anniversary. (National Library of Indonesia)

Figure 207. Girls at an Islamic boarding school. While Muslim leaders maneuvered for political influence, Islamic teachers in rural areas continued to mobilize their students. (Beryl Bernay)

front KAP-Gestapu and in issuing the NU's October 5 statement demanding the dissolution of the PKI. The NU's women's organizations, Muslimat and Fatayat, also played an early and active role in the anti-Communist actions.

The tensions between these two NU factions reached a crisis point in late October, when members of Ansor reportedly kidnapped Chalid, held him for two days, and, according to a US diplomatic cable, "persuaded him to take [an] oath on [the] Koran to stand up to [the] president."[1] For his part, Sukarno worked to buttress the position of the accommodationists and to weaken the militants. In late November, he summoned NU leaders Chalid and Zuhri to a meeting at which he offered Zuhri the position of fourth deputy prime minister, on the condition that Subchan would be sent abroad and Subandrio would be permitted to retain his post. And in the run-up to the Special Session of the parliament in June 1966, Sukarno reportedly offered Subchan a cabinet post in an effort to win his cooperation. While not wholly successful in sidelining the militant wing, these efforts served for a time to keep the internal conflict alive and in that way to blunt NU efforts to sideline Sukarno.

## 62. Floods in Central Java

In March 1966, torrential rains in the Surakarta residency of Central Java resulted in disastrous flooding. The inundations began in Wonogiri, a very poor district to the south, on March 1. Two weeks later, the Solo River overflowed its banks and the city of Surakarta was submerged under more than six feet of water. Ninety people died as a direct result of the floods, more than three hundred thousand people were displaced from their homes, and officials estimated total property damage to be 1 billion rupiah. In response to the flooding, the commander of the Diponegoro Regional Military Command, Major General Suryosumpeno, declared Surakarta a "closed city," and Governor Mochtar requested

Figure 208. Sutarto, a local journalist, photographed soldiers using inflatable boats in the flooded streets of Surakarta, March 1966. (Sutarto)

that it be declared a national disaster area. On March 22, Suharto skipped a scheduled meeting with Sukarno to fly to Surakarta so that he could assess the situation, and he promised 1 million rupiah in emergency relief.

There were reports that the killing of leftists ceased in some areas as a result of the floods, but when the *Washington Post* correspondent Stanley Karnow visited Yogyakarta and parts of Central Java in April, he found that nightly killings were still being carried out.

Government officials welcomed Japan's promise to provide twenty thousand tons of rice to help with relief efforts in Central Java, but their real interest was to meet the need for sixty-five thousand tons of rice per month for civil servants and military personnel. As a result, Suharto's government became increasingly receptive to the idea of a "Western club" that would help to stabilize government finances, but on the condition that it be led by Japan.

## 63. Suharto's Civilian Partners

Suharto had emerged as the preeminent leader of the campaign to destroy the PKI and undermine Sukarno's authority. In late March, following the installation of a new cabinet, Suharto declared, "With [the] support of [the] people, I have banned [the] PKI and taken steps against [a] number of ministers and other officials who were either connected with Gestapu/PKI, hesitant in sincerely supporting President, or lived immorally or anti-socially in luxury, thereby placing [a] burden on [the] shoulders of [the] people."[2]

In the weeks after Supersemar and the transfer of executive power, there was much concern about Sukarno's ability to cause trouble, as well as speculation about how and when the army would fully remove him from the presidency. A telegram from the US embassy reported, "Though Sukarno's wings have been clipped and he has no come-back capability, he can be a trouble maker. Thus one of [the] main tasks before Suharto-Sultan-Malik will be to keep the old man from interfering in important State affairs. This can be time-consuming and irritating. Yet his power is constantly declining, and a program . . . is now being drawn up to reduce Sukarno and Sukarnoism even further. Within several months it is hoped that Sukarno will just decide to pack up and go on a long trip abroad."[3]

Neither Suharto nor his allies had an interest in reviving the party system, but they recognized the need for mechanisms through which they could channel popular support. US officials also noted that "none of the dominant 'Triumvirate' of Suharto, the Sultan and Malik are oriented toward political Islam but, at present, the Moslems are the only element to emerge from the September 30 affair and its aftermath with significant political organization. The Triumvirate, accordingly, would probably like to erect organizational counter-weights to the Moslems."[4]

Foreign observers held vastly different assessments of Suharto, the sultan of Yogyakarta, and Adam Malik. Western governments praised Suharto's resolve in overseeing the killing of hundreds of thousands of leftists but continued to underestimate his political ambitions.

Figure 209. Sultan Hamengkubuwono IX of Yogyakarta, dressed in an honorary military uniform, April 5, 1966. (Rory Dell/ Camera)

Figure 210. Foreign Minister Adam Malik with US ambassador Marshall Green. (Beryl Bernay)

Malik was generally held in high regard for his diplomatic skills and his realistic assessment of the domestic situation. The sultan, by contrast, was viewed as the "weak link," lacking technical expertise, organizational skills, and the ability to mobilize popular support.[5]

## 64. Hundreds of Thousands of Detainees

By early 1966, there were hundreds of thousands of detainees across the vast archipelago. Some were held in regular prisons, others in properties seized by the military, and still others in makeshift camps or even open fields. The *Washington Post* journalist Stanley Karnow, who visited Central Java, East Java, and Bali in April 1966, briefed US embassy officials on his findings:

> Karnow [was] told by a number of local officials that killings of PKI prisoners were continuing on a systematic basis although the rate of killings was now sharply reduced over that of late 1965. One *lurah* (district official) reported that 80 prisoners had been killed in his area only last week. There are also large numbers of PKI prisoners being held. In Salatiga, for example, approximately 1,500 prisoners are being held in four locations in the town (one was the old PKI headquarters building). In Solo [Surakarta], Karnow was told that 1,000 prisoners were being held in a wing of the *kraton* [palace]. Karnow, like a number of other Western newsmen who have visited Indonesia recently, believes that estimates usually cited in the Western press based on diplomatic or Indonesian military sources are far too low.[6]

Local officials often expressed concern about their ability to feed the prisoners. In some areas the army used the lack of resources as an excuse to carry out further executions, and in other places as a threat that if resources were not made available, the prisoners would be handed over to civilians. Because of this lack of resources and the appalling conditions of detention, it was common for detainees' relatives to bring them food each day.

"High-value" prisoners, including those in Kopkamtib's Category A and Category B, were often moved from one prison to another. The journalist Dimyathi Saleh provided the following account of detainees in Boyolali: "There were 2,300 prisoners. They were partly captured during our operations, partly handed over by the people. They were housed in detention camps in the town. A special investigation team interrogated them. Those who were not guilty and not involved in the September 30 affair were returned to the community, followed by indoctrination by the authorities. Those who were clearly involved were subjected to legal measures in accordance with their crime. Some of them have been sent to Nusakambangan [a penal colony on an island off the south coast of Java]. Today there are only 500 prisoners."[7] In major cities, military searches for high-ranking Communists continued to bear fruit, including the arrest of several prominent leftist women. Among those detained was Suwardiningsih, one of the few female members of the PKI Central Committee. On the morning

Figure 211. Women bringing food to relatives detained in Wirogunan Prison in Yogyakarta, June 1966. Among those detained at Wirogunan was the artist Mia Bustam, a member of the leftist cultural organization LEKRA. Arrested by soldiers at her home in Yogyakarta in November 1965, she was held without trial for twelve years, half of them at Wirogunan.

of October 1, 1965, she had flown to Palembang, South Sumatra, where she remained active in the Communist underground and contributed to a publication called *Mimbar Rakyat* up until her arrest in July 1966. Several Gerwani figures also evaded arrest. While moving from one hiding place to another in Jakarta, Vice Chairwoman Sulami contributed to an underground publication called *Supporters of President Sukarno's Command*. She and a friend named Sudjinah eventually fled to East Java but were captured in 1967 and brought to Bukit Duri Women's Prison in Jakarta for what the army called "judicial interrogation," intended to establish guilt.

## 65. Chinese Indonesians and China

The transfer of executive authority from Sukarno to Suharto on March 11, and the subsequent arrest of many of Sukarno's former ministers, was a victory for the army. While operations to detain leftists continued in many regions, the army took measures to exercise far greater control over killings. It was in this context that a new round of anti-Chinese violence erupted in early April 1966. These attacks were particularly severe in East Java, where the anti-Communist action fronts seized Chinese chambers of commerce and schools in Probolinggo, Djember, and other second-tier cities. In East Java's capital city, Surabaya, there were even reports that anti-Communist Chinese planned to occupy the Baperki office.

These actions prompted the government of China to lodge a formal complaint with Indonesia on April 12. In doing so, however, China claimed that the victims were Chinese nationals, based on the legal concept of *jus sanguinis*, thereby distorting the reality that for a decade Baperki had fought for the right

Figure 212. Anti-Communist Chinese-Indonesians demonstrate on April 15, 1966. The banner on the left says "Crush! Radio Peking." (Bettman-Corbis Collection/Getty)

of stateless Chinese to become Indonesian citizens. The statement began,

> Since October 1965 the Indonesian rightwing reactionary forces have launched massive campaigns against the Chinese nationals in an organized and planned way.
>
> In all parts of Indonesia they have organized large numbers of hooligans for the unbridled persecution of innocent Chinese nationals. The houses and shops of thousands of Chinese nationals have been ransacked or burned up. Many associations and schools of Chinese nationals have been smashed up or seized. Large numbers of Chinese nationals have been beat up or unwarrantedly arrested. Many have been murdered in cold blood, or even beheaded, disemboweled, dismembered, or burned alive.[8]

Figure 213. Soldiers enter the Chinese embassy in Jakarta after it was ransacked by an anti-Communist mob, April 18, 1966. (TopFoto)

This view was fodder for the army's own campaign. Days later, the army mobilized ethnic Chinese to stage rallies opposing Communist China. In Jakarta, a mob consisting primarily of NU supporters stormed the Chinese embassy while security forces stood by watching. In Medan, North Sumatra, where there were tens of thousands of ethnic Chinese refugees, the All-Sumatra military commander was compelled to issue an order forbidding "acts of racialism," and in early May, the army organized a mass rally of more than twenty thousand Chinese. The US consul in Medan reported, "Carrying signs reading "Long Live Suharto," "Dissolve Peking Regime," "Expell [*sic*] Chinese Communist Organizations," demonstrators marched to All-Sumatra and North Sumatra Military Headquarters, where they presented donations for Army, Central Java flood victims, and Medan hospital. Demonstrators also presented several resolutions including demand for breaking diplomatic relations with CPR and request that GOI [Government of Indonesia] allow stateless Chinese [to] become Indo[nesian] citizens."[9]

While China and the domestic Chinese were a favorite target of demonstrators, and while there was destruction and seizure of property, only a few thousand were killed in 1965–66, and these because of their alleged affiliation with leftist organizations, not solely because of their ethnicity.

## 66. Changing Student Demands

The political atmosphere changed dramatically in the months after March 11, as the more militant student and youth groups demanded the removal of Sukarno and called for a complete break with the "Old Order." These anti-Sukarno forces were strongly supported by elements of the banned Indonesian Socialist Party and the Islamist Masyumi, and by some elements of the army. But the political situation in these months was fraught with conflicts, which gave Sukarno some room to maneuver and complicated efforts to remove him from power.

There were serious tensions within the armed forces, especially between the army and the other service branches and between supporters and critics of Sukarno within the army itself. Even after March 11, Sukarno still had substantial army backing in Central and East Java and within the other services. Sukarno sought to use that support to reassert his authority—for example, by meeting leaders of the air force, navy, and marines and by resisting demands for the arrest of Foreign Minister Subandrio. Conscious of these divisions, and fearful of unleashing serious intra-military conflict, Suharto and his army colleagues adopted a cautious, and outwardly deferential, posture toward Sukarno, deflecting demands for his ouster.

Suharto's cautious approach accentuated lingering tensions between the army leadership and the more militant youth groups. Paradoxically, those tensions laid the groundwork for a further extension of army power and a weakening of Sukarno's position. Backed by anti-Sukarno elements within the army (notably RPKAD commander Colonel Sarwo Edhie and Kostrad chief of staff Brigadier General Kemal Idris), the more militant youth groups began to pressure Suharto to move more forcefully against Sukarno and his allies. To press their case, on March 16, they kidnapped several members of Sukarno's cabinet and took them to the Kostrad headquarters. In the following days, they staged large demonstrations in Jakarta and Bandung. Then, on March 18, RPKAD forces led by Edhie arrested fifteen cabinet ministers, all of them Sukarno loyalists. Nine days later, a new cabinet was appointed that bore the clear imprint of Suharto's influence.

There were also conflicts among the various anti-Communist youth and student groups. In May, for example, the Muslim university student group HMI was expelled from the broader university students' action front, KAPPI, on the grounds that it had tried to monopolize the movement and for its "racist and anti-Sukarno tendencies."[10] When a crowd of HMI followers tried to storm a KAPPI meeting in Jakarta later that

Figure 214. Cartoon depicting the "Generation of '66" carrying a scroll with the state ideology Pancasila, destroying "immorality," "sycophancy," "economic and political dynasties," "feudalism," and the "cult of individuals." (*Trisakti*)

Figure 215. Student demonstration in Bandung, ca. June 1966. (Co Rentmeester/Getty)

Figure 216. The photojournalist Beryl Bernay with members of the anti-Communist Indonesian University Students' Action Front (KAMI), Jakarta. (Beryl Bernay)

Figure 217. Demonstration of the PNI-affiliated Indonesian National University Students' Movement in Bali, mid-1966. The banner reads, "Long Live Pak Harto! Long Live Bung Karno!" The German photojournalist Horst Faas is on the right. (Horst Faas/AP Images)

month, marines opened fire, killing one and wounding five others.

There were similar conflicts, and even some physical clashes, between the NU's Ansor and PNI followers in Yogyakarta, Surabaya, and elsewhere. These conflicts stemmed mainly from the groups' differing positions toward Sukarno and the army, with PNI followers remaining loyal and Ansor adopting a stridently anti-Sukarno and pro-army posture. In some areas, activists sought to fudge the difference. In Bali, for example, followers of the regional branch of the PNI-affiliated university student organization waved a banner expressing support for both the army and Sukarno, which read: "Long Live Pak Harto! Long Live Bung Karno!"

## 67. Salemba Prison

By mid-1966, hundreds of thousands of leftists were being held in hundreds of prisons and lockups across the country. Among these was the Salemba Special Detention Center, located in the heart of Jakarta. Conditions in Salemba were notorious, with chronic overcrowding, inadequate food, and poor medical facilities. A handful of photographs taken by foreign journalists at the prison in May and June 1966 provide a hint, but only a hint, of the terrible conditions in which the prisoners lived.

Built by Dutch colonial authorities in 1936 to house 750 prisoners, in 1965–66 Salemba held as many as 2,000 political prisoners, with up to five people crammed into cells of just 1.5 by 2 meters. One former prisoner described the colonial-era cells as similar to the

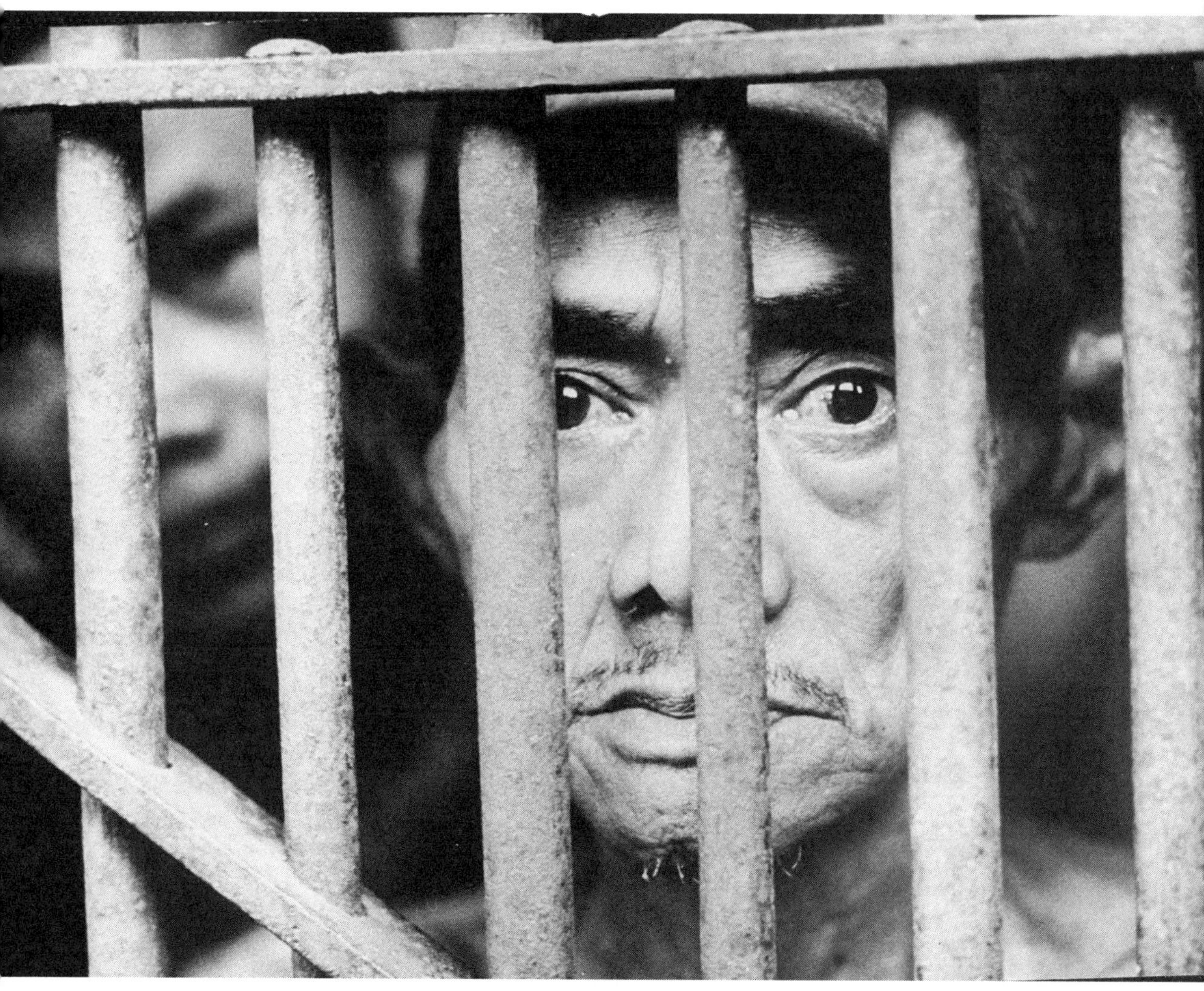

Figure 218. Man behind bars, Salemba Prison, Jakarta, 1966. (Co Rentmeester/LIFE Picture Collection)

Figure 219. Prisoners doing calisthenics, Salemba Prison, Jakarta, 1966. Published in *Time* magazine, this photograph was accompanied by the caption, "Communists arrested during weeks of trouble chant, 'We are keeping healthy in Salemba Prison,' during supervised calisthenics." (Harry Redl/*Time*)

cages at a zoo, but smaller. The lack of basic sanitation facilities in the cells compounded the problem of overcrowding. One prisoner who was transferred to Salemba in 1969 wrote that the inmates looked like they had been living on the streets—dressed in rags, their emaciated bodies covered in sores and lice—and that their putrid smell was unbearable.

Comprising several "blocks," each containing dozens of cells, the prison was encircled by two massive walls a meter thick. Between those walls was a strip of land where prisoners were put to work growing vegetables and fruit. A photograph by Co Rentmeester published in *Life* magazine in July 1966 shows several men working in this area, with one of the prison walls visible in the background. What the photo does not reveal is that this labor was neither voluntary nor paid, that the best of the produce went directly to army officers, and that the food given to the prisoners themselves was completely inadequate.

The inadequacy of prison food was compounded by extremely limited medical facilities. There was a rudimentary clinic but little or no medicine. The predictable consequence was that many prisoners suffered malnutrition and chronic illness. Their condition can be glimpsed in a photograph taken by Harry Redl and published in *Time* magazine in July 1966. This rare color image shows emaciated prisoners doing calisthenics under armed guard. Revealing as it is, the photo does not show the even more dire condition of one of Salemba's most important inmates, Colonel Abdul Latief. Shot and stabbed with a bayonet at the time of his arrest in October 1965, Latief suffered serious wounds that festered for almost two years while he languished

Figure 220. Prisoners working in the garden, Salemba Prison, Jakarta, 1966. (Co Rentmeester/LIFE Picture Collection)

in his cell. At one stage his wounds were so badly infected that they were teeming with maggots.

Most of the inmates in Salemba were Category B prisoners. In 1965–66, they included a number of esteemed cultural figures, such as the author Pramoedya Ananta Toer, and a good many army officers, including Latief. They were routinely subjected to religious and political indoctrination sessions by army officers. One former prisoner recalled that an army captain told him and his fellow inmates that they had been condemned by God because of their atheism, and that his role was to cure their outmoded ways of thinking. "I consider you all to be like people suffering a mental illness," he told them, "because you have been infected by Old Order and atheist thinking, and I am like the doctor who is going to cure you."[11]

## 68. The Indonesian Economy and Foreign Aid

The dire economic situation of 1965 continued through 1966. A devaluation of the Indonesian rupiah in December 1965 resulted in a dramatic rise in the price of rice and other commodities, accentuating the already desperate conditions for ordinary people. A series of photographs taken by the German war photographer Horst Faas in June–July 1966 captured the acute poverty in Jakarta and Bali. At the same time, these images revealed very little about the wider context of political maneuvering and violence in which it played out.

Figure 221. Woman returning from a market in Jakarta, June 1966.

Figure 222. Scene in a backstreet, Jakarta, ca. June 1966. (Horst Faas)

Figure 223. Women with milk aid provided by the US government, June 1966. (Horst Faas)

The army saw a swift economic recovery as crucial to its political goals. Its approach was driven largely by a group of University of Indonesia economists trained at the University of California, Berkeley, and later dubbed the "Berkeley Mafia." In a series of policy papers and seminars, they argued for a policy of dramatically reducing government expenditures while simultaneously guaranteeing the supply of strategic goods, such as rice and cotton. That strategy required, above all, a speedy rescheduling of Indonesia's crushing foreign debt—which was estimated to be US$2.5 billion in May 1966. It also called for foreign credits to pay for vital imports, thereby lowering prices and reducing the budget deficit. Rice, the essential staple of most Indonesians' diets, was a crucial piece of the puzzle. If the army could supply rice and bring the price down, its political position would be strengthened.

Whatever its merits, this strategy was politically very risky. After all, Indonesia's economic policy was based on the principle of "self-reliance" (Berdikari) and a powerful rejection of foreign assistance. In 1964, Sukarno had famously told the United States to "go to hell with your aid!" Any sign that the army was now begging Western governments for aid could easily backfire and provide Sukarno with a political cudgel with which to beat back his critics. Accordingly, with army agreement, Western powers initially provided assistance on a purely covert basis, often through third parties. In late December 1965, for example, the US embassy coordinated with Catholic Relief Services and the army to distribute food and other assistance. That setup, the US ambassador wrote, would "minimize risks of possible adverse political notice."[12] As this and many similar arrangements made clear, foreign assistance had a distinctly political purpose: to support the army in crushing the PKI, removing Sukarno, and establishing a regime sympathetic to Western interests.

With Suharto's usurpation of executive authority in March 1966, foreign aid and credit from Western powers began to flow more freely, and by mid-1966, large economic assistance programs were underway. In quick succession, the United States, Japan, the United Kingdom, and other powers provided Indonesia with millions of dollars in bilateral food aid and other support, as well as generous loans. In July, for example, US ambassador Green proposed the provision of one hundred thousand bales of cotton and up to five hundred thousand tons of rice, and in August he promised Suharto $500 million in bilateral aid. Meanwhile, key Western governments began to meet with Indonesian officials to develop a multilateral plan for economic recovery and "modernization." That plan—which led to the creation in 1967 of a multilateral aid consortium called the Inter-Governmental Group on Indonesia—entailed a major program of debt rescheduling, long-term commitments of economic and military aid, and a significant relaxation of restrictions on foreign investment.

In the long term, those arrangements led to a stabilization of the national economy. But in the short term, Indonesia continued to be gripped by poverty. Moreover, the massive flow of foreign aid and investment set in motion at this time served to bolster the army regime and to obscure the grotesque campaign of violence through which it came to power.

## 69. Reorienting Indonesian Foreign Policy

Even as his authority was coming under increasing attack from the army, in December 1965 Sukarno had insisted that Indonesian foreign policy would remain unchanged. "There will not be [the] slightest change in our determination to carry out Confrontation. . . . Malaysia is a threat to our safety and sovereignty . . . we will not be encircled or contained. I will continue to help [the] people of Malaya, Singapore, Sarawak, Sabah and Brunei to become free."[13] What Sukarno didn't know was that the army, working through its intelligence agency, had already initiated secret talks with Malaysia to bring an end to Confrontation. And in May 1966, the new foreign minister, Adam Malik, openly stated that Indonesia would do exactly that. Soon after, army units that had been posted to North Sumatra and West Kalimantan as part of the Confrontation campaign were withdrawn and returned to their home regions.

Figure 224. Soldiers disembark in Jakarta after serving in West Kalimantan as part of the Confrontation campaign against Malaysia, June 20, 1966. (United Press International)

For the United States, the United Kingdom, and other Western powers, ending Confrontation was only a first step in the longer process of realigning Indonesian foreign policy away from Sukarno's strident anti-imperialism. In Indonesia, however, the army and its civilian backers continued to view the US with some suspicion. A particularly sensitive issue was the undeclared US war in Vietnam, where in early 1965 there had been a massive buildup of troops and the onset of Operation Rolling Thunder. Ambassador Green wrote, "Indonesian attitudes on Vietnam are still ambivalent. For[eign] Min[ister] Malik has privately supported our stand but, for domestic political reasons, has felt it necessary to criticize publicly [US] bombings in Hanoi-Haiphong area. In information media, where attitudes are in process of transition, wide range of opinion is expressed, much of which [is] still unfavorable to US."[14]

Furthermore, as early as January 1966, Green had identified the need "to include Indonesia in some type of regional framework." Ruling out the Southeast Asia Treaty Organization on the grounds that it was too "tainted' by its pro-Western origins and stance, Green concluded, "What is needed when the time is appropriate is a new concept to include both pro-Western and neutral states of Southeast Asia and possibly Australia to turn Indonesia's energies outward in a more responsible manner."[15] This conception eventually led to the formation of the Association of Southeast Asian Nations (ASEAN) in August 1967.

## 70. Militarization and Demobilization

The mobilization of civilians was a central element in the army's attack on the PKI and involved a diverse range of actors, activities, and aims. In urban areas, anti-Communist action fronts inflamed passions and spread the call for the destruction of the PKI, but they were only rarely involved in more than the destruction of property or the detention of leftists. In rural areas, by contrast, it was youth groups associated with political parties—the NU's Ansor and Banser, the PNI's Pemuda Marhaenis and Banra, IPKI's Pemuda Pancasila, and the Catholic Party's Pemuda Katolik—that took directions from and acted in coordination with army troops in the worst of the violence.

Though it was less visible to many observers, during this same period the army was equally busy overseeing an entirely different form of militarization. This effort began in October and November 1965 with the purge of suspected leftists from the civil defense force (Pertahanan Sipil, or Hansip), which was directly under the local military commanders, and the People's Resistance (Perlawanan Rakyat, or Wanra), which was under local civil authorities. Following the early purges in Java and parts of Sumatra, in late November 1965 the ministers of defense and the interior sent instructions for the recruitment of new Hansips, with a target of one platoon in every village, one company in every subdistrict, one battalion in every district, and one brigade in every province.

Militarization served different aims for different actors. For the leaders of the anti-Communist political parties and mass organizations, paramilitary forces were a way to demonstrate their power and lobby for influence with the emerging army elite. For many youths, participation in paramilitary groups was an expression of identity, and at times even a form of protection against accusations that one had leftist affiliations, tendencies, or relatives. For the army, rural militarization was generally strategic, while urban militarization provided the spectacle of threat and the consolidation of power. During the first half of 1966, the military was eager to provide civilians with paramilitary training. In some instances, the training included the use of weapons, but more often it was simply calisthenics and marching with bamboo staves or mock wooden guns. These activities wed new actors to the military and helped to fill out parades and "shows of force," especially in the lead-up to the Special Session of the parliament in June 1966.

Following the Special Session, however, the military increasingly sought to tighten its control over the many civilian forces, especially in areas like East Java

*opposite*

Figure 225. Army units, in full combat gear, were on display in major urban centers in the lead-up to the Special Session of the parliament in June–July 1966. (Horst Faas)

Figure 226. Man posing with a machete, Jakarta, 1966. (Co Rentmeester/LIFE Picture Collection)

Figure 227. Catholic nuns and students serving refreshments to army personnel, probably Jakarta, mid-1966. (National Library of Indonesia)

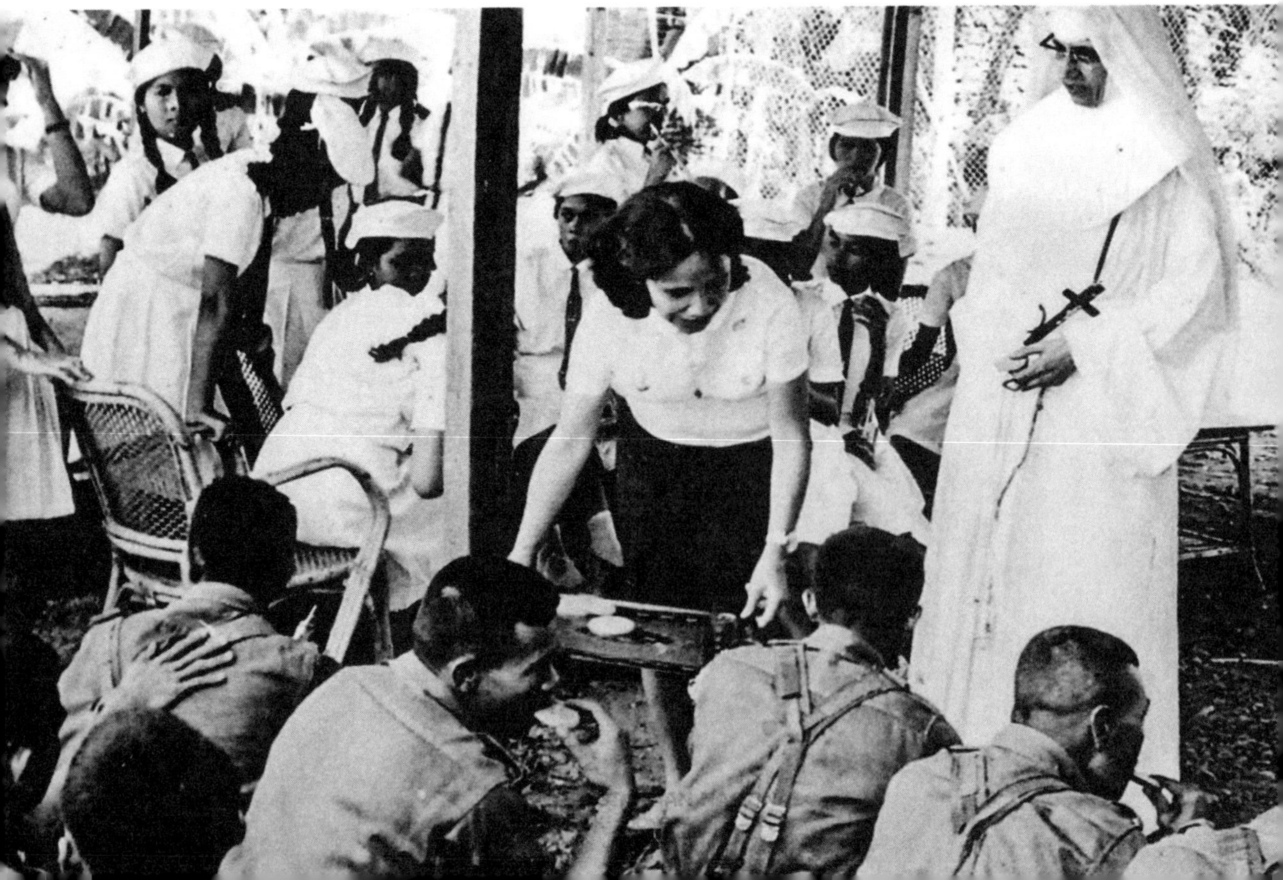

Figure 228. Original AP caption: "Speak softly and carry a gun: Indonesia's graceful girls are moving in a new style these days; they march. From pre-teenagers to matronly types, thousands of females in this Asian country are in uniform." (Horst Faas)

Figure 229. Students from a secretarial school drill with guns in Jakarta, mid-1966. (Co Rentmeester/LIFE Picture Collection)

Figure 230. Women in uniform marching with guns, ca. July 1966. (Horst Faas)

where fighting broke out among rival anti-Communist organizations. Some paramilitaries were recruited into the Hansip and Wanra, but others were ordered to disband. For example, the regional military commander in East Java issued an order in September 1966, suspending all paramilitary training as a way to demobilize the many student and youth regiments, which by mid-1966 were becoming less useful and more of a liability.

## 71. KAMI Caricatures Attacking Officials

In its campaign to overthrow Sukarno and his Old Order, the Indonesian University Students' Action Front (KAMI) employed a range of tactics and methods, including protest marches, demonstrations, strikes, and violence. It also made its case through visual media, including poster-sized cartoons and caricatures. Similar in style to the political cartoons printed in army-controlled newspapers of the day, they were drawn or painted on large canvasses or cardboard, sometimes measuring several feet, for display in public places. Few if any of these poster-cartoons have

Figures 231–234. Posters produced by KAMI's Parman Battalion show officials abusing their authority in the name of the people. (National Library of Indonesia)

survived, but a handful of photographs taken at the time offer a glimpse of their messages and visual themes.

Reflecting the preoccupations of KAMI activists, the posters typically attacked government officials for corruption, immorality, duplicity, selfishness, or greed, and juxtaposed the depraved behavior of officials with the suffering of ordinary people. One poster, for example, depicts a government official holding a bundle of cash in one hand and a bottle of alcohol in the other while consorting with an attractive young woman. Offstage a poorly dressed man and woman sit silently, holding out their empty bowls. The caption reads, "Attention, meeting in progress." Another poster is a scathing attack on the president himself, focusing on his alleged selfishness and duplicity. In it, an angry Sukarno stands at a microphone saying, "Me, me, I, me" alongside a caption that reads, "False myths must be banished."

The visual language of these posters is intentionally easy to read. Officials are fat and well dressed, often in jacket and tie and shoes, and they stand in arrogant postures, their mouths open, one hand raised with finger pointed in a hectoring manner. Meanwhile, the suffering people are dressed in little more than tattered briefs, shoeless and unshaven, sitting or lying on the ground. In a typical example, a fat man in a suit and tie lectures a poor man who lies abjectly on his back, wearing only a pair of patched shorts, his protruding ribs clearly visible.

The posters of which there are photographs were created by members of KAMI's "Parman Battalion," based in Bandung, West Java. They appear to

Figure 235. Students with a hand-drawn poster showing Sukarno saying, "Me, me, I, me." It is labeled, "False myths must be banished." (National Library of Indonesia)

Figure 236. Youths reading the daily newspaper *Harian KAMI*. (Beryl Bernay) have been part of a public exhibition held in the city sometime in mid-1966. KAMI held a similar exhibition in Jakarta in August 1966, at which more than one hundred cartoons were displayed. Although in that case, the army instructed the students to withdraw eight cartoons it regarded as overly critical of Sukarno, these exhibitions and others like them undoubtedly had army approval.

## 72. The Special Session of the Parliament

By mid-1966, then, the army and its allies had made substantial progress in their campaign to annihilate the PKI and sideline Sukarno, but that progress was far from secure. They now sought to consolidate their gains by convening a Special Session of the parliament. Chaired by Sukarno's nemesis, General Nasution, the session lasted from June 20 through July 5. While the session did not remove Sukarno from office, and indeed revealed that he still had many supporters, it rejected his nine-point accountability speech (titled "Nawaksara") and provided a pseudo-constitutional veneer for the army's power grab. This seriously undermined the president and his allies.

Figure 237. Sukarno delivers a speech to officials, early July 1966. Suharto (seated) disdainfully feigns sleep. (Algemeen Nederlands Persbureau)

Figure 238. Students belonging to KAMI Bandung stage a protest in Jakarta, July 2, 1966. One demonstrator standing atop the leading truck is dressed to look like Sukarno, who is the target of the students' animosity.

Figure 239. Political flyer attacking Sukarno, mid-1966. Sukarno is shown declaring that Indonesia is a beacon to the world. Below, the text reads, "The Old Order: Prestige and arrogance built on lies! The New Order: Truth based on common sense." The stamp in the lower right corner shows that the poster was produced by a Bandung-based art group. (Beryl Bernay)

In its most important move, the parliament formalized Sukarno's letter of March 11, which granted Suharto extensive authority to "restore order." It also stripped Sukarno of his title of president for life and ordered him to report again to the parliament on the causes of the September 30th Movement and the reasons for the country's moral and economic decay. The parliament also signaled a major departure from Sukarno's foreign policy, declaring a commitment to ending Confrontation and returning to the UN. In one of its most consequential decisions, the MPRS formalized the ban on the PKI and its

Figure 240. Political poster attacking Sukarno, who had declared himself the "mouthpiece of the people." The caption reads, "Mouthpiece of the people Old Order–style." (Beryl Bernay)

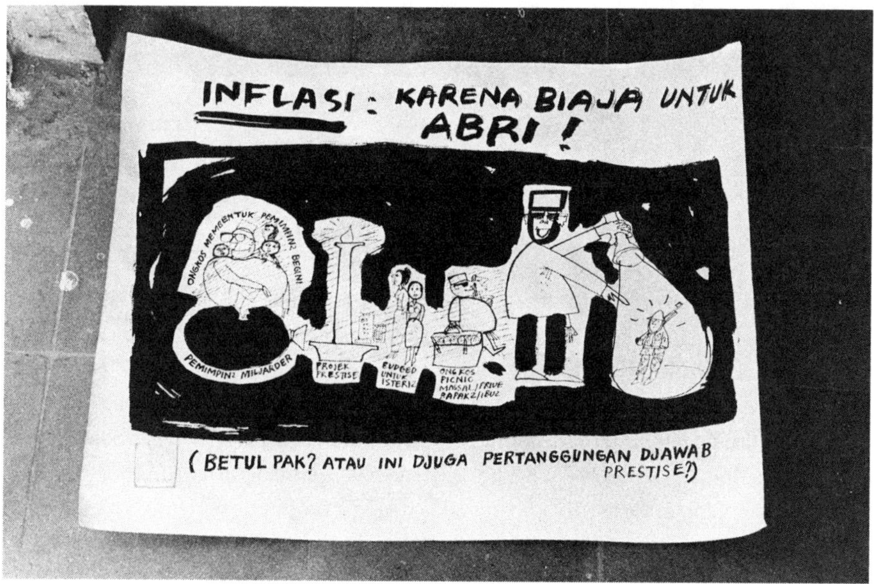


Figure 241. The caption at the top presents a Sukarno-era explanation: "Inflation is caused by military expenditures!" The caption at the bottom presents the New Order critique: "Is that true? Or is this how the prestigious take responsibility?" (Beryl Bernay)

affiliates and outlawed the dissemination of Marxism, Leninism, and Communism. That decree (TAP MPRS XXV/1966) became the "legal" foundation for years of repressive actions against the Left, and it remains in effect today.

At the same time, the Special Session of the parliament made clear that the contest between Sukarno and the army was far from straightforward. In the streets outside the meeting hall, tens of thousands of students and Muslim youths, brandishing hand-drawn posters, angrily denounced Sukarno and called for his resignation. Inside the hall, the mood was less categorical.

Figure 242. Suharto (in military uniform) at an official presentation of the new government's program intended to achieve political, social, and economic stabilization, mid-1966. The term "Ampera"—a portmanteau of "Demands of the People's Suffering" (Amanat Penderitaan Rakyat)—was coined by Sukarno, but by mid-1966 it had been co-opted by Sukarno's critics and was used as the name for the new bundle of policies and the new cabinet. (Beryl Bernay)

With the PNI leader Osa Maliki and the NU figure Subchan elected vice chairs, there was certainly no sympathy for the PKI. But there was a reluctance to embrace the more strident attacks on Sukarno. In debates and committee meetings, PNI and NU delegates resisted the most drastic measures and voiced continued, albeit muted, support for the president.

For its part, the army leadership understood that Sukarno retained support within the PNI and the NU, both of which had large mass bases, and within the armed forces, especially in East and Central Java. Underscoring the continued support for the president within the armed forces, on July 1 several truckloads of marines who had come from East Java to Jakarta drove past the parliament building, shouting, "Long live Bung Karno!" Wary of sparking a backlash from these elements and the political parties, the army leadership adopted a more cautious approach than the students and some Muslim leaders demanded.

Paradoxically, Sukarno seems to have interpreted the army's caution as a sign of weakness, and in the following weeks he sought to reassert his authority. Ultimately, however, the Special Session marked a crucial turning point in the struggle for political power. The new cabinet that was formed a few weeks after the Special Session, although ostensibly selected by Sukarno, bore the army's clear imprint. Twelve of its twenty-seven members were military officers, and key Sukarno loyalists were removed and replaced by well-known anti-Sukarnoists.

Figure 243. Sukarno (left) points an accusing finger at his nemesis, Suharto, August 24, 1966. (Agence France Press)

## 73. "Sukarno Is Still President!"

In his Independence Day address on August 17, 1966, Sukarno directly challenged Suharto and the army:

> This year of 1966—they say—at last, at last, at long last. President Sukarno has been grabbed by his own people; there has been a coup against President Sukarno; President Sukarno has been stripped of all his power; President Sukarno's hands have been tied by a "triumvirate" consisting of General Suharto, Sultan Hamengkubuwono, and Adam Malik. . . .
>
> At first, and indeed for a certain period of time, the 11th March Order made them exult joyfully. They thought the 11th March Order was a "transfer of authority." In fact it was not. The 11th March Order is a security order. . . .
>
> They had it all wrong! And now, too, on this Proclamation day, they are wrong again!! Hey, Sukarno is still President! Sukarno is still Great Leader of the Revolution! Sukarno is still Mandatory of the Provisional MPR! Sukarno is still Prime Minister! Sukarno is again standing on this rostrum![16]

Suharto and Nasution not only ignored Sukarno's speeches; they used his words against him. They mocked Sukarno for having said that the murder of the generals on October 1 was nothing more than "a ripple in the ocean of the Revolution." A final showdown was looming.

# VII. The New Order Emerges

## 74. Declaring the New Order

A week after Sukarno's August 17, 1966, Independence Day address, the army began a weeklong seminar in Bandung at which it adopted the term "New Order" to distinguish between the emerging regime and that of Sukarno. The term was by no means new. In a telegram sent to Washington, DC, in March 1966, Ambassador Green had referred to the struggle for influence in the "new order." Soon thereafter, the student action fronts started using the same phrase to distinguish between Sukarno's government, now termed the "Old Order," and the newly emerging regime. And in July, in a speech to the American Men's Club in Jakarta, Adam Malik had explained, "Since October last year a great process of political transition has been taking place, from what is popularly now called the Old Order to the New Order."[1] The army seminar recommended that before general elections were held in 1968, Suharto should "take executive action to regroup political and social forces in parliament" and "guarantee the role of the armed forces" so that in the postelection period, the New Order would flourish.[2]

Figure 245. General Nasution (left) and General Suharto, in full dress uniforms, attending the army conference in Bandung, September 1966. (*New York Times*)

In the months after the army adopted the term "New Order," student activists once again took to the streets. They now began to call openly for Sukarno's ouster and demanded that he be tried before the Extraordinary Military Tribunal. The timing of their actions was no coincidence. As on earlier occasions, these demonstrations were encouraged and coordinated by army leadership, with Suharto's approval. In September 1966, the US embassy reported, "The students themselves were having great difficulty mobilizing sentiment against Sukarno himself for a variety of reasons. . . . By early September, however, it was reliably reported that Suharto had given his approval to a nation-wide campaign geared to the theme of 'New Order vs. Old Order,' and a series of Action Command briefings got underway in the effort to begin accelerating activities."[3]

But the army's alliance with the students was an unstable one, with students pushing hard for immediate and drastic action against Sukarno, while the army—ever conscious of the president's continued popularity within certain branches of the armed forces and in some regions—sought to ease him more gradually from power.

Figure 246. Political cartoon showing Sukarno trying to stamp out what he called the "October 1st Movement" (Gestok), unable to see that beneath the surface it was really the September 30th Movement, the PKI, and those engaged in "guerrilla politics." (*Harian KAMI*)

Figure 247. Demonstration in Jakarta demanding that Sukarno be brought to trial before the Extraordinary Military Tribunal (Mahmillub), October 24, 1966. (Gamma-Keystone/Getty)

Figure 248. Apocryphal drawings of naked Gerwani women torturing the generals on October 1, 1965, produced by KAMI Bandung, September 1966. (Beryl Bernay collection)

As street demonstrations accelerated and student demands became more strident, the army's desire to control the process became increasingly clear. It now indicated that it expected "constitutional processes" to replace popular agitation as the preferred means to remove Sukarno and manage the transition to the New Order. Several top army officials (including Nasution and Jakarta regional commander Major General Amir Machmud) made public statements to that effect, and army crackdowns on student demonstrations in some areas made it clear that the new line had been passed down to the provinces.

Suharto's hand in these machinations was unmistakable and well known. As the US embassy reported in mid-October 1966, "While Suharto's attitude toward student demonstrations may ease after [a] cooling off period, odds are that henceforth he will keep [a] much tighter rein on [the] anti-Sukarno campaign and that direct assaults on [the] palace will not be permitted."[4]

## 75. Political Trials Continue

The number of political trials in the Extraordinary Military Tribunal intensified during the last quarter of 1966. On September 27, Suharto hand-delivered the indictment against Foreign Minister Subandrio to the court in Jakarta. After thirteen days of questioning, the prosecutor requested that the judges impose the death penalty. The following day, Subandrio read his defense statement, denying that he had any involvement in the September 30th Movement and breaking into tears. On October 25, the panel of judges sentenced him to death.

Further trials were soon held in the provinces, including North Sumatra, Yogyakarta, and Central Java. The trial of former air force commander Omar Dhani began in Jakarta on December 5 and concluded on December 24, with a verdict of guilty and a sentence of death. By the end of 1966, a total of sixteen individuals had been brought before the Extraordinary Military Tribunal, of whom three were given life sentences and the rest the death penalty.

These trials were not simply about individuals accused of involvement in the September 30th Movement. They were, in the words of Harold Crouch, also a "means of discrediting the president

*(above)* Figure 250. Foreign Minister Subandrio listening to the presiding judge read out his sentence following his trial, October 25, 1966. (Netherlands National Archives)

*(left)* Figure 249. Former air force commander Omar Dhani on trial, Jakarta, December 18, 1966. He was sentenced to death but was later pardoned and finally released from prison in 1995.

by proxy and demonstrating his lack of power to save his most loyal colleagues."[5] During Dhani's trial, evidence was presented to suggest that Sukarno had conspired with the plotters on the morning of October 1, 1965.

## 76. Sukarno's Last Speech

In mid-December 1966, the army intensified its pressure on Sukarno to account for his actions on October 1, 1965, and to condemn the September 30th Movement. A series of tense meetings ensued over a two-week period. Sukarno finally relented, and on January 10 he spoke grimly before the military commanders. He said the September 30th Movement had caught him completely by surprise; he said that his favored term, the "October 1st Movement" (Gestok), referred to the assassinations of the generals that morning; and he blamed the PKI leaders for their "confusion." But he still hoped to salvage his position.

Military hard-liners and the most militant student action fronts were still not satisfied, and they intensified their attacks in the streets and via the media. In response, and almost certainly acting

Figure 251. Cartoon with caption "Your statement of accounts is demanded," showing Sukarno under spotlights representing the parliament (MPRS), the action fronts, the press, and the people. (*Merdeka*)

Figure 252. Sukarno delivering his final public speech, titled "Supplement to the Nine Points" (Pelengkap Nawaksara), at the presidential palace in Jakarta, January 10, 1967. (National Library of Indonesia)

Figure 253. High school students demanding that Sukarno be put on trial. (Agence France Press)

Figure 254. Cartoon showing time running out on Sukarno. (*Sinar Harapan*/Beryl Bernay collection)

Figure 255. Men sleeping at the base of a monument with graffiti featuring the statement "Sukarno is the Great Gestapu" and a crudely drawn hammer and sickle. (Beryl Bernay)

on instructions from the army, the parliament passed a resolution calling for a special session to remove Sukarno from the presidency. The military mobilized eighty thousand troops in the capital in preparation.

As part of its campaign, the military further restricted Sukarno's movements and closely vetted whom he could meet. Allowing him to meet with officials from China provided further evidence of Sukarno's "Communist sympathies" and thus could be used against him.

## 77. Suharto Becomes President

The Special Session of the parliament began on March 7, 1967, and five days later Suharto was installed as acting president—one year and one day after Sukarno's March 1966 executive order transferring authority to Suharto. Eighteen months of mass violence and student demonstrations demanding that Sukarno be placed on trial had served their purpose. But Suharto had no interest in an actual trial that would give Sukarno a chance to speak and mobilize his supporters. In a speech the day after becoming acting president, Suharto explained, "For the time being we will treat him as a president who no longer has power, as a president who has no authority of any kind in the fields of politics, the state, and government."[6]

Remarkably, two months later, the press reported that at the time of the Special Session, the security apparatus had uncovered a plot to assassinate Suharto and nineteen members of his government. Real or manufactured, this news provided yet another opportunity for arrests of former high-ranking officials, and soon after, Suharto evicted Sukarno from the palace in Jakarta and banished him to a state property in Bogor, two hours' drive to the south.

Figure 256. Sukarno was forced to endure the ceremony at which Suharto was installed as acting president. (Associated Press)

Figure 257. Suharto posing on March 12, 1967, after being installed as acting president. (Associated Press)

## 78. Supardjo and Sudisman Trials

The political trials of high-profile figures accused of involvement in the September 30th Movement continued into 1967. Among the most important were the trials of Brigadier General Supardjo, a Sukarno loyalist tried in February and March, and Sudisman, the fourth-ranking member of the PKI Politburo, who was tried in July. Like those that preceded them, these were show trials, one element of the political campaign to remove Sukarno from power and to destroy the PKI.

Supardjo's arrest and trial occurred against the backdrop of the army's final push to remove Sukarno from power. He was arrested on January 12, 1967, just two days after Sukarno had defied the parliament by denying any involvement in the September 30th Movement. The most senior army officer involved in the movement, Supardjo was captured at the home of an army officer near Lubang Buaya, where the generals' bodies had been dumped down an unused well. He reportedly had in his possession a letter of protection from Sukarno.

At his trial, Supardjo defended Sukarno and insisted that there really had been a Council of Generals, which had necessitated action by the September 30th Movement. But far from saving the president, the trial served only as a stage prop in his ouster. As the trial drew to a close in early March, the parliament met under heavy security to orchestrate Sukarno's removal. In a speech on March 7, Suharto obliquely accused Sukarno of complicity in the alleged coup. As if in a hurry to remove any contradictory evidence, two days later, Supardjo was sentenced to death; three years later he was executed by firing squad in Cimahi, West Java. He was dressed in white, his request to

Figure 258. Brigadier General Supardjo on trial, Jakarta, February 1967. Supardjo was sentenced to death by the court, and in May 1970 he was executed. (Bill Lord/Camera Press)

Figure 259. PKI Central Committee member Sudisman escorted into court, Jakarta, July 1967. He was sentenced to death and later executed. (Perpustakaan Online Genosida 1965–1966)

wear his military uniform having been denied.

If Supardjo's trial was part of a campaign to remove the president, Sudisman's trial was intended primarily to drive a nail into the coffin of the PKI. At the time of his arrest on December 6, 1966, Sudisman was one of only two top PKI figures still alive and the assumed successor to Aidit. Sudisman's trial began on July 7, 1967, and lasted just under three weeks. A key witness at trial was Sjam Kamaruzaman, who claimed to be the head of the PKI's Special Bureau, tasked with recruiting army members to the party, but who may well have been a double agent working for army intelligence. Whoever Sjam was and whatever his agenda, he became the army's star witness during this and later trials—testifying that the September 30th Movement and the Revolutionary Council it established were the brainchildren of the PKI.

Compared to the earlier political trials, press coverage and foreign embassy interest in the Sudisman trial were slight. The only foreigner on hand for the final days of the trial was a young academic, Benedict Anderson, who later translated Sudisman's defense statement, "Analysis of Responsibility." In that statement, given before the court on July 21, 1967, Sudisman denied that the PKI had masterminded the alleged coup, and he offered an eloquent critique of the army and its New Order. He was sentenced to death on July 27, his forty-seventh birthday, and executed by firing squad three years later.

## 79. The Chinese and China, 1967

Suharto's regime passed a series of new anti-Chinese policies. The Chinese-language press was forced to close down in October 1965, and the extensive system of private Chinese-language schools was officially closed in May 1966. Ethnic Chinese were encouraged to assimilate by changing their names. The regime also adopted the use of the pejorative term *Cina* in place of the neutral, Hokkien-derived words *Tiongkok* (originally meaning "Middle Kingdom") and *Tionghoa* (Chinese).

The "Chinese" issue exploded once again in April 1967. The trigger was an announcement by Jakarta regional commander Major General Amir Machmud that Chinese-language pamphlets circulating in Jakarta called for ethnic Chinese to resist oppression. A week later, a Chinese man named Ling Siang Yu, who was accused of being a spy for China, died in detention. Tens of thousands of stateless ethnic Chinese turned out for Ling's funeral, which became a protest against discriminatory state policies. Two days later, several thousand youths staged a counterdemonstration and marched into the city's Chinatown, north of Merdeka Square, where they attacked residents.

Indonesian-Chinese relations rapidly deteriorated. In response to the demonstration and riot, the Indonesian government expelled the Chinese consul general and trade representative, accusing them of subversive activities, and announced that it would expedite the repatriation of Chinese who did not have Indonesian citizenship. The Chinese government retaliated, expelling two Indonesian diplomats. Soon after, the

Figure 260. Chinese youth rescued from violent demonstrators, April 22, 1967. (Bettman-Corbis Collection/Getty)

Figure 261. Members of the Pandjaitan student battalion protest against China, August 1967. The poster in the middle says, “Stop, there’s no road to Peking!” and appears to show a pedicab or rickshaw pulled by someone who might be Sukarno being stopped by military personnel. (National Library of Indonesia)

Indonesian government established a Special Staff for Chinese Affairs, which reported directly to Suharto’s cabinet, and a Contact Body for Chinese Affairs. Both bodies aimed to exert executive control over the ethnic Chinese population.

The tit for tat between Indonesia and China continued for several months. In Jakarta, the military arrested ethnic Chinese whom it accused of subversive activities, while also encouraging the Pancasila Youth and other anti-Communist organizations to stage demonstrations opposing China. On October 1, 1967—the second anniversary of the September 30th Movement—anti-Communist demonstrators again attacked the Chinese embassy, this time seizing property. Finally, on October 9, the Indonesian government suspended diplomatic relations with China.

## 80. US Support for the New Order

Despite its success in destroying the PKI and sidelining Sukarno, it was not obvious that Suharto’s New Order would survive or thrive. A crucial factor ensuring that it did so was the economic and political backing the regime received from the United States and its allies.

After a period of cautious and largely covert backing, in mid-1966 US support for Suharto and his New Order became more open and enthusiastic. The earliest signs of such backing took the form of a substantial program of multilateral economic assistance. The program entailed the swift rescheduling of Indonesia’s foreign debt and the provision of hundreds of millions of dollars in loans for the import of essential goods such as rice and textiles. Developed by the International Monetary Fund and the World Bank together with the regime’s

Figure 262. US vice president Hubert Humphrey laying flowers on the grave of General Yani in Kalibata Cemetery, Jakarta, November 1967.

US-trained economists—the so-called Berkeley Mafia—the plan was backed by a consortium of donors that came to be known as the Inter-Governmental Group on Indonesia. The United States pledged at least one-third of the total assistance package, making its aid program to Indonesia one of the largest in the world at the time.

These moves led to a radical reorientation of Indonesia's economy away from Sukarno's program of self-reliance and toward an openly pro-Western liberalization, in which the free flow of capital would, in theory, stimulate economic stabilization and recovery. A crucial aspect of that shift was the opening of Indonesia to direct foreign investment. A new law on foreign investment drafted in 1966–67, with the assistance of a US consultant, led to a rush of foreign investment, especially in extractive industries, as companies like Freeport Sulphur (later Freeport McMoRan), Mobil, and the Japanese Petroleum Exploration Company signed deals for the exploitation of Indonesia's vast reserves of oil, natural gas, and minerals.

The United States also sought to buttress the New Order regime through open political backing. That move reflected a conscious endorsement of the military as the country's central political power and of Suharto as leader. As Ambassador Green later recalled in his memoir, US officials "agreed that for the military to withdraw from a major and active role in political life would be disastrous for Indonesia at that time. . . . I felt we should be doing everything possible to help Suharto."[7]

US political backing was conveyed through its diplomatic recognition of the new regime and a series of high-profile meetings with influential American political figures. In October 1967, Green flew to Washington to brief President Lyndon Johnson and his cabinet on the situation in Indonesia. His briefings provided a glowing account of Suharto and made a strong case for expanding US economic and political support for the New Order. As he later wrote, he told the cabinet "how Indonesia had escaped a communist take-over, and how Sukarno was being replaced by a sound, friendly leader who had ended Confrontation with Malaysia and rejoined the U.N., had converted to a free-market economy and welcomed foreign investment, and had helped form a new Southeast Asian regional organization [ASEAN]."[8] Shortly

Figure 263. US ambassador Marshall Green at Suharto's home, December 1, 1967. A photograph of Sukarno installing Suharto as army commander on October 16, 1965, is on the wall. (Larry Burrows/LIFE Picture Collection)

thereafter, according to Green, Johnson sent Suharto a "warm personal letter . . . congratulating him and his government on Indonesia's solid achievements over the past year in its stabilization effort and reassuring him that the U.S. would 'continue to have an active, supportive interest in Indonesia's needs.'"[9]

Green's briefings in Washington set the stage for a politically important three-day visit by Vice President Hubert Humphrey in November 1967. During his visit, Humphrey had several meetings with Suharto, as well as a palace banquet, and also made a point of visiting and laying flowers on the grave of General Yani, one of the six generals killed on October 1, 1965. The visit sent a powerful message of US support for the new regime and laid the groundwork for many years of economic and political cooperation.

## 81. Students and the New Order Regime

The student activists involved in the urban action fronts expected to be rewarded for their role in assisting the army's campaign against the PKI and Sukarno. Those from Islamic organizations, especially the HMI, hoped the new regime would allow for meaningful representation of Islam. While a handful of student leaders did receive official positions in the bureaucracy and subsequently rose to national prominence, it quickly became apparent that the army leadership had no intention of allowing independent voices within the emerging New Order regime. For the architects of the regime, inclusion meant co-optation and control, not representation.

One result of this lack of inclusion was the rise of new, critical undertones in student activism. This shift was particularly apparent following Suharto's installation as acting president in March 1967. A few days later, three thousand students held a large demonstration in

Figure 264. Demonstrators demanding the "rule of law," Jakarta, March 1967. (United Press International)

Jakarta with placards demanding that the new regime "uphold" the rule of law and hold national elections the following year. While these demands may have sounded straightforward, they were in fact the subject of dispute as well as a good deal of confusion. Over the previous year, the slogan "rule of law" had been shorthand for the demand that Sukarno be put on trial for his involvement in the events of October 1, 1965; now at least some demonstrators understood the phrase as muted criticism of the gross violations of the law perpetrated by the army and the emergence of a new authoritarianism that excluded the very students who had supported regime change. The army's response to the demonstration was telling: more than five hundred shots were fired into the air in order to break up what was clearly a protest.

Figure 265. Cartoon in a student newspaper showing a poster that reads, "Corrective critique [is a form of] social control." The call is ignored by leaders, presumably intended to depict Suharto, two generals, and a technocrat. (*Mahasiswa Indonesia*)

*opposite*
Figure 266. By 1968, social activism also reflected global trends, including both Western counterculture and opposition to the US war in Vietnam. In this photograph from February 1968, an Indonesian hippie cites the "San Francisco declaration," perhaps referencing a famous 1966 article in the *San Francisco Oracle* titled "A Prophesy of a Declaration of Independence." (United Press International)

MAKE LOVE
NOT
WAR!!!
SAN FRANCISCO DECLARATION

## 82. The "Night-time PKI"

Even after the worst of the killings had subsided in mid-1966, the army and the New Order regime remained concerned about what they referred to variously as "Gerpol" (a portmanteau of "guerrilla" and "politics") and "PKI Malam" (literally "Night-time PKI," meaning the Communist underground). While these terms gained prominence in 1967, both terms were already in use by mid-1966. In fact, in an address at the presidential palace on September 13, 1966, Sukarno had directly addressed the accusations leveled against himself and his wife Hartini: "There's a tendency [to think] that Bung Karno is, so to speak, part of the PKI Malam, of the underground PKI. That it is Bung Karno who is going along with PKI guerrilla politics. That even Bung Karno's wife engages in guerrilla politics. That's the tendency."[10]

Figure 267. Mbah Suro, the Javanese mystic accused of leading the "Night-time PKI" (PKI Malam), after his arrest in 1967. (Ramelan, *Mbah Suro nginggil*)

The most remarkable reporting about the PKI Malam involved a long-haired mystic in Ngawi District, on the border of East and Central Java, named Mbah Suro. In 1966, the press reported that "remnants of the Gestapu/PKI adventurers" and some ethnic Chinese had traveled to Mbah Suro's rural home to ask for predictions about the future. Reporting about the mystic escalated over the following months, and it was soon claimed that Mbah Suro had five thousand followers, among whom were Communists from Jakarta, Surabaya, and other major cities. After repeated approaches by the military had been rebuffed, the army launched operations involving three battalions and special forces personnel in March 1967. The operation resulted in Mbah Suro's capture and the arrest of thousands of his followers in the vicinity of Purwodadi. Two years later, the Dutch-Indonesian human rights activist Poncke Princen and the journalist Jopie Lasut published a report on the "Purwodadi Affair," revealing that several hundred, and perhaps as many as one thousand, of Mbah Suro's followers had in fact been massacred while in detention. The pro-regime press vilified the authors for stirring up a hornets' nest, and the two were arrested.

In the eyes of the military, the troubles in Purwodadi were not an isolated incident but further evidence of a much wider underground threat, which the army hyperbolically called the People's Resistance Army (Tentara Perlawanan Rakyat). In Central Java alone, the regional military command identified PKI cells in the Merapi-Merbabu mountain complex, around Mount Lawu, Mount Sindoro, Mount Muria, and several other upland areas. These, the army claimed, had ties to PKI cells in East Java, especially in the Blitar region as well as the volcanic uplands to the east of Malang, and in West Java, particularly in the greater Cirebon-Majalengka-Indramayu area.

Concern about the PKI underground was by no means restricted to Java. Across Sumatra, the military conducted cleanup operations throughout 1967, 1968, and 1969. In Lampung, for example, a three-month military operation in May 1969 netted sixty alleged Gestapu/PKI fugitives. Concern also lingered that Communists and ex-Communists were hiding in plain sight in the civil service and the military, leading to localized campaigns to purge state institutions of their influence. The motivation for these anti-Communist witch hunts varied from place to place. In some areas, authorities believed that the scope of the anti-Communist purges in 1965–66 had been insufficient and that a real threat remained. Elsewhere, military officers felt compelled to launch operations in order to prove their own anti-Communist credentials. And still elsewhere, political rivalries and ambitions led to accusations, on which the authorities felt compelled to act. One of the most remarkable of these was in Buton, in Southeast Sulawesi, where in March 1969 accusations against the local district head led to a string of arrests and a purge of civil servants.

While the actual threat posed by members of the now-banned PKI and its affiliates was minimal, reporting on the PKI Malam and the arrest of its members was useful for propaganda purposes. It served to keep the threat alive and to justify the ever-greater reach of the army into all facets of civilian life.

## 83. Rebellion and Mass Violence in West Kalimantan

In August 1966, the Indonesian and Malaysian governments signed an accord formally ending Confrontation. In keeping with the accord, the army instructed "volunteers" who had been mobilized to participate in Confrontation to return their weapons. But any hope that this agreement would be the end of the issue was misplaced. In early 1966, having evaded arrest since the previous October, the leader of the West Kalimantan branch of the PKI, Said Achmad Sofyan, who was of mixed Arab and Madurese descent, established a base in the mountains northeast of the provincial capital, Pontianak. This location put him in close proximity to the large population of rural and mostly stateless ethnic Chinese and within easy distance of the coastal towns where support for leftist organizations had been centered. From this new base, the PKI built an extensive underground organization and even established a "city committee" in Singkawang.

In early 1967, Sofyan met with leaders of the Sarawak People's Guerrilla Force (Pasukan Gerilya Rakyat Sarawak, or PGRS), which was the armed wing of the banned Sarawak Communist Party, and the even smaller North Kalimantan People's Force (Pasukan Rakyat Kalimantan Utara, or Paraku), whose members had fled Brunei following the abortive 1962 uprising there. The PGRS and Paraku had made common cause against the federal government of Malaysia. Now, with Indonesia and Malaysia coordinating their counterinsurgency efforts along the border, PGRS/Paraku and Sofyan's underground PKI were prepared to cooperate. In July 1967, these forces attacked the small Indonesian Air Force base located in Sangau Ledo, capturing 150 weapons.

Shocked by the attack, the Indonesian Army moved into high gear. Suharto summoned the regional commanding officers in Kalimantan to Jakarta, and plans were made for an offensive. But military assessments of the "gang of Chinese communists," as Jakarta referred to them,[11] varied wildly; some officials claimed that Sofyan had no more than ninety followers, others that his organization had as many as five hundred members. On the other side of the border, it was estimated that PGRS/Paraku had several thousand troops. West Kalimantan was declared an "operations area" and new units from Java (including the RPKAD) and Sumatra were sent to begin operations. But with little concrete intelligence and a vast, heavily forested

Figure 268. Soldiers burning a house in West Kalimantan, ca. 1968. (Bettman-Corbis Collection/Getty)

Figure 269. Soldier teaching a Dayak youth to use a gun, ca. December 1968. (Keystone-France/Getty)

area stretching to the border with Malaysia, military commanders first settled on a strategy of removing the rural Chinese population on which Sofyan's forces relied for supplies and support.

As had been the case in Java, Bali, and elsewhere, the army's strategy in West Kalimantan was premised on mobilizing civilians to attack alleged Communists. That strategy was rendered more difficult by the long history of amicable ties between the ethnic Dayaks and the ethnic Chinese, who numbered 450,000 in the province. To overcome this impediment, units from the RPKAD carried out a series of small-scale atrocities against ethnic Dayaks that they blamed on the "gang of Chinese communists." In one case, nine Dayaks were kidnapped and killed; in another, a Dayak leader was killed and, according to stories, left castrated with a note written in Chinese characters claiming responsibility. The army then called on Dayaks to take revenge on the Chinese population at large for these acts. When these efforts failed, RPKAD troops stepped up operations, resulting in several massacres. While the armed forces newspapers proudly credited the army for military successes, military authorities in West Kalimantan blamed these massacres on the Communists, with the aim of inciting Dayaks to take revenge. The result was that in the last months of 1967, ethnic Dayaks operating under instructions from the army (and at times alongside it) killed several thousand Chinese villagers. Tens of thousands of Chinese fled from the interior to the coast, where many were forced into detention camps surrounded by barbed wire and armed guards.

The regional military commander, Brigadier General Soemadi, later wrote

Figure 270. Ethnic Chinese detainees behind barbed wire, Singkawang, West Kalimantan, ca. 1967. (Keystone-France/Getty)

with pride about the role the army had played in instigating ethnic Dayaks to attack the Chinese: "With each victory of the Dayak people in these kampungs, we always held traditional victory feasts with dancing and drinking of rice liquor from the skulls of PGRS-Paraku members killed by the local people."[12]

## 84. Refuge and Violence in South Blitar

At the height of the attack on the PKI in 1965–66, Communists and other leftists had sought refuge in the anonymity of big cities such as Jakarta, Semarang, and Surabaya. But as military sweeps and new efforts to register residents intensified, even moving from one safe house to another became untenable. In late 1966, surviving PKI leaders in East and Central Java started scouting rural areas for new hideouts. One location they identified as promising was the southern part of Blitar, in East Java. The limestone karsts and relative lack of fresh water along the southern coast made this a poor area. Support for the PKI in Blitar had been strong prior to October 1, 1965, with the Pemuda Rakyat claiming to have twenty-five thousand members; after October 1, there were reports of clashes between party supporters and the military as well as alleged PKI sabotage. But in a conversation with the outgoing US consul in Surabaya in late November, the regional military commander "discounted Blitar as a place

Figure 271. Wanted poster from ca. 1968 issued by the Malang District Military Command, near Blitar, East Java. The poster calls on the public to detain the "Gestok/PKI fugitives" and turn them over to the army. (Etnohistori Collection)

Figure 272. Poster reading, "Beware . . . don't be used as bait," showing a fiendish PKI member manipulating a naive villager, labeled "the people." Posters like this appeared in many villages in the course of the army's 1968 military operation in Blitar. (Etnohistori Collection)

of trouble."[13] Blitar had not suffered from mass killings and in late 1966 was not a focus of military attention.

PKI leaders viewed southern Blitar first and foremost as a place of refuge, and secondarily as a possible experiment in reviving the party and establishing a Yenan-style guerrilla base. Meanwhile, individuals from a range of backgrounds and with a variety of motives were attracted to the area. They included deserters from the army, those seeking to reunite with family members, and still others simply seeking safety. Party cells were established and efforts made to reach out to former party members. But activism risked drawing unwanted attention, and weapons were scarce.

Beginning in mid-1967, there were increasing reports of attacks—including robbery, kidnapping, and even murder—on members of the NU throughout East Java. Blitar soon came to the attention of the NU's armed wings, Ansor and Banser, and Islamic leaders argued that the area was a Communist haven and that the PKI was attempting to rebuild. It was not until May 1968, however, that East Java regional military commander Brigadier General Jasin decided to launch a major campaign named Operation Trident (Operasi Trisula) involving five thousand troops from six infantry battalions. Between June and early September, the southern part of Blitar was cordoned off and checkpoints were established to monitor movement in and out of the region. Army troops rounded up villagers and searched houses and the extensive network of caves in the karst landscape. A Western journalist who was allowed to visit the area reported that "every village

Figure 273. Military personnel during operations in Blitar, 1968. (National Library of Indonesia)

Figure 274. Soldiers search a cave in Blitar for Communists, 1968. (National Library of Indonesia)

Figure 275. Captured alleged Communists in Blitar, 1968. (National Library of Indonesia)

Figure 276. Army officers interrogate captured alleged Communists in Blitar, 1968. (National Library of Indonesia)

Figure 277. An army officer addresses villagers in Blitar, 1968. (National Library of Indonesia)

Figure 278. Army officer showing seized evidence to an unidentified Associated Press journalist in Blitar, 1968. (National Library of Indonesia)

Figure 279. Military checkpoint in Blitar, 1968. (National Library of Indonesia)

is plastered with colorful posters, which depict the party as a cruel fairy-tale ogre enticing the poor peasant to his lair." One militia leader boasted to the journalist, "We don't take many prisoners. If there's the slightest doubt about someone, we shoot first."[14]

In the course of the military campaign in southern Blitar, an estimated two thousand people were captured or killed. It is doubtful that those killed and arrested ever represented a serious threat to national security, or that such a massive military operation was in any way necessary. More than anything else, the operation was an effort by the army to demonstrate its power and to sow terror among populations that had yet to accept its authority.

## 85. Burying Sukarno

New investment laws passed in 1968 spurred a rush of natural-resource extraction. Concessions for timber and minerals were doled out to political cronies and army officers. Suharto and his wife, Tien (who became known as "Mrs. Ten Percent" for the kickbacks she received), quickly amassed a vast fortune.

In 1970, after four years under house arrest in Bogor, Sukarno died. Five years earlier, he had told the journalist Cindy Adams that he wanted a simple funeral and headstone: "When I die, bury Bapak in accordance with Islam, and on a plain little stone write simply: Here lies Bung Karno, the mouthpiece of the Indonesian people."[15] Suharto ensured that the state funeral, held in distant Blitar, was simple because he wished to bury not only Sukarno but Sukarnoism as well.

In 1971, the New Order held its first legislative elections. Hundreds of thousands of former prisoners were denied the right to vote. The regime's new electoral vehicle, Golkar, won 68 percent of the vote, and the following year the People's Consultative Assembly dutifully selected Suharto to serve another term as president.

*above*
Figure 280. Cartoon in which Suharto and his wife, carrying bags of money, ride away from a mass grave. (*TAPOL Bulletin*)

*right*
Figure 281. State funeral for Sukarno in Blitar, East Java, on June 22, 1970. (Bettman-Corbis Collection/Getty)

# VIII. Long-Term Detention

## 86. Release of Category C Prisoners

In 1969, Suharto's government sought a long-term solution for the tens of thousands of people detained since October 1965. Senior officials discussed the possibility of releasing Category C prisoners on Independence Day. But in an address before the national legislature on August 16, Suharto rejected the proposal on security grounds and instead chose to move forward with the transportation of thousands of Category B prisoners to newly established Exile Camps, the centerpiece of which was Buru Island, in the Moluccan Islands.

Over the next few months, further discussions ensued about the fate of Category C prisoners. There were conflicting reports about their total number. Attorney General Sugih Arto stated in October 1969 that twenty-six thousand would be released. The following month, the Diponegoro Regional Military Command announced that it was holding a total of twenty-four thousand political prisoners in Central Java, of whom six thousand were in Category C.

Mass releases began in early 1970: 85 prisoners released in Tangerang in January; 1,295 prisoners released in Central Java in February; and so on. By the end of 1970, tens of thousands of prisoners had been freed.

But there were also new arrests. In North Sumatra, for example, 478 suspected "pro-Peking" Communists were detained in 1969 alone. As the attorney general explained, "It was not possible for the government to give the exact number [of political detainees] since it was like a floating rate, like the yen vis-à-vis the dollar: every day it changes."[1]

Figure 283. Release of Category C political prisoners in Semarang, Central Java, 1970. (National Library of Indonesia)

## 87. Detention in West Kalimantan

Long-term imprisonment in West Kalimantan differed greatly from that in the rest of Indonesia. With the army focused primarily on Java, Bali, and Sumatra, and with the resolution of Confrontation dragging into mid-1966, few real or alleged Communists were detained in West Kalimantan in 1965–66. It was only in late 1967, in the context of the campaign against Communist remnants and the Malaysian PGRS/Paraku rebels, that the violence erupted on a large scale.

The result was the relocation of tens of thousands of rural ethnic Chinese who were targeted because they were Chinese, not because of actual leftist affiliations. Some fled out of fear, others under military escort. Within a month of the army-instigated massacres of ethnic Chinese, there were sixty thousand "refugees" in Pontianak and other coastal towns, of whom about half were living with relatives or simply squatting; the other half were being held in official "camps" run by the military. By August 1968, the official numbers had fallen to 12,500 refugees living with families (a gross underestimate) and 15,500 in the

Figure 284. Military officers explaining the security situation in West Kalimantan to visiting journalists, 1971. (Peter Schumacher)

Figure 285. Ethnic Chinese prisoner in West Kalimantan, 1971. (Peter Schumacher)

guarded camps. Numbers fluctuated, of course, and over the next several years an additional 25,000 ethnic Chinese were forced out of rural areas to the coast.

Conditions in the military detention centers were horrific. The Australian scholar Herbert Feith, who visited West Kalimantan in 1968, described extreme overcrowding, shortages of food, and a lack of medical care. Malaria and other diseases were common, and death rates were high. Sexual abuse of female prisoners was also rampant.[2]

To address the eyesore of impoverished refugees, provincial authorities drew up plans for permanent resettlement—9,000 families in Pontianak, 4,000 families in Sambas District, and 1,500 families in Ketapang District—but little came of this proposal. Instead, those who were not detained sought work as laborers, fishermen, and traders

Figures 286 and 287. Ethnic Chinese prisoners, Pontianak, 1971. (Peter Schumacher)

Figure 288. Ethnic Chinese man in a cell, Pontianak, 1971. (Peter Schumacher)

in and around the coastal towns, while others made their way to Jakarta or elsewhere.

The Dutch photojournalist Peter Schumacher arrived in Jakarta a few weeks before the 1971 general election, the first to be held under the New Order. Schumacher was invited to join a group of journalists accompanying Foreign Minister Malik on a campaign tour of West and South Kalimantan. While in Pontianak, the regional military commander provided Schumacher and the other journalists with an overview of the security situation in the province, complete with maps showing where operations were ongoing.

Schumacher asked the regional military commander, Brigadier General Soemadi, if he could visit a detention center for political prisoners on the outskirts of Pontianak. The initial reply was that there was not enough time, and in any case permission would be needed from Jakarta. The next morning, to his surprise, Schumacher was taken to the camp and given permission to roam freely and take photographs for twenty minutes. The prisoners in the open-air compound were mainly ethnic Chinese, including a number of women who, he was told, had been couriers for the Communists. The cells below held men who, it was said, were the real, hard-core Communists. Schumacher later wrote, "The light was bad, but I still took photographs, although I had no flash. We could exchange a few words with them, but because there were soldiers escorting us, they did not say much. Yes, they were treated quite well, but they were never allowed out of their cells to be aired. The authorities confirmed this."[3]

## 88. Buru Island Prison

The largest and most notorious of the long-term prison camps was located on remote Buru Island, in Indonesia's Moluccan archipelago. Starting in 1969,

Figure 289. Entrance to Wanapura Unit X, Buru Island, November 1971. The sign on the right reads, "Toward a new life." (Peter Schumacher)

Figure 290. Barracks in Wanapura detention camp, Buru Island, November 1971. (Peter Schumacher)

Figure 291. Soldiers arriving at one of the Buru detention camps, 1971. (Visual Documentation Project)

as many as fourteen thousand political prisoners were sent to the island, where they were made to carry out forced labor and suffered extreme hardship and isolation. Most remained until the late 1970s, when an international human rights campaign finally led to their conditional release.

The camp was officially run by the office of the prosecutor general and was described as a "rehabilitation project" (Proyek Instalasi Rehabilitasi Pulau Buru). In reality, Buru was a penal colony staffed and managed by the army. Official statements made clear that it was devised as a solution to the "problem" of Category B prisoners who could not be charged or tried due to lack of evidence. Among the detainees held at Buru were many of Indonesia's leading intellectuals and cultural figures.

The Buru facility was made up of eighteen separate, numbered sites, each encircled by barbed-wire fencing and kept under heavy military guard. The sites were connected by rough trails that had been cut through the jungle by the prisoners themselves. Routinely subjected to harsh treatment by camp guards, many prisoners died or suffered serious illness due to overwork, poor nutrition, and inadequate medical care.

Following Dutch colonial practice, the Buru Island camp was designed not only to punish political detainees but to isolate them. Under pressure from human rights organizations, the media, and some foreign governments, the authorities permitted occasional visits by the International Committee of the Red Cross (ICRC) and foreign journalists. These visits were tightly controlled by the army. Detainees were warned not to speak critically or to share compromising information with visitors and suffered collective punishment when they did. Despite those restrictions, reports and photographs from Buru eventually reached a wider public.

Figure 292. Group of prisoners on Buru Island, 1971. (Visual Documentation Project)

Figure 293. The filmmaker Basuki Effendi, Buru Island, November 1971. (Peter Schumacher)

## 89. Buru: Journalists and Other Visitors

Access to Buru Island was extremely limited from the outset and was further restricted following the publication of critical media reports in the early 1970s. Still, the authorities did permit highly controlled visits by some domestic and foreign journalists and ICRC delegations. Despite official efforts to limit what these visitors saw and heard, their reports and photographs offered an invaluable glimpse into the workings of the Buru regime and the conditions under which detainees lived.

Among the most important of these visits was one by Peter Schumacher in

Figure 294. Basuki Effendi (left) with the photojournalist Peter Schumacher, Buru Island, November 1971. (Peter Schumacher)

1971. His black-and-white photographs of the camp barracks and of detainees breaking rocks, digging ditches, and working in the hot sun were then and remain among the most detailed and compelling images available of the camps. His intimate photographs of the filmmaker Basuki Effendi and the writer Pramoedya Ananta Toer, clad in numbered prison uniforms, underscored the reality that many of the country's leading cultural figures were languishing in a concentration camp. These images became a central element of Amnesty International's successful campaign to free Indonesia's political prisoners.

In a troubling twist, the authorities also invited some leading Indonesian psychologists to visit the island to assess the mental state, and political disposition, of the detainees. Over the course of two days, the psychologists from the University of Indonesia and Gajah Mada University conducted personality tests and interviewed detainees before sharing their conclusions with army officers and journalists who had accompanied them on the visit. The prisoners, they said, were doing very well and were well on their way to shedding their Communist sympathies and embracing the state ideology, Pancasila.

## 90. Buru: Forced Labor

Government and military officials insisted that the goal of the Buru camp was to rehabilitate political prisoners, in part by allowing them to undertake productive work. Prisoners have the "right" to work, they said, and work is good for body and soul. In practice, Buru was a penal colony in which prisoners were required to perform all kinds of arduous and unpaid labor, under armed guard and constant threat of punishment, just to stay alive.

Among other tasks, prisoners built the crude barracks in which they lived, the watchtowers and fences that surrounded their camps, and the offices and quarters of the officers who guarded them. They constructed the miles of trails and roads connecting the eighteen

Figure 295. Prisoners with agricultural tools on an irrigation dyke, Buru Island, November 1971. (Peter Schumacher)

Figure 296. Prisoners working wood, Buru Island, November 1971. (Peter Schumacher)

camp facilities, a job that involved clearing dense tropical forest and grasslands with simple hand tools such as sickles, machetes, and axes. As photographs taken in the early 1970s show, they also dug miles of irrigation ditches, felled and removed huge trees, broke rock into gravel, and made salt from the sea. All prisoners were required to carry out this work, regardless of age, health, or

Figure 297. Prisoners crushing rocks, Buru Island, November 1971. (Peter Schumacher)

physical condition, and many suffered injury and exhaustion as a result.

To supplement the meager rations provided by their captors, most prisoners grew crops on land they had carved out of the jungle, and some raised chickens and other small farm animals. All too often, however, this produce was confiscated by army officers for their own use or to sell at a profit in the market in the nearby town of Namlea. Army officers also required prisoners to work in the officers' houses and offices, labor for which they received little or no compensation. It was not without reason that the International Labor Organization lodged a formal complaint about Buru in 1973–74 and Amnesty International began to call the scheme what it was: a system of forced labor.

Figure 298. Political prisoners on Buru gather for the funeral of their friend Sukotjo, ca. 1975. (Visual Documentation Project)

## 91. Buru: Wives and Children

The deliberate isolation of the Buru detainees took a heavy psychological toll on them and on their families. Official attempts to resolve the problem by relocating families to the camp only made matters worse.

From the moment they arrived on the island, the detainees had virtually no contact with their families. In theory, they could send one postcard to their loved ones each month, but in practice those cards seldom reached their destinations. The separation from families contributed to the detainees' sense of hopelessness and despair, and for many it created a rupture in family ties that was impossible to repair when they were finally released.

In response to mounting criticism, and to discourage detainees from returning home upon their release, in 1972 the army began to transport their wives and children to Buru. Describing the plan as a program of permanent resettlement that would benefit the families in the long run, they pressured detainees and families alike to take part. Despite their reluctance to do so, by 1977 some two hundred families had been sent to the island, where they lived under the same restrictive regime as their husbands and fathers.

Figure 299. Woman and child on board a ship bound for Buru Island, where they would join her husband, July 1972. (United Press International)

## 92. Pramoedya Ananta Toer on Buru

Many of those held on Buru Island were journalists, writers, teachers, and artists known for their critical views or their association with LEKRA, the left-wing cultural organization loosely affiliated with the PKI. Among the best known of those prisoners was Pramoedya Ananta Toer, then and still today one of Indonesia's most renowned and widely translated writers and cultural critics.

Pramoedya was arrested at his Jakarta home in October 1965, less than two weeks after the alleged coup. As he was taken away and soldiers looked on, an angry anti-Communist mob that had gathered outside the house seized his books and manuscripts, threw them into the yard, and set them on fire. For the next four years, he was held in various prisons in and around Jakarta, and then in 1969 he was transported to Buru, where he remained for the next ten years. He was never charged or tried, and after his release in late 1979, he was

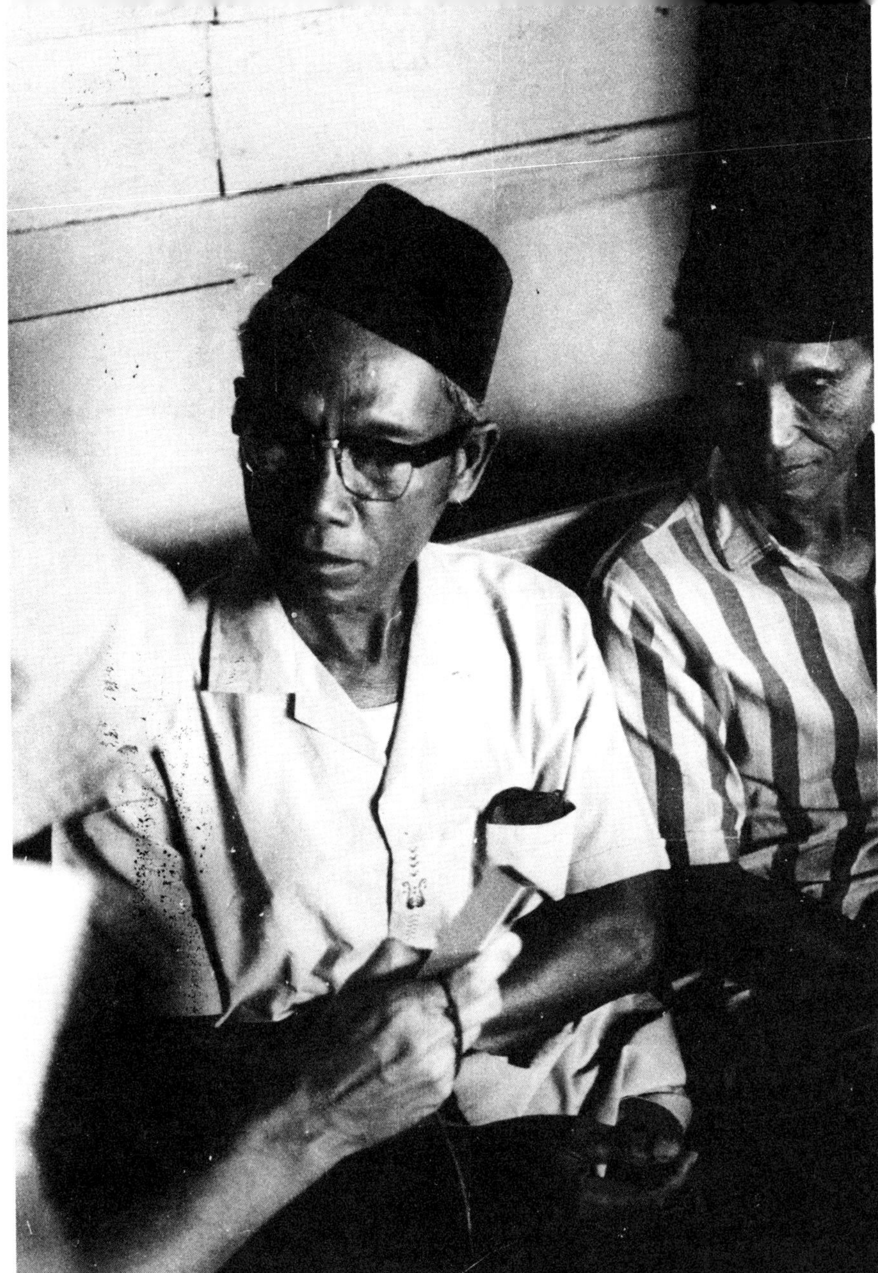

Figure 300. Pramoedya Ananta Toer interviewed by journalists, Buru Island, November 1971. (Peter Schumacher)

subjected to constant restrictions and his works were banned. For a time, those found in possession of his books were subject to arrest and imprisonment.

Pramoedya's experience on Buru, and that of his fellow detainees, was documented by Peter Schumacher. The critical reporting that followed that 1971 visit angered the Indonesian authorities and led them to close the camp to all but a handful of outside observers for the next five years. In that time, Schumacher's photographs were among the only visual evidence of conditions in the camp. Indeed, his photograph of Pramoedya was printed in virtually every Amnesty International document on the subject and became something like an

Figure 301. Pramoedya Ananta Toer's wife, Maemunah Thamrin, and children in Jakarta, 1971. (Peter Schumacher)

emblem of the organization's campaign on behalf of Indonesia's political prisoners through the 1970s.

Like other detainees on Buru, Pramoedya was subjected to harsh conditions, including forced labor, inadequate food, severe punishments, and minimal medical care. But beyond the normal torments, he suffered a fate unique to writers: he was denied access to pens or paper and was forbidden to write. For several years, he made do with whatever was available, using indigo and charcoal as ink and cement bags as paper. Finally, following a visit and intervention by the ICRC in the mid-1970s, he was given paper and pens and permitted to write again.

But access to writing materials was only part of the problem; whatever he wrote was subject to arbitrary confiscation by the authorities. At one point, army officials seized nine notepads he had filled with notes for a novel about Indonesia's early nationalist movement and never returned them. To avoid a repeat of that fate, Pramoedya took to hiding his manuscript in a hole disguised as a toilet. With the help of a fellow inmate, the journalist Oei Hiem Hwie, he secretly shared his drafts and ideas with other writers in the camp. And when he learned that Oei was scheduled for release in 1978, he entrusted the manuscripts to him. A few years later, the first volume of Pramoedya's four-part masterpiece about Indonesia's early nationalist movement was published. Fittingly, it became known as *The Buru Quartet*, a work that has now been translated into dozens of languages.

Figure 302. Female prisoners pose with military officers in Bukit Duri Prison, Jakarta. (MetroTV)

## 93. Women's Prisons

From the earliest days of October 1965, the army took special interest in politically active women, and particularly those affiliated with Gerwani. Army propaganda (falsely) claimed that Gerwani members present at Lubang Buaya on the morning of October 1 had danced naked before engaging in an orgy with the generals, castrating them with razors, and gouging out their eyes. In the ensuing months, the press kept up a steady stream of sensational reporting about the treachery of women affiliated with the PKI. One result of these stories was that military authorities were eager to identify and detain Gerwani members. Many female detainees—including some who were still teenagers—were held in designated women's prisons, the most infamous of which were the Bukit Duri Special Prison for Women in Jakarta, a women's wing within Wirogunan Prison in Yogyakarta, and Bulu Women's Prison in Semarang.

As the number of female detainees rose, army authorities decided there was a need for a new, long-term solution. In July 1969, instructions were issued for the establishment of a temporary detention center for Category B female prisoners on the site of a former leprosy center in Plantungan Village in Kendal District, Central Java. The initial target was that the facility would house five hundred women between 1969 and 1974, though it did not open until April 1971 and remained in operation until the last prisoners were released in 1979. Located in a rural setting, the facility included prison dorms, kitchen facilities, workshops, and gardens in which the prisoners were required to work. Remarkably, some of the women transferred to Plantungan had in fact already been processed and approved for release.

In addition to the hardship of a strict regimen, poor rations, inadequate health care, and sexual abuse, female prisoners also struggled to stay in touch with their families. Occasional family visits

Figure 303. Female prisoners in Plantungan Prison, Central Java, with stamp showing that the photograph was approved for circulation. (*Pameran foto mengenang yang dilupakan*)

Figure 304. Female prisoners in Plantungan Prison study the Koran, 1977. (David Jenkins)

were allowed, but these often created extra burdens on the prisoners and their families. It was not uncommon for family members who did visit to be harassed by prison officials or by authorities in their home village. In Bukit Duri, there was a strict policy that photographs of family members were not allowed. In Plantungan, by contrast, some women maintained connections to relatives by asking the prison warden to send photographs, but these had to be to be "approved" for circulation, which was indicated by an official stamp. For authorities, the primary concern was to ensure that the prisoners be portrayed as healthy and well treated. The photographs that were approved of women in their best clothes did not reflect the day-to-day reality.

Photographs also gave detainees occasional glimpses of life outside the prison walls, but those images were not always reassuring. In 1968, for example, the daily newspapers prominently displayed a photograph of the battered corpse of Olan Hutapea, a member of the

Figure 305. Female prisoners at a Christian church service, Plantungan Prison, 1977. (David Jenkins)

PKI Politburo who had been killed by the army during its operations in Blitar, East Java. Years later, Carmel Budiardjo, who was then a political prisoner in Jakarta, recalled her feelings upon seeing the photo: "The sight of Hutapea's body transfixed me. I would have preferred not to look but I could not help studying the photo because I wanted to convince myself that it was really him. What must his wife and children have thought when they saw it? I knew him in the old days as a very confident man, always optimistic about the future, but now it had come to this."[4]

## 94. North Sumatra Prison Camps

The prisons in which alleged Communists were held were initially called Special Prisons, then were renamed Exile Camps, and finally were redesignated as Rehabilitation Installations.

In North Sumatra, long-term political prisoners were divided by classification. Category C prisoners were held at a center in the provincial capital, Medan; Category B prisoners were remanded to a detention center located in Tanjung Kasau, Tebing Tinggi District; and Category A prisoners were in more isolated camps in Sidikalang, Dairi District. In 1977, the government began a phased release program. In December of that year, 886

Figure 306. Detention center for political prisoners in North Sumatra. The printing on the wall reads, "Special Authority of Kopkamtib, North Sumatra, Sukamulia Rehabilitation Installation." (Indonesian Department of Information)

Figure 307. Prisoners at the gates of a detention camp in Sidikalang, North Sumatra, on the occasion of Admiral Sudomo's visit in 1978. (Zakaria M. Passe/ Tempo)

prisoners were released from Tanjung Kasau. The following year, Admiral Sudomo, the head of Kopkamtib, visited Sidikalang in preparation for further releases and the distribution of land on which prisoners would be allowed to settle.

## 95. East Kalimantan Prison Camps

In East Kalimantan during the 1950s and early 1960s, under the leadership of a Dutch-educated aristocrat of Arab descent, Sayid Fahrul Baraqbah, the PKI developed significant support among workers in the oil sector. The party's growth was facilitated by Fahrul Baraqbah's close relations with the regional military commander, Brigadier General R. Soeharjo, who was a staunch Sukarnoist. In early 1965, however, Soeharjo was replaced by a new, hard-line commander, depriving the party of political protection.

Following the events of October 1, 1965, Fahrul Baraqbah and other leftists were arrested and held without trial. While some of them were members of the PKI or its affiliated unions, others were arrested for simply participating in cultural or sporting activities organized by leftists. In some cases, individuals were released after a year or two in detention and then rearrested without knowing the exact charges or receiving any official documentation of their legal status.

In many parts of the outer islands, legal proceedings against detained Communists were delayed, and many detainees were never formally processed. In East Kalimantan, it was not until 1970 that systematic legal efforts to address the fate of detainees were set in motion. That year, a number of individuals were put on trial in Balikpapan and a spree of further arrests were made. At the same time, efforts were made to screen those already in detention, resulting in the release of more than 175 alleged Communists and their families, who were resettled in a forested area under the watchful eye of the military.

Meanwhile, the military built a number of new detention centers in East Kalimantan to house some 2,500 prisoners. One of these was Camp Sumberejo, which the Australian journalist David

Figure 308. Prisoner barracks, Amborawang, East Kalimantan, 1976. (Syarif Hidayat/Tempo)

Figure 309. Prisoners with their possessions, Sumberejo prison camp, Balikpapan, East Kalimantan, 1977. (David Jenkins)

Figure 310. Prisoners on the veranda, Sumberejo prison camp, Balikpapan, East Kalimantan, 1977. (David Jenkins)

Jenkins was allowed to visit in 1977, consisted of eleven barracks. These were initially open halls built of rough-hewn planks, hardwood saplings, and bamboo, with walls made of plaited palm fronds and simple corrugated tin roofs. Over time, as the prisoners felled trees and the wood was milled, the inmates constructed more permanent structures. Inside the barracks, on a raised wooden platform, each prisoner was allocated a meter-wide space for a sleeping mat and personal possessions.

In a visit to the camp in December 1977, the regional military commander of East Kalimantan announced that the prisoners were to be relocated, with each to receive a house and two hectares of land. Initial hopes that this plan meant release were quickly dashed, however. Instead the prisoners were moved to a forested site in Amborawang, designated Agrosari, where a few model houses had been constructed. They were given machetes and axes with which to clear the forest and construct their own houses. This initiative was presented as an extension of Indonesia's transmigration program, but the men remained under military control and were used as laborers for designated projects. Formal permission was required to leave the village.

## 96. Release of Long-Term Detainees

The army's plan, dating from documents prepared in late 1965, was to put all Category A political prisoners on trial. A decade later, however, only about a quarter of the 1,700 Category A prisoners had been tried, and many more Category B prisoners languished

Figure 311. Prisoner release, Surabaya, East Java, 1977. (Slamet Urip Prihadi/Tempo)

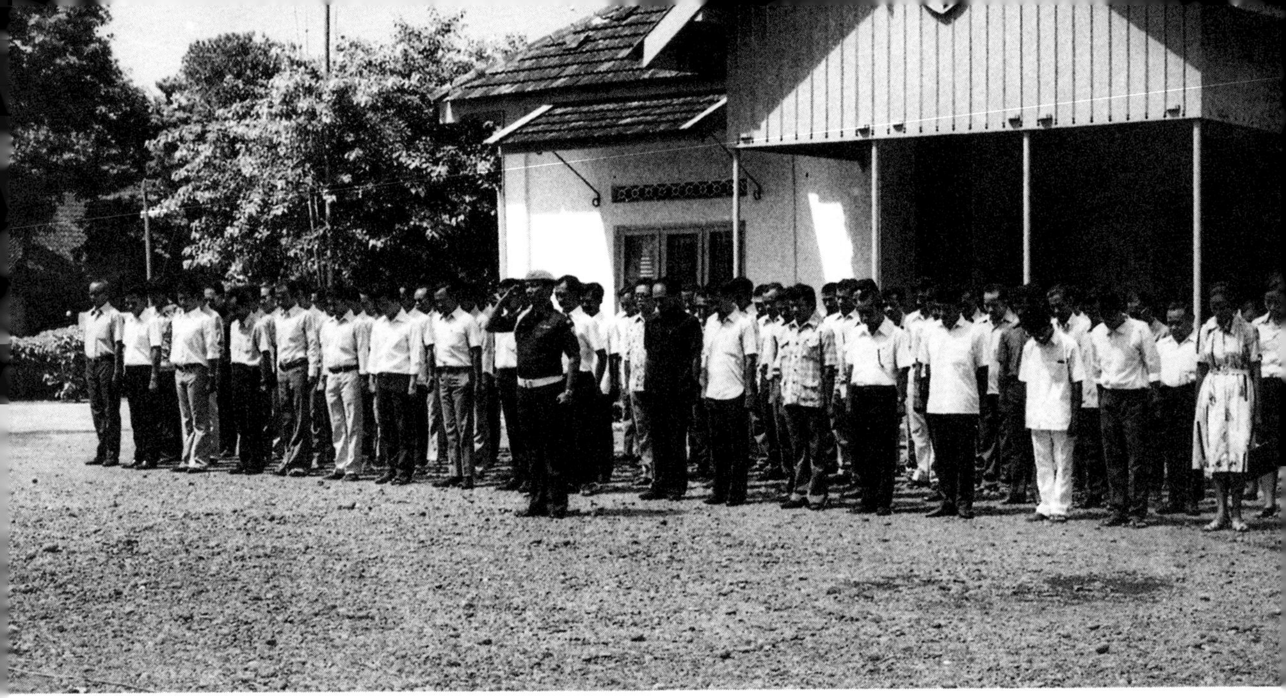

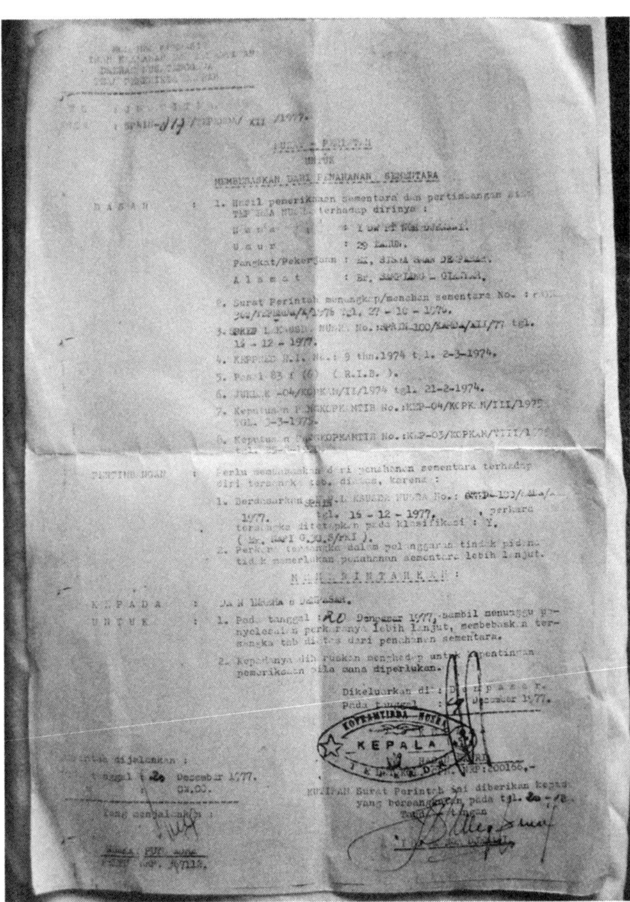

MEMBEBASKAN DARI PENAHANAN SEMENTARA

DASAR : 1. Hasil pemeriksaan sementara dan pertimbangan [illegible] terhadap dirinya :

Umur : 29 tahun.

Alamat : Br. [illegible]

2. Surat Perintah menangkap/menahan sementara No. : [illegible] tgl. 27 - 10 - 1976.

3. [illegible] tgl. 15 - 12 - 1977.

4. KEPPRES R.I. No. : 9 thn.1974 tgl. 2-3-1974.

5. Pasal 83 f (6) ( R.I.B. ).

6. [illegible] -04/KOPKAM/II/1974 tgl. 21-2-1974.

7. Keputusan [illegible] No. :KEP-04/KOPKAM/III/1975 [illegible]

8. Keputusan [illegible] No. :KEP-03/KOPKAM/VIII/[illegible]

PERTIMBANGAN : Perlu membebaskan dari penahanan sementara terhadap diri tersangka tsb. diatas, karena :

1. Berdasarkan [illegible] 1977. tgl. 15 - 12 - 1977, perkara tersangka ditetapkan pada klasifikasi : Y.

2. Perkara tersangka dalam pelanggaran tindak pidana tidak memerlukan penahanan sementara lebih lanjut.

MENERINTAHKAN :

KEPADA : [illegible]

UNTUK : 1. Pada tanggal : 20 Desember 1977, sambil menunggu penyelesaian perkaranya lebih lanjut, membebaskan tersangka tsb diatas dari penahanan sementara.

2. Kepadanya diharuskan menghadap untuk kepentingan pemeriksaan bila mana diperlukan.

Dikeluarkan di : D e n p a s a r.

Pada tanggal : [illegible] Desember 1977.

KEPALA

NRP:200166,-

Perintah dijalankan :

tanggal : 20 Desember 1977.

Yang menjalankan :

[illegible] Surat Perintah ini diberikan kepada yang bersangkutan pada tgl. 20 - 12.

Figure 312. Ceremony for the release of political prisoners who had never been legally tried, in Denpasar, Bali, December 20, 1977. Six prisoners who had been tried were made to sit inside during the ceremony. (Putu Setia/Tempo)

Figure 313. I Dewa Putu Ngurah Djenawi's letter of release, 1977. (Courtesy of Djenawi)

in provincial prisons. In December 1976, Admiral Sudomo, the commander of Kopkamtib, announced plans for the staggered release of Category B prisoners, emphasizing that such releases were being done thanks to the magnanimity of the Indonesian people in accepting the prisoners back into the "big family of the Indonesian nation."

In Bali, authorities at Pekambingan Prison informed the detainees that they were going to be released in December 1977. In preparation, the prisoners were provided with "spiritual guidance." The release ceremony was held at the military police office in the regional military command. Several dozen prisoners who had never been tried—both male and female, and Balinese, Javanese, and ethnic Chinese—were made to stand at attention for the official ceremony. Meanwhile, six men who had been tried and sentenced were held inside the military police office. Among them, I Dewa Putu Ngurah Djenawi had been a high school student at the time he was arrested in 1968, and two years later he was sentenced to six years in prison. When his sentence ended in 1976, however, he was informed that he would remain in prison under "temporary detention," though he was never provided legal counsel or given a court document regarding his case. His letter of release at the time of the December 1977 ceremony stated that he was reclassified Category Y—"an ex-G.30.S/PKI prisoner."

Figure 314. Release of 668 Category B political prisoners in Yogyakarta, attended by Kopkamtib commander Admiral Sudomo, December 8, 1979. (National Library of Indonesia)

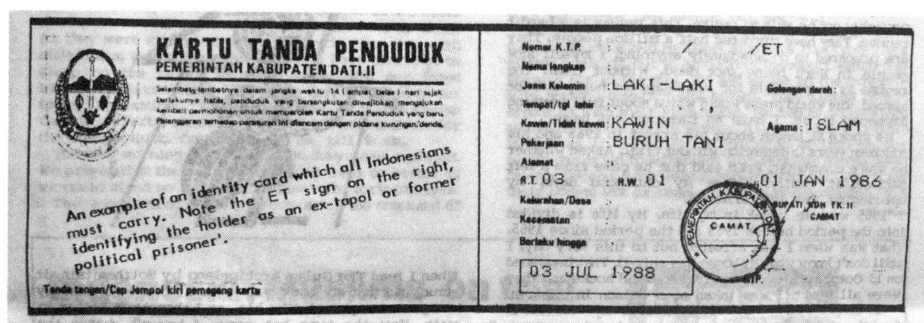

**KARTU TANDA PENDUDUK**
PEMERINTAH KABUPATEN DATI.II

Selambat-lambatnya dalam jangka waktu 14 (empat belas) hari sejak berlakunya habis, penduduk yang bersangkutan diwajibkan mengajukan kembali permohonan untuk memperoleh Kartu Tanda Penduduk yang baru. Pelanggaran terhadap peraturan ini diancam dengan pidana kurungan/denda.

An example of an identity card which all Indonesians must carry. Note the ET sign on the right, identifying the holder as an ex-tapol or former political prisoner'.

Tanda tangan/Cap Jempol kiri pemegang kartu

Nomor K.T.P. : / /ET
Nama lengkap :
Jenis Kelamin : LAKI-LAKI
Golongan darah :
Tempat/tgl lahir : ,
Kawin/Tidak kawin : KAWIN
Agama : ISLAM
Pekerjaan : BURUH TANI
Alamat :
R.T. 03 : R.W. 01
01 JAN 1986
Kelurahan/Desa :
Kecamatan
BUPATI KDH TK.II
CAMAT
Berlaku hingga :
03 JUL 1988
PEMERINTAH KABUPATEN DATI
CAMAT

Figure 315. Identity card marked with "ET," which stands for "Eks-Tapol" (former political prisoner). (*TAPOL Bulletin*)

# IX. Epilogue

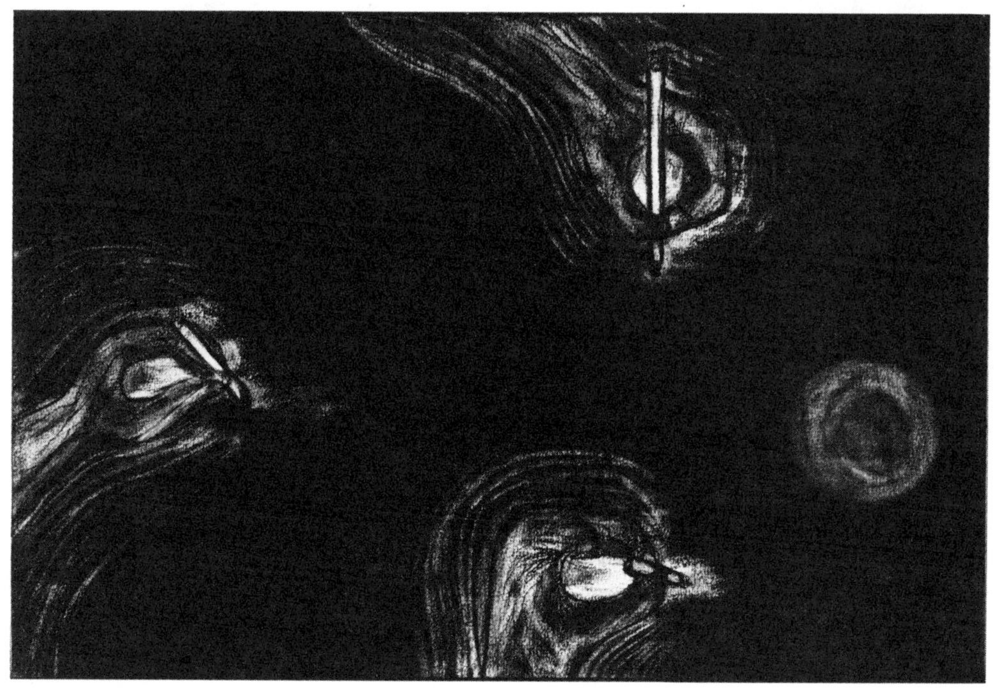

Figure 317. Poster for the official propaganda film, *Destruction of the Treacherous G30S/PKI*. (Wikimedia Commons)

## 97. Propaganda and Fear

In the years after the violence subsided, the army worked hard to ensure that its account of the alleged coup and its aftermath prevailed. As in the period of violence itself, a crucial element of that effort involved the production and dissemination of images—photographs, cartoons, posters, and films—that portrayed the PKI as treacherous, brutal, and inhuman, and the army as heroic and patriotic.

The visual propaganda campaign was set in motion within days of the alleged coup, with the publication of photos and footage of the generals' muddy and decomposed bodies being exhumed from the well at Lubang Buaya. In the 1970s, the Army History Bureau (Dinas Sejarah Angkatan Darat) undertook to create a visual record of the destruction of the Left by publishing a series of photo books. The purpose of these books was evident from their content. In page after page they depict, on the one hand, the inhumanity of the PKI and, on the other, the heroism of the army. Notably, each picture was supplied with a caption that, beyond a description, tells the reader how to interpret the image.

The visual propaganda strategy reached its apogee in the early 1980s, when the army's Film Bureau commissioned a feature-length docudrama that purported to tell the true story of the alleged coup. The result was the grotesquely violent propaganda film *Destruction of the Treacherous G30S/PKI* (*Penumpasan pengkhianatan Gerakan 30 September/PKI*). For many Indonesians, this film was the sole or main

Figure 318. Suharto family shooting pistols, December 1, 1967. (Larry Burrows/LIFE Picture Collection)

source of their knowledge about the events that precipitated the army's onslaught.

In short, visual images—and especially this film—were a crucial element of the New Order's propaganda campaign, a campaign that was designed not only to shape public attitudes about the alleged coup and to entrench a false historical narrative about army heroism, but also to terrorize the population into silence.

## 98. The Past before Us

Despite its long dominance and its power, the New Order's account of the political violence against the PKI has not gone unchallenged. Especially since the fall of Suharto in 1998, Indonesian scholars, journalists, survivors, and artists have engaged in a serious reexamination of that history and a search for something like truth and justice. Among the most powerful avenues for challenging official narratives have been visual media, including political cartoons, artworks, and films.

Some political cartoons were produced during the Suharto years, but as the possession or distribution of such artwork was severely punished, their public circulation was limited. That situation changed after Suharto's fall in 1998, in part because of a new skepticism about official history that emerged out of the anti-Suharto movement and in part because of growing access to the internet. Some of these cartoons are explicit representations of the violence,

Figure 319. Elisabeth Ida Mulyani photo montage, depicting the New Order legacy of regimentation and militarization of Indonesian society. The graffiti on the elevated highway reads, "Why crush the Communists?" (Elisabeth Ida Mulyani and Derek Bacon)

and their purpose is clearly didactic. They are also a form of visual testimony, both in the sense of providing "evidence" of wrongdoing and also in the sense of bearing witness to past crimes.

In addition to cartoons, the past two decades have seen a flourishing of works of art depicting the violence of 1965, subverting official narratives, or expressing solidarity with its victims. These include the remarkable paintings by Dadang Christanto, whose works have been exhibited around the world but not yet inside Indonesia. Much of his art is explicit and intentionally shocking. He aims to portray the grim reality of the violence in order to expose the "truth" that has been suppressed or obscured for so long.

Other artists have adopted a less direct visual language, aiming to provoke reflection and questioning rather than shock and revulsion. These include Andreas Iswinarto, whose haunting

Figure 320. Theatrical poster for Joshua Oppenheimer's film *The Look of Silence*. (Final Cut for Real)

Figure 321. Cartoon depicting the mass execution of some 4,500 alleged Communists at Grubuk Cave near Yogyakarta over a period of thirty days in late 1965. The blindfolded prisoner about to be executed cries out, "Long Live the People!" (Yayak Yatmaka et al., *Sejarah gerakan kiri Indonesia untuk pemula*)

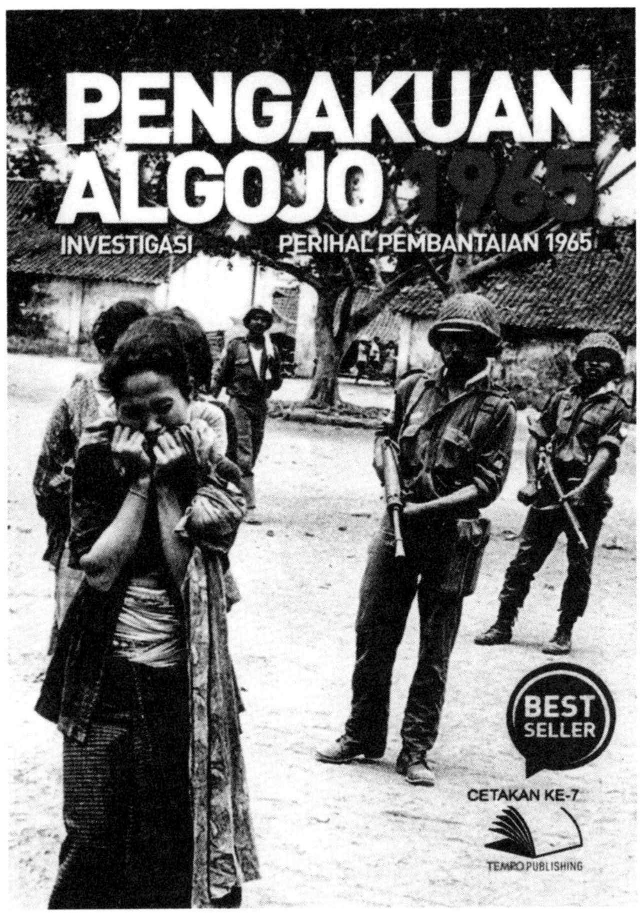


Figure 322. Cover of the best-selling book *Confessions of a 1965 Killer: Tempo's Investigation into the 1965 Massacres.*

Figure 323. Dadang Christanto's untitled painting depicting the slaughter in 1965–66.

charcoal sketches are based on historical photographs, and Elisabeth Mulyani, a visual artist who grew up during the Suharto years. Her art is an attempt to deconstruct and critique the official memory of 1965 and to posit an alternative. The visual imagery she employs is notably free of explicit violence. She does not want to use the same brutal visual language that she and others were subjected to as children, but instead confronts us with paradoxically beautiful images that conceal a violent past.

Equally important in challenging official narratives are the dozens of films about 1965 that have been produced since the fall of Suharto. These include documentaries in which witnesses and survivors speak directly to the camera and several feature films that portray the events of 1965 with some sympathy for the victims. By far the best known, and most controversial, of the films to emerge about this period are the award-winning documentaries by the Danish-American director Joshua Oppenheimer: *The Act of Killing* and *The Look of Silence*. These films follow some of the perpetrators as they discuss and

reenact the shocking acts of violence they themselves committed in 1965—an approach that is both provocative and powerful. Internationally, the films have stimulated vastly more public and scholarly attention than any of the books or articles that have been written about 1965 over the past fifty years. But it is inside Indonesia that they have had their most profound effect. Shown on college campuses and in private screenings across the country, they have given rise to a new awareness of the mass violence against the political Left—and to powerful new demands for justice and a rectification of the historical record.

In different ways, all of these visual representations have begun to disrupt the monolithic official version of history that was so long enforced by the government and to lay the foundation for new and alternative historical narratives and social memories.

## APPENDIX

# Figure Information: Photographers, Credits, and Original Captions

**1.** (Page 19) Itji Tarmizi, woodblock print titled "Maju terus, djangan mundur sedjaripun!" (Keep advancing, don't retreat even an inch!)

*Harian Rakjat*, May 3, 1964.

**2.** Sukarno and Mao, Beijing, summer 1956

Keystone/Photopress-Archiv.

**3.** President Sukarno at a Soviet naval base, 1956

Photographer unknown.
Handwritten in Russian on back: "Sukarno. Sukhumi-Sochi. Cruiser 'Kutuzov.'"

**4.** Sukarno with Premier Khrushchev, February 1960

Photographer unknown.

**5.** Sukarno with President John F. Kennedy, September 13, 1961

William Allen. Associated Press.

**6.** President Sukarno with aide Lieutenant Colonel Sabur at United Nations, September 30, 1960

Associated Press. Bettman-Corbis Collection, Getty Images.

**7.** Cartoon: "Indonesia's interior decorator"

*Philadelphia Inquirer*, August 30, 1965; republished in the *New York Times*, September 5, 1965.

**8.** D. N. Aidit at campaign rally, 1955

Howard Sochurek. The LIFE Picture Collection, Getty Images.

**9.** Hammer and sickle on palace wall, Central Java

Keystone Press Agency. Keystone Pictures USA/ Alamy Stock Photo.

**10.** PKI campaign statue and poster in the 1958 Jakarta regional elections

Sam Waagemaar. Camera Press.

**11.** Indonesian troops arrive in Hollandia/ Jayapura, 1963

No official source.

**12.** President Sukarno, with Major General Suharto and Lieutenant Colonel Untung, inspecting the 454th Airborne Battalion, February 19, 1963

Indonesian Press Photo Service (IPPHOS), reproduced in Ken Conboy, *Kopassus: Inside Indonesia's Special Forces* (Jakarta: Equinox, 2003), 152c.

**13.** Women rally in support of Konfrontasi, April 23, 1964.

United Press International

**14.** Demonstration against neocolonial stooges

National Library of Indonesia.

**15.** Members of the Nationalist Party jab bamboo spears into an effigy of Malaysian prime minister Abdul Rahman

United Press International.

**16.** Volunteers with bamboo spears

United Press International, November 2, 1964.

**17.** Army training former sex workers, December 23, 1964

TopFoto.

**18.** Cartoon: Sukarno declaring Malaysia will be crushed, late 1964

Arsib Negara, Malaysia.

**19.** Indonesian Peasants' Front demonstration

Nugraha Bookstore, Facebook, April 29, 2020, https://www.facebook.com/nugrahabookstore/posts/parade-aksi-barisan-tani-indonesia-bti-organisasi-underbow-pki-saat-konflik-land/260451028655020/.

**20.** Rally against US ambassador Jones, August 19, 1964

Bettman-Corbis Collection, Getty Images.

**21.** Demonstrator with sign reading "Kick Out Jones," August 19, 1964

Thomas Hoepker. Magnum.

**22.** Protest against foreign military bases

John Bulmer and Harry Redl, *Illustrated London News*, March 13, 1965.

**23.** Demonstration against US ambassador Marshall Green, July 26, 1965

Associated Press. Reproduced from Marshall Green, *Indonesia: Crisis and Transformation, 1965-68* (New York: Compass, 1990), 48.

**24.** Ambassador Green in Jakarta, ca. August 1965

Beryl Bernay. Courtesy of Carol Gonzalez.

**25.** Anti-British demonstration, Jakarta, September 16, 1963

Associated Press.

**26.** NZ/UK high commission letter

Cover note to document from Mr. M. J. C. Templeton, New Zealand High Commission in London, to Mr. Peck, British Foreign Office, "The Succession to Sukarno," December 18, 1964, DH 1015/112, FO 371/175251, UK National Archive.

**27.** Singing Soeprapto: Official encouraging peasants, 1962

United Press International.

**28.** Woman selling rice in market, Jakarta, September 6, 1965

No official source.

**29.** Becak and beggar in front of anti-imperialist banner, Jakarta, 1965

John Bulmer and Harry Redl, *Illustrated London News*, March 13, 1965.

**30.** Rural scene, likely on the outskirts of Jakarta, mid-1965

Beryl Bernay. Courtesy of Carol Gonzalez.

**31.** General Achmad Yani, January 31, 1964

John Bulmer. Camera Press.

**32.** Army Special Forces Regiment marching in Jakarta, January 1965

No official source.

**33.** Female volunteers, January 1965

No official source.

**34.** IPKI members march in North Sumatra, 1965

Beryl Bernay. Courtesy of Carol Gonzalez.

**35.** Muslimat women training, July 1965

*Sejarah Muslimat Nahdlatul Ulama* (Jakarta: P.P. Muslimat N.U., 1979), 74.

**36.** Female police volunteers march in Menteng, Central Jakarta, July 8, 1965

United Press International.

**37.** Women parade on Independence Day, August 17, 1965

Rory Dell. Camera Press.

**38.** Volunteers demonstrate against the formation of Malaysia on the occasion of Sukarno laying the cornerstone for a nuclear reactor in Serpong, West Java, January 21, 1965

United Press International.

**39.** US diplomatic telegram regarding Indonesian intention to purchase atomic bomb

Airgram A-100, American Embassy Jakarta to Secretary of State, Washington, DC, August 9, 1965, POL2-1 INDO, National Archives and Records Administration.

**40.** Crowd gathered in Bali to see Sukarno and Cambodian prime minister Sihanouk, August 1965

Beryl Bernay. Courtesy of Carol Gonzalez.

**41.** Sukarno in crowd

Beryl Bernay. Courtesy of Carol Gonzalez.

**42.** President Sukarno addressing May Day rally, 1965

Bettman-Corbis Collection, Getty Images.

**43.** Festive demonstration, Yogyakarta

Moelyono. Courtesy of Upik Asriati.

**44.** Demonstrators with Uncle Sam effigy, Jakarta, February 1965

No official source.

**45.** Political graffiti in North Sulawesi, 1965
Beryl Bernay. Courtesy of Carol Gonzalez.

**46.** Demonstrators burn US publications, Jakarta, August 16, 1965
ANP.

**47.** Communist demonstrators protest "capitalist-bureaucrats" and Islamic University Students' Association, Jakarta, September 9, 1965
Keystone Pictures USA/Alamy Stock Photo.

**48.** Members of the Islamic University Students' Association protest against the Indonesian Communist Party, September 13, 1965
National Library of Indonesia.

**49.** Cindy Adams posing with members of the Presidential Guard, Jakarta
Cindy Adams, *Sukarno, My Friend* (Singapore: Gunung Agung, 1971), between pages 104 and 105.

**50.** Beryl Bernay with President Sukarno, September 1965
Beryl Bernay. Courtesy of Carol Gonzalez.

**51.** (Page 59) Iswinarto drawing of prisoners on a truck
Courtesy of Iswinarto.

**52.** Cartoon: September 30th Movement knocks out the CIA-backed Generals' Council
*Harian Rakjat*, October 2, 1965.

**53.** Lieutenant Colonel Untung
Associated Press.

**54.** Colonel Abdul Latief
Tribunnews, https://www.tribunnewswiki.com/2021/09/02/kolonel-abdul-latief.

**55.** Brigadier General Supardjo
Kumpulan Kisah dan Sejarah, https://kumpulankisahdansejarah.blogspot.com/2015/11/hari-hari-terakir-brigjen-soepardjo.html.

**56.** Sjam Kamaruzaman
National Library of Indonesia.

**57.** Suharto and his wife enjoying a picnic with Untung, no date
Electronic file courtesy of Stanley Adi Prasetyo.

**58.** Convoy of army paracommandos in Central Jakarta, October 1, 1965
Beryl Bernay. Courtesy of Carol Gonzalez.

**59.** Armored vehicles in the Hotel Indonesia roundabout, Jakarta, October 1, 1965
No official source.

**60.** Soldiers running with guns on street in central Jakarta, October 2, 1965
No official source.

**61.** Soldiers with armored vehicle in background, Jakarta, October 1, 1965
TopFoto.

**62.** General Nasution speaking to reporters, October 1, 1965
Beryl Bernay. Courtesy of Carol Gonzalez.

**63.** Major General Suharto in front of a jeep, Jakarta, October 1965
National Library of Indonesia.

**64.** Army trucks carrying coffins, Jakarta, October 5, 1965
Stamped *Paris Match/Marie Claire*, October 20, 1965.

**65.** Soldiers carrying coffins, Kalibata Cemetery, Jakarta, October 5, 1965
National Library of Indonesia.

**66.** Photograph of the exhumation of the generals
Beryl Bernay. Courtesy of Carol Gonzalez.

**67.** Major General Suharto with senior officers, Kalibata Cemetery, Jakarta, October 5, 1965
Associated Press.

**68.** Cartoon: Chinese tentacles around Sukarno
Bill Mauldin for the *Chicago Sun-Times*, 1965, republished in *Dagens nyheter* (Sweden), October 2, 1965.

**69.** US ambassador Marshall Green and military attaché Willis Ethel at Kalibata Cemetery, October 5, 1965
Carol Goldstein.

**70.** Letter from British ambassador Gilchrist to Foreign Office, London, October 5, 1965
DH 1015/187, FO 371/180317, UK National Archive.

**71.** Young men reading Army daily *Berita Yudha,* Jakarta, October 10, 1965
ANP.

**72.** Front page of *Angkatan Bersendjata*, October 9, 1965

**73.** Cartoon: Eradicate down to the roots
*Angkatan Bersendjata*, October 8, 1965.

**74.** Image of a rubber tapping tool published in army newspaper
*Berita Yudha*, October 13, 1965.

**75.** Alleged "eye gougers"
Stamped *Paris Match/Marie Claire*, October 20, 1965.

**76.** Cartoon: G30S with skull and dripping blood
*Angkatan Bersendjata*, October 8, 1965.

**77.** Cartoon: Crocodiles eat generals
Beryl Bernay. Courtesy of Carol Gonzalez.

**78.** Graffiti: "Down with PKI"
National Library of Indonesia.

**79.** Graffiti: "Relakah djenderal2 kita gugur"
Carol Goldstein. Keystone Pictures USA/Alamy Stock Photo.

**80.** Graffiti: "Aidit otaknja 30 Sept"
Keystone Pictures USA/Alamy Stock Photo.

**81.** Graffiti reading "PKI go to hell," Hayam Wuruk Street, Jakarta
Beryl Bernay. Courtesy of Carol Gonzalez.

**82.** Anti-PKI demonstration, Jakarta, October 8, 1965
No official source.

**83.** Demonstrators with poster reading "Gerwani is immoral"
Beryl Bernay. Courtesy of Carol Gonzalez.

**84.** Anti-PKI demonstration with women wearing veils
Beryl Bernay. Courtesy of Carol Gonzalez.

**85.** Anti-PKI demonstration with Muslims and Catholics
Beryl Bernay. Courtesy of Carol Gonzalez.

**86.** PKI headquarters burned by mob, Jakarta, October 8, 1965
Bettman-Corbis Collection, Getty Images.

**87.** Scene of explosion near PKI headquarters, Jakarta, ca. October 8, 1965
Stamped Michel Le Tac, *Paris Match/Marie Claire*, October 20, 1965.

**88.** Soldier in front of PKI Jakarta branch sign, October 1965
Agence France Press.

**89.** Soldier guarding scene of attack on PKI office, October 13, 1965
United Press International.

**90.** Man painting "PKI" on fence
Beryl Bernay. Courtesy of Carol Gonzalez.

**91.** President Sukarno announcing the establishment of Kopkamtib, October 10, 1965
Keystone Pictures USA/Alamy Stock Photo.

**92.** Army troops guarding prisoners on a truck, Jakarta, October 10, 1965
Bettman-Corbis Collection, Getty Images.

**93.** Soldiers guarding detainees on a truck, Jakarta, October 10, 1965
Getty Images.

**94.** Prisoner jumping off a truck, Jakarta, late October 1965
No official source.

**95.** Lieutenant Colonel Untung captured, October 12, 1965
*Sejarah Pengabdian Corps Polisi Militer Angkatan Darat, 1945–1978* (Jakarta: Yayasan Gajah Mada, 1981).

**96.** Cartoon: "Chased by the facts"
*Angkatan Bersendjata*, October 9, 1965.

**97.** Banner reading "Hang Aidit and his cronies," Jakarta
National Library of Indonesia.

**98.** Njoto's house ransacked, October 1965
Carol Goldstein, Keystone.

**99.** Man painting "Hang Njoto" with guards, ca. October 1965
Beryl Bernay. Courtesy of Carol Gonzalez.

**100.** Children in house next to LEKRA hall in Manggarai, Jakarta, October 13, 1965
National Library of Indonesia.

**101.** Attack on leftist bookstore, Jakarta, October 14, 1965
Carol Goldstein, Keystone. Getty Images.

**102.** Men removing portraits of Dutch governors general
Henri Cartier-Bresson. Copyright Fondation Henri Cartier-Bresson/Magnum.

**103.** Looters with portraits of Sukarno, October 14, 1965
Carol Goldstein, Keystone. Getty Images.

**104.** Attack on Res Publica University, Jakarta, October 15, 1965
No official source.

**105.** Chinese man cowers from attackers, Jakarta, October 15, 1965
Bettman-Corbis Collection, Getty Images.

**106.** Graffiti reading "Baperki bankrolls the PKI," Jakarta
Beryl Bernay. Courtesy of Carol Gonzalez.

**107.** President Sukarno announces appointment of Major General Suharto as army chief of staff, October 14, 1965
Keystone Pictures USA/Alamy Stock Photo.

**108.** President Sukarno installs Major General Suharto as army chief of staff, October 16, 1965
National Library of Indonesia.

**109.** (Page 95) Iswinarto drawing, woman cowering.
Courtesy of Iswinarto.

**110.** Colonel Sarwo Edhie.
Beryl Bernay. Courtesy of Carol Gonzalez.

**111.** Troops search for Communists in Solo, 1965
Sutarto/Antara.

**112.** Men with poster supporting the September 30th Movement, Solo, Central Java
Sutarto/Antara.

**113.** Soldiers removing poster supporting the September 30th Movement, Central Java
Sutarto/Antara.

**114.** Burning PKI logo in Djajengan, Surakarta
Sutarto/Antara.

**115.** Military personnel instructing youths in Grobogan, Central Java, 1965
National Library of Indonesia.

**116.** Ansor drum band, Java, 1965
Idayu collection. Reproduced from Sulastomo, *Hari-hari yang Panjang, 1963-1966* (Jakarta: Kompas, 2002).

**117.** Anti-Communist militia near Mount Merapi, Central Java, November 17, 1965
Bettman-Corbis Collection, Getty Images.

**118.** Certificate presented by the Army Paracommando Regiment to Gajah Mada University, Yogyakarta, dated December 25, 1965
Photographed by Abdul Wahid.

**119.** Certificate of appreciation from regent of Sleman District, Yogyakarta, to an individual who provided a loan to support campaign against the PKI, September 1969.
Wikimedia Commons, https://commons.wikimedia.org/wiki/File:Certificate_of_Gratitude_for_Financial_Loan_for_the_Elimination_of_PKI,_Sleman_%28dated_09-1969%29.jpg.

**120.** Detainees sitting in field, Central Java
National Library of Indonesia.

**121.** Detainees in teak forest, Central Java
Kopkamtib, *Gerakan 30 September Partai Komunis Indonesia* (Jakarta: Komando Operasi Pemulihan Keamanan dan Ketertiban, 1978), 292.

**122.** Detainees sitting in ditch, Central Java
United Press International, no date.

**123.** Detainees lying by a ditch, Central Java
*Lukisan pemberontakan PKI di Indonesia dan penumpasannya* (Bandung: Disjarahad, 1979), 135.

**124.** Detainees led under guard, Central Java, late 1965
National Library of Indonesia.

**125.** BTI leader with injury near Mount Merapi, Java, late 1965
National Library of Indonesia.

**126.** Moelyono, journalist from Yogyakarta, late 1965
Moelyono. Courtesy of Moelyono family.

**127.** Detainees with armed guards in Klaten, Central Java, late 1965
Moelyono. Courtesy of Moelyono family.

**128.** Two alleged Communist youths, late 1965
Moelyono. Courtesy of Moelyono family.

**129.** PKI leader Aidit wearing white, Central Java, November 1965
Soebekti, *Hari-hari terakhir Aidit* (Jogjakarta: Kedaulatan Rakjat, 1966).

**130.** PKI leader Aidit blindfolded, Central Java, November 1965

*TAPOL Bulletin*, no. 39 (May 1980): 4.

**131.** Cartoon: Progressive-revolutionary masses curse the September 30th Movement

*Api Pantjasila*, October 25, 1965.

**132.** Suharto handwritten memo on the revolution, October 27, 1965

*Angkatan Bersendjata*, November 23, 1965.

**133.** Cartoon with the heading "Same Methods" depicting Pesindo/PKI as the perpetrators in 1948 and the People's Youth/PKI as the perpetrator of "Gestapu" in 1965

*Api*, no date, November 1965.

**134.** Cartoon with caption "This is what's wanted!" depicting those who undermine the economy, Gestapu/PKI, and subversives as rats being hung

*Angkatan Bersendjata*, December 26, 1965.

**135.** Cartoon: "Calm won't be restored until the 'Gestapu-PKI' devils have been eradicated"

*Api*, October 29, 1965.

**136.** Young militia member with machete, Yogyakarta, December 1965

United Press International.

**137.** Severed head of Communist displayed with ammunition, Central Java, 1965

Sutarto/Antara.

**138.** A detainee arrives at a military base, Jakarta, November 1, 1965

National Library of Indonesia. Image reproduced from Pierre Labrousse, "Les bouleversements de 1965-1966 dans la documentation de la Fondation Idayu," *Archipel* 42 (1991): 121–31.

**139.** Communist youths under police guard, ca. October 30, 1965

No official source.

**140.** Soldiers entering a high school, Jakarta, late 1965

Beryl Bernay. Courtesy of Carol Gonzalez.

**141.** Res Publica University in Jakarta ransacked, November 13, 1965

Bettman-Corbis Collection, Getty Images.

**142.** Cartoon: "Price manipulators are the 'hidden Gestapu'"

*Angkatan Bersendjata*, December 17, 1965.

**143.** Detainee with hands behind head, Jakarta, November 26, 1965

Bettman-Corbis Collection, Getty Images.

**144.** Detainee squatting, Jakarta, November 26, 1965

Rory Dell for Camera Press. Redux.

**145.** Communist detainees in Tangerang, November 1965

National Library of Indonesia.

**146.** Jakarta commander Brigadier General Umar Wirahadikusumah visiting prison in Tangerang, November 1965

National Library of Indonesia.

**147.** Communist prisoners seated behind bars, Tangerang, November 1965

National Library of Indonesia.

**148.** PKI members and sympathizers disbanding local branch, North Jakarta, December 1965

National Library of Indonesia.

**149.** Cartoon: West Java authorities disbanding the PKI

*Api*, late 1965.

**150.** Detainees with SOBSI sign, Tanjung, Borneo

United Press International. TopFoto.

**151.** Demonstrators in Makassar, October 15, 1965

*Lukisan pemberontakan PKI di Indonesia dan penumpasannya* (Bandung: Disjarahad, 1979), 137.

**152.** Army paracommando officer posing in photo studio in Bali, 1965

Reproduced from Wong Sangar, September 29, 2013, https://wong-sangar.blogspot.com/2013/09/wong-solo-dalam-pusaran-g30s.html.

**153.** Members of anti-Communist militia in Bali, late 1965

National Library of Indonesia.

**154.** Detainees under guard in Bali, late 1965

National Library of Indonesia.

**155.** Militia member with a machete in Bali, late 1965

National Library of Indonesia.

**156.** Woman with child, Bali, late 1965

National Library of Indonesia.

**157.** (Page 133) Iswinarto drawing, faces
Courtesy of Iswinarto.

**158.** Fact-Finding Commission contact sheet 1
Dr. Soemarno photo collection, in National Library of Indonesia.

**159.** Fact-Finding Commission contact sheet 2
Dr. Soemarno photo collection, in National Library of Indonesia.

**160.** Commissioner Oei Tjoe Tat and military officer
Dr. Soemarno collection, image #21, National Library of Indonesia.

**161.** Military personnel display evidence
Dr. Soemarno collection, image #23, National Library of Indonesia.

**162.** Detainees in Sasono Mulyo, Surakarta
Dr. Soemarno collection, image #13, National Library of Indonesia.

**163.** Military personnel question Sasono Mulyo detainees
Dr. Soemarno collection, image #12, National Library of Indonesia.

**164.** Detainees listening to official briefing in Sasono Mulyo
Dr. Soemarno collection, image #27, National Library of Indonesia.

**165.** Detainees respond to questioning
Dr. Soemarno collection, image #15, National Library of Indonesia.

**166.** A young woman detainee answering a military officer
Dr. Soemarno collection, image #16, National Library of Indonesia.

**167.** Sign in Kamp Balaikota, Solo
Dr. Soemarno collection, #9, National Library of Indonesia.

**168.** Gerwani members in Kamp Balaikota, Solo
Dr. Soemarno collection, #11, National Library of Indonesia.

**169.** Djojudo (left), from Klaten, who the military claimed was a September 30th Movement "general"
*Kedaulatan Rakjat*, November 19, 1965.

**170.** Detainees assembled in a village in Klaten
Dr. Soemarno collection, image #18, National Library of Indonesia.

**171.** Detainees listening to army officer, Kamp Klaten
Dr. Soemarno collection, image #17, National Library of Indonesia.

**172.** Child kissing officer's hand, Kamp Klaten
Dr. Soemarno collection, image #28, National Library of Indonesia.

**173.** Exhumation in Jambukidul, Klaten
Dr. Soemarno collection, image #29, National Library of Indonesia.

**174.** Reburial in Jambukidul, Klaten
Dr. Soemarno collection, image #30, National Library of Indonesia.

**175.** (Page 147) Iswinarto drawing, men in ditch
Courtesy of Iswinarto.

**176.** Map of RPKAD victory tour through Central Java, late December 1965

**177.** Colonel Sarwo Edhie sitting on jeep, January 4, 1966
National Library of Indonesia.

**178.** Soldiers and armored vehicles, January 4, 1966
National Library of Indonesia.

**179.** Anti-Communist demonstration in Bogor, West Java, January 1966
Getty Images.

**180.** Commanders' statement, January 16, 1966
National Library of Indonesia.

**181.** PKI Politburo member Njono led into court, February 14, 1966
United Press International radiotelephoto. TopFoto.

**182.** Lieutenant Colonel Untung in court, March 7, 1966
Camera Press.

**183.** Cartoon showing "defenders of the Communist Party"
*Trisakti*, February 27, 1966.

**184.** Sukarno speaking with guests, ca. March 1966
Stamped *Paris Match/Marie Claire*.

**185.** Army and marines guard the presidential palace, February 25, 1966
United Press International.

**186.** Marines attack anti-Communist demonstrators in Jakarta, February 25, 1966
No official source.

**187.** Fact-Finding Commission death totals
*Laporan tentang Fact-Finding Commission KOTI*, January 10, 1966, 3.

**188.** Swedish Ambassador Edelstam in Jakarta to Foreign Minister Nilsson, February 21, 1966
Department of Foreign Affairs Archive, Series HP, Group 1, Case XI, National Archives of Sweden.

**189.** Demonstration against Foreign Minister Subandrio, with effigy, March 2, 1966
Harry Redl, *Time*.

**190.** Demonstrators at University of Indonesia, March 2, 1966
Bettman-Corbis Collection, Getty Images.

**191.** HMI protesters with an effigy of Uncle Sam, early March 1966
Stamped *Paris Match/Marie Claire*, March 7, 1966.

**192.** Women running a "public kitchen" to feed student demonstrators, Jakarta
Beryl Bernay. Courtesy of Carol Gonzalez.

**193.** Suharto declaring the nationwide ban on the PKI, March 12, 1966
Bettman-Corbis Collection, Getty Images.

**194.** Suharto behind Sukarno after the transfer of executive authority, March 11, 1966
Beryl Bernay. Courtesy of Carol Gonzalez.

**195.** Armored vehicles parade past civilians, March 12, 1966
Stamped *Paris Match/Marie Claire*.

**196.** Army tank convoy, March 12, 1966
Stamped *Paris Match/Marie Claire*.

**197.** Army tank and civilians from above, March 12, 1966
Stamped *Paris Match/Marie Claire*.

**198.** Army tank and crowd, Hotel Indonesia roundabout, March 13, 1966
United Press International radiophoto, dated March 14, 1966.

**199.** Civilians riding on army tank, March 12, 1966
Stamped *Paris Match/Marie Claire*.

**200.** Student convoy in Pasar Baru, Jakarta, March 1966
National Library of Indonesia.

**201.** (Page 171) Iswinarto drawing, victims and balloons
Courtesy of Iswinarto.

**202.** General Nasution with Tjipto Sukardhana, leader of the Bandung Institute of Technology student regiment, 1965
National Archive of the Republic of Indonesia.

**203.** A soldier teaching university students how to operate a machine gun, March 1966
No official source.

**204.** Soldier teaching a youth to shoot a gun
Photograph by Beryl Bernay. Courtesy of Carol Gonzalez.

**205.** NU militant Subchan ZE, on bed with books and submachine gun, 1966
Co Rentmeester. The LIFE Picture Collection, Getty Images.

**206.** General Nasution with Dr. Idham Cholid during NU anniversary
National Library of Indonesia.

**207.** Girls at an Islamic boarding school
Photograph by Beryl Bernay. Courtesy of Carol Gonzalez.

**208.** Soldiers using inflatable raft in Solo, Central Java, March 1966
Photograph by Sutarto. Reproduced from an album posted on the internet (site discontinued).

**209.** Sultan of Yogyakarta in military uniform, April 5, 1966
Rory Dell. Camera Press.

**210.** Foreign Minister Adam Malik with Ambassador Green
Beryl Bernay. Courtesy of Carol Gonzalez.

**211.** Women taking food to prisoners in Yogyakarta, June 1966
No official source.

**212.** Chinese-Indonesians rally in Jakarta against the PRC, April 15, 1966
Bettman-Corbis Collection, Getty Images.

**213.** Soldiers enter the Chinese embassy in Jakarta, April 18, 1966
TopFoto.

**214.** Cartoon depicting the Generation of '66 carrying a scroll with the state ideology
*Trisakti*, April 11, 1966.

**215.** Student demonstration in Bandung, ca. June 1966
Co Rentmeester. Getty Images.

**216.** Beryl Bernay with KAMI demonstrators, 1966
Beryl Bernay. Courtesy of Carol Gonzalez.

**217.** Student union demonstration in Bali, ca. June 1966
Horst Faas. AP Images.

**218.** Man behind bars, Jakarta, 1966
Co Rentmeester. The LIFE Picture Collection, Getty Images.

**219.** Prisoners doing calisthenics, Salemba Jail, Jakarta, 1966
Harry Redl, *Time*.

**220.** Prisoners working in the garden, Salemba Prison, Jakarta, 1966
Co Rentmeester. The LIFE Picture Collection, Getty Images.

**221.** Woman returning from a market in Jakarta, June 1966
No official source.

**222.** Back street in Jakarta, June 1966
Horst Faas.

**223.** Women with dried milk powder donated by the US, June 1966
Probably by Horst Faas.

**224.** Soldiers returning from Confrontation service in Kalimantan, mid-1966
United Press International, dated June 20, 1966.

**225.** Soldiers with semiautomatic weapons, ca. July 1966
Horst Faas.

**226.** Man with machete, Jakarta, 1966
Co Rentmeester. The LIFE Picture Collection, Getty Images.

**227.** Catholic nuns serving refreshments to army soldiers, probably Jakarta, mid-1966
National Library of Indonesia.

**228.** Girls with bamboo practice marching, ca. July 1966
Horst Faas.

**229.** Students from a secretarial school drill with guns, Jakarta, ca. June 1966
Co Rentmeester, The LIFE Picture Collection, Getty Images.

**230.** Uniformed women marching with guns, ca. July 1966
Horst Faas.

**231.** Caricature of Sukarno ranting at the poor
National Library of Indonesia.

**232.** Caricature of students rolling back Communism
National Library of Indonesia.

**233.** Caricature of a corrupt official and poor man
National Library of Indonesia.

**234.** Caricature of an official meeting
National Library of Indonesia.

**235.** Students with a poster showing Sukarno saying, "Me, me, I, me"
National Library of Indonesia.

**236.** Youths reading *Harian KAMI* daily newspaper
Beryl Bernay. Courtesy of Carol Gonzalez.

**237.** President Sukarno speaking at Sidang Istimewa MPR, July 1966
Algemeen Nederlands Persbureau, licensed via Newscom.

**238.** KAMI Bandung members protest in Jakarta, July 2, 1966
No official source.

**239.** Poster: Old Order, New Order
Beryl Bernay. Courtesy of Carol Gonzalez.

**240.** Poster: Mouthpiece of the People
Beryl Bernay. Courtesy of Carol Gonzalez.

**241.** Poster: Inflation
Beryl Bernay. Courtesy of Carol Gonzalez.

**242.** General Suharto at Ampera strategy presentation
Beryl Bernay. Courtesy of Carol Gonzalez.

**243.** President Sukarno pointing at General Suharto
Agence France Press.

**244.** (Page 207) Iswinarto drawing, tree and buried faces
Courtesy of Iswinarto.

**245.** Generals Nasution and Suharto, late September 1966
*New York Times*.

**246.** Cartoon: Sukarno trying to stamp out what he called the "October 1st Movement"
*Harian KAMI*, October 30, 1966.

**247.** Demonstrators demand that President Sukarno be put on trial
Gamma-Keystone. Copyright Getty Images.

**248.** Drawings of naked Gerwani women torturing the generals on October 1, 1965, part of dossier produced by KAMI Bandung, September 30, 1966.
Beryl Bernay collection. Courtesy of Carol Gonzalez.

**249.** Air Force commander Omar Dhani listening to the death sentence, December 18, 1966
Photographer unknown.

**250.** Subandrio on trial, Jakarta, October 1966
Archive ANP (222), in Netherlands National Archives.

**251.** Cartoon: "Your statement of accounts is demanded," showing President Sukarno under spotlights
*Merdeka*, December 1966. Republished in *New York Times*, December 31, 1966.

**252.** President Sukarno giving his last public speech, January 10, 1967
National Library of Indonesia.

**253.** Anti-Sukarno demonstrators, March 11, 1967
Agence France Press.

**254.** Cartoon: Time running out on Sukarno
*Sinar Harapan*, ca. March 1, 1967; reproduced in *New York Times*, March 7, 1967. Beryl Bernay collection. Courtesy of Carol Gonzalez.

**255.** Men sleeping at base of monument with graffiti: "Sukarno Gestapu"
Beryl Bernay. Courtesy of Carol Gonzalez.

**256.** Sukarno with Suharto, March 12, 1967
Associated Press.

**257.** Suharto posing as president, March 12, 1967
Associated Press.

**258.** Brigadier General Supardjo on trial, February 1967
Bill Lord. Camera Press.

**259.** PKI Central Committee member Sudisman escorted to court in Jakarta, July 1967
Perpustakaan Online Genosida 1965–1966, https://19651966perpustakaanonline.wordpress.com/2020/12/31/hidup-dalam-djuang-djuang-dalam-hidup-pena-sudisman-anggota-politbiro-pki-di-tahap-akhir-perjuangan-dan-kehidupannya/.

**260.** Chinese youth rescued from violent demonstrators, April 22, 1967
Bettman-Corbis Collection, Getty Images.

**261.** Pandjaitan student battalion protest against the People's Republic of China, August 1967
National Library of Indonesia.

**262.** Vice President Hubert Humphrey laying flowers on the grave of General Yani, November 1967
No official source.

**263.** US ambassador Green visiting General/President Suharto, December 1, 1967
Photograph by Larry Burrows. The LIFE Picture Collection, Getty Images.

**264.** Demonstrators demanding the rule of law, Jakarta, March 1967
United Press International radiophoto.

**265.** Cartoon of man with a poster reading, "Corrective critique [is a form of] social control"
*Mahasiswa Indonesia*, week 3, August 1967.

**266.** Indonesian hippie, 1968
United Press International, dated February 2, 1968.

**267.** Mbah Suro after arrest
Ramelan, *Mbah Suro nginggil* (Djakarta: Matoa, 1967).

**268.** Soldiers burning a house, West Kalimantan, ca. 1968
Bettman-Corbis Collection, Getty Images.

**269.** Soldier teaching a Dayak youth to use a gun, ca. December 1968
Keystone-France, Getty Images.

**270.** Chinese detainees behind barbed wire, Singakwang, West Kalimantan, ca. 1967
Keystone France, Getty Images.

**271.** Document: Malang District Military Command wanted poster
Etnohistori Collection.

**272.** Document: Army poster: Don't become bait for the Communists
Etnohistori Collection.

**273.** Blitar 1: Military personnel during operations in south Blitar
National Library of Indonesia.

**274.** Blitar 2: Soldiers searching cave
National Library of Indonesia.

**275.** Blitar 3: Captured Communists
National Library of Indonesia.

**276.** Blitar 4: Army officers interrogating villagers
National Library of Indonesia.

**277.** Blitar 5: Army officer addressing villagers
National Library of Indonesia.

**278.** Blitar 6: Western journalist
National Library of Indonesia.

**279.** Blitar 7: Checkpoint search
National Library of Indonesia.

**280.** Cartoon: Suharto and wife walking away from a grave with riches
*TAPOL Bulletin*, no. 40 (July 1980): 13.

**281.** Sukarno's state funeral in Blitar, East Java, June 22, 1970
Bettman-Corbis Collection, Getty Images.

**282.** (Page 235) Drawing of prisoner behind bars
*TAPOL Bulletin*, no. 83 (October 1987): 20.

**283.** Release of Category C prisoners in Semarang, Central Java, 1970
National Library of Indonesia.

**284.** Army officers explaining the security situation, Pontianak, West Kalimantan, 1971
Courtesy of Peter Schumacher.

**285.** Ethnic Chinese prisoner at gate, Pontianak, West Kalimantan
Courtesy of Peter Schumacher.

**286.** Male prisoners lined up, Pontianak, West Kalimantan, 1971
Courtesy of Peter Schumacher.

**287.** Female prisoners, Pontianak, West Kalimantan, 1971
Courtesy of Peter Schumacher.

**288.** Chinese man in a cell, Pontianak, West Kalimantan, 1971
Courtesy of Peter Schumacher.

**289.** Entrance to Wanapura Unit X, Buru Island, November 1971
Courtesy of Peter Schumacher.

**290.** Barracks in Wanapura detention camp, Buru Island, November 1971
Courtesy of Peter Schumacher.

**291.** Soldiers arriving at one of the Buru detention camps, 1971
Visual Documentation Project, https://visualdocumentationproject.wordpress.com/foto/pulau-buru/.

**292.** Group of prisoners on Buru Island, 1971
Visual Documentation Project, https://visualdocumentationproject.wordpress.com/foto/pulau-buru/.

**293.** The filmmaker Basuki Effendi, Buru Island, November 1971
Courtesy of Peter Schumacher.

**294.** Peter Schumacher with Basuki Effendi, Buru Island, November 1971
Courtesy of Peter Schumacher.

**295.** Prisoners on dyke, Buru Island, November 1971
Courtesy of Peter Schumacher.

**296.** Prisoners working wood, Buru Island, November 1971
Courtesy of Peter Schumacher.

**297.** Prisoners crushing rocks, Buru Island, November 1971
Courtesy of Peter Schumacher.

**298.** Sukotjo's funeral, Buru Island, ca. 1975
Visual Documentation Project, https://visualdocumentationproject.wordpress.com/foto/pulau-buru/.

**299.** Woman with child on a ship to join her husband on Buru Island, July 1972
United Press International.

**300.** Pramoedya Ananta Toer interviewed by journalists, Buru Island, November 1971
Courtesy of Peter Schumacher.

**301.** Pramoedya Ananta Toer's wife and children in Jakarta, 1971
Courtesy of Peter Schumacher.

**302.** Bukit Duri Women's Prison, Jakarta
MetroTV, October 20, 2015, http://hiburan.metrotvnews.com/read/2015/10/20/182222/tetap-senyum-menjelang-fajar-di-balik-penjara (site discontinued). Can be found at Buah Tangan dari yang Terbuang, https://edward-akip33.blogspot.com/2012/02/penjara-yang-telah-hilang-di-indonesia.html.

**303.** Plantungan Women's Prison, Central Java
Reproduced from flyer for exhibit *Pameran foto mengenang yang dilupakan*, Yogyakarta, 2006.

**304.** Women studying the Koran in Plantungan Prison, 1977
Courtesy of David Jenkins.

**305.** Women at a church service in Plantungan Prison, Central Java, 1977
Courtesy of David Jenkins.

**306.** Sukamulia Rehabilitation Installation, North Sumatra, no date
Indonesian Department of Information. From *Long Road to Democracy: A Photographic Journey of the Civil Society Movement in Indonesia, 1965-2001* (Jakarta: YAPPIKA, 2002), 10.

**307.** Sidikalang prison camp, North Sumatra, 1977
Zakaria M. Passe. *Tempo*.

**308.** Prisoner barracks, Amborawang, East Kalimantan, 1976
Syarif Hidayat. *Tempo*.

**309.** Prisoners with their possessions, Sumberejo prison camp, Balikpapan, East Kalimantan, 1977
Courtesy of David Jenkins.

**310.** Men on veranda in Sumberejo prison camp, Balikpapan, East Kalimantan, 1977
Courtesy of David Jenkins.

**311.** Prisoner release, Surabaya, 1977
Slamet Urip Prihadi. *Tempo*.

**312.** Prisoner release in Bali, December 1977
Putu Setia. *Tempo*.

**313.** I Dewa Putu Ngurah Djenawi's release letter
Courtesy of Djenawi, photographed December 24, 2018.

**314.** Release of Category B prisoners, Central Java and Yogyakarta, December 1979
National Library of Indonesia.

**315.** Example of identity card, with the letters "ET" in top right corner
*TAPOL Bulletin*, no. 87 (June 1988): 19.

**316.** (Page 263) Iswinarto drawing, writing
Courtesy of Iswinarto.

**317.** Poster for the film *Destruction of the Treacherous G30S/PKI*
Wikimedia Commons, https://en.wikipedia.org/wiki/Pengkhianatan_G30S/PKI.

**318.** Suharto family shooting pistols, December 1, 1967
Larry Burrows. The LIFE Picture Collection, Getty Images.

**319.** Elisabeth Ida Mulyani photo montage
Courtesy of Elisabeth Ida Mulyani and Derek Bacon.

**320.** Poster for Joshua Oppenheimer's film *The Look of Silence*
Final Cut for Real, https://www.finalcutforreal.dk/the-look-of-silence.

**321.** Cartoon from Yayak Yatmaka et al., *Sejarah gerakan kiri Indonesia untuk pemula*
(Bandung: Ultimus, 2016), 379.

**322.** *Pengakuan Algojo 1965: Investigasi Tempo Perihal Pembantaian 1965* (Tempo, 2013).

**323.** Untitled painting by Dadang Christanto
Courtesy of the artist.

# Notes

### Introduction

1 Hua Hsu, "Corky Lee's Photographs Helped Generations of Asian-Americans See Themselves," *New Yorker*, January 30, 2021, https://www.newyorker.com/culture/postscript/corky-lees-photographs-helped-generations-of-asian-americans-see-themselves.

2 Boerhan and Soebekti, *Gerakan 30 September* (Jakarta: Lembaga Pendidikan Ilmu Pengetahuan dan Kebudajaan Kosgoro, 1966), 77–79.

3 Dinas Sejarah Tentara Nasional Indonesia Angkatan Darat, *Lukisan pemberontakan PKI di Indonesia dan penumpasannya* (Jakarta: Disjarahad—AD & Sumber Jaya Offset Bandung, 1979), 149.

4 A selection of these works is discussed in the bibliographical essay at the end of this book.

5 As Hua Hsu writes of the white men who posed in 1869 for a photo commemorating the completion of the transcontinental railway, which had been built largely by Chinese coolies: "It's a kind of double entitlement—a sense that you are allowed to manipulate the levers of history, and that you're in control of your posture and expression as you pose for the commemorative picture." Hsu, "Corky Lee's Photographs."

6 With thanks to Karen Strassler for kindly providing the transcript of her interview with Moelyono, May 5, 1999.

7 Djoko Pekik, interview by Karen Strassler, February 21, 2000.

8 Roger Paget, interview by Douglas Kammen, February 19, 2016.

9 Nancy K. Florida, "A Proliferation of Pigs," *Public Culture* 20, no. 3 (2008): 502n14.

10 Dinas Sejarah Tentara Nasional Indonesia Angkatan Darat, *Lukisan pemberontakan PKI*, 127, 128.

11 In 2017 the military announced that it would resume mandatory screenings of the film for all members of the military. This prompted a new spree of anti-Communist hysteria.

12 See Benedict Anderson, "How Did the Generals Die?," *Indonesia* 43 (April 1987): 109–34.

13 Some of these photos were published in the army's *Lukisan pemberontakan* and credited to the Koleksi Dinas Sedjarah Angkatan Darat (Army History Service Collection). See, for example, *Lukisan pemberontakan*, 125, 128, 130, and 131.

14 "Potret-Potret Palsu Plantungan," *Pameran foto: Mengenang yang dilupakan* (Yogyakarta and Jakarta: Syarikat & Komnas Perempuan, 2006).

15 The exhibition, "Three Orders of Yogyakarta Solo Photojournalists," was held at a gallery in Yogyakarta from April 10 to 18, 1999. Karen Strassler, *Refracted Visions: Popular Photography and National Modernity in Java* (Durham, NC: Duke University Press, 2010), 230.

16 Strassler, *Refracted Visions*, 239–41.

17 Indonesian journalists who covered the events of 1965–66 in some depth included Salim Said for the army daily, *Angkatan*

*Bersendjata*; Yuli Ismartono, a student intern with *Angkatan Bersendjata*; and Dimyathi Saleh, who worked as an informant to Stanley Karnow of the *New York Times*.

18 In addition to photographers, a number of foreign journalists were active in Indonesia during this period. They included Neil Sheehan, Seymour Topping, and Seth King of the *New York Times*; Stanley Karnow of the *Washington Post*; Frank Palmos with the *Sydney Morning Herald*, who served as head of the foreign correspondents' association in Jakarta; Don North, who traveled through Java by car with Palmos in late 1965; Frank de Jong, cofounder of the Djakarta Foreign Correspondent's Club; Cindy Adams, the fashion model turned correspondent who befriended Sukarno in early 1965 and ghostwrote his autobiography; Walter Dommen, who reported for the *Los Angeles Times*; Deens Warner, a correspondent for the *Sydney Morning Herald*; Antoine Yared and John Leggoe, who filed stories for the Associated Press and Reuters that appeared in the *Washington Post*; the Sri Lankan journalist Tarzi Vittachi; and John Hughes, correspondent with the *Christian Science Monitor*, who later published a book about his experiences, titled *Indonesian Upheaval* (David McKay, 1967).

19 James Reston, "A Gleam of Light in Asia," *New York Times*, June 19, 1966; "Indonesia: Vengeance with a Smile," *Time*, July 15, 1966, 26.

20 Orhan Pamuk, *Istanbul: Memories and the City*, trans. Maureen Freely (New York: Alfred A. Knopf, 2017).

**Part I: Sukarno's Indonesia**

1 Memorandum for the Joint Chiefs of Staff from Department of the Navy, "Sino-Soviet Bloc Assistance to Indonesia," March 28, 1958, Declassified Documents Catalogue, 1982, #2384.

2 "'Go to Hell with Your Aid,' Sukarno tells U.S.," *Washington Post*, March 26, 1964.

3 Telegram 240A, American Embassy Jakarta to Department of State, April 5, 1965, POL RELS US-INDON, National Archives and Records Administration (hereafter NARA), College Park, MD.

4 Ida Bagus Gde Putra, "Pelaksanaan landreform dan keresahan masyarakat di Kabupaten Karangasem (1960–1965)" (PhD diss., Udayana University, 1986), 105.

5 I Gusti Putu Yasa Arimbawa, interview by Geoffrey Robinson, December 20, 1986, Banjar Bongan Tengah, Tabanan, Bali.

6 *Sukarno: An Autobiography*, as told to Cindy Adams (Hong Kong: Gunung Agung, 1966), 294.

7 Draft letter from CIA Director W. F. Raborn to the President, July 20, 1965. Personal archive of George McT. Kahin.

8 George Ball Telephone Conversation (telcon) with McGeorge Bundy, August 16, 1965, George W. Ball Papers, Seeley G. Mudd Manuscript Library, Princeton University, Princeton, NJ.

9 Telegram A-135, American Embassy Djakarta to Department of State, August 21, 1965, POL 2–1 INDON, NARA.

10 Cover note to document from Mr. M. J. C. Templeton, New Zealand High Commission in London, to Mr. Peck, British Foreign Office, "The Succession to Sukarno," December 18, 1964, DH 1015/112, FO 371/175251, UK National Archive.

11 Quoted in Brian May, *The Indonesian Tragedy* (London: Routledge & Kegan Paul, 1978), 125–26.

12 Ruth McVey, "The Great Fear," unpublished manuscript, 2–3.

13 Translation of Sukarno speech on August 17, 1965, enclosure to Airgram A-830, American Embassy Djakarta to Department of State, May 7, 1965, p. 28, POL 15–1 INDON, NARA.

14 Translation of Sukarno speech to PNI thirty-eighth anniversary celebration, enclosure to Airgram A-94, American Embassy Djakarta to Department of State, August 9, 1965, POL 12 INDON, NARA.

15 Sukarno, "Reach to the Stars! A Year of Self-reliance," speech, August 17, 1965, enclosure to Airgram 134, American Embassy Djakarta to Secretary of State, Washington, DC, August 20, 1965, POL 15–1 [INDON], NARA.

16 Airgram A-830, American Embassy Djakarta to Department of State, May 7, 1965, POL 15–1 INDON, NARA.

17 Telegram A-5, American Consulate Surabaya to State Department, September 16, 1965, POL 13–6 INDON, NARA.

**Part II: Crisis in Jakarta**

1 "Initial Statement of Lieutenant Colonel Untung," in Benedict Anderson and Ruth McVey, *A Preliminary Analysis of the October 1, 1965 "Coup" in Indonesia* (Ithaca, NY: Modern Indonesia Project, 1971), 164–66.
2 Boerhan and Soebekti, *Gerakan 30 September* (Jakarta: Lembaga Pendidikan Ilmu Pengetahuan dan Kebudajaan Kosgoro, 1966), 77–79.
3 Telegram 105A, American Embassy Djakarta to Department of State, October 2, 1965, POL 15-1 INDON, NARA.
4 Telegram 856, American Embassy Djakarta to Department of State, October 5, 1965, POL 23-9 INDON, NARA.
5 Telegram 851, American Embassy Djakarta to Department of State, October 5, 1965, POL 23-9 INDON, NARA.
6 Howard Jones, "Indonesian Coup Was a Red Bobble," *Washington Post*, October 10, 1965.
7 Telegram 452, State Department to American Embassy Jakarta, October 13, 1965, NSF CO File Indonesia Vol. 5, Lyndon Baines Johnson Library, Austin, TX.
8 Telegram A286, American Embassy Djakarta to Department of State, October 20, 1965, POL 6 INDON, NARA.
9 Telegram 1959 American Embassy Djakarta to Department of State, October 1965, POL 23-9 INDON, NARA.
10 Mansuruddin Bogok, an associate of the then foreign minister Adam Malik, interview with Ruth McVey, October 2, 1966, New York, box 2, file 31c, McVey Papers, Montisi, Italy.
11 Telegram 857, American Embassy Djakarta to Department of State, October 5, 1965, POL 23-9 INDON, NARA.
12 Komando Operasi Tertinggi, Seksi Penerangan, "Tjatatan kronologis disekitar peristiwa 'Gerakan 390 September,'" section titled "Pernjataan ORPOL2 dan ORMAS2 penentang 'Gerakan 30 September,'" 18.
13 Telegram 375A American Embassy Djakarta to Department of State, October 8, 1965, POL 23-9 INDON, NARA.
14 "Surat Keputusan Nomer: 1147/10/1965," in Kopkamtib, *Himpunan surat2 keputusan jang berhubungan dengan Kopkamtib 1965 s./d 1969* (n.p.: issued by Sekretariat Kopkamtib, 1970).
15 "Indonesia Special," *Wordt vervolgd*, March 1973, 12.
16 Telegram 535A, American Embassy Djakarta to Department of State, October 12, 1965, POL 23-9 INDON, NARA.
17 Telegram 956, American Embassy Djakarta to Department of State, October 11, 1965, POL 23-9 INDON, NARA.
18 Telegram 915A, American Embassy Djakarta to Department of State, October 20, 1965, POL 23-9 INDON, NARA.
19 Telegram 717A, American Embassy Djakarta to Department of State, October 15, 1965, POL 23-9 INDON, NARA.

**Part III: Onslaught**

1 Telegram 1360, American Embassy Djakarta to Department of State, November 6, 1965, POL 23-9 INDON, NARA.
2 Telegram 736A, American Embassy Djakarta to Department of State, November 19, 1965, POL 23-9 INDON, NARA.
3 Quoted in John Hughes, *The End of Sukarno: A Coup That Misfired, a Purge That Ran Wild* (London: Angus & Robertson, 1968), 151.
4 Telegram 1438, American Embassy Jakarta to Department of State, November 13, 1965, POL 23-9, Indonesia, NARA.
5 Joshua Oppenheimer, dir., *The Act of Killing* (Denmark: Final Cut for Real and DK Films, 2012).
6 Karen Strassler, *Refracted Visions: Popular Photography and National Modernity in Java* (Durham, NC: Duke University Press, 2010), 239.
7 Strassler, *Refracted Visions*, 239.
8 Strassler, *Refracted Visions*, 238.
9 Dinas Sejarah TNI Angkatan Darat, quoted and translated in Robert Cribb, ed., *The Indonesian Killings, 1965–1966* (Clayton, Victoria: Monash Papers on Southeast Asia, 1990), 165.
10 Taguchi Mitsuo, "Aiditto ansatsu no shinsō: Gungokuhi hōkoku wa kataru" [The truth about Aidit's assassination: Top secret military report reveals], *Sekai shūhō* [Weekly world report], January 25, 1966.
11 "Aidit segera akan dapat ditangkap," *Angkatan Bersendjata*, November 25, 1965.
12 "Berita dari Djawa Tengah Gembong PKI D.N. Aidit di 'oprak' Rakjat," *Berita Yudha*, November 28, 1965.

13 Telegram 938A, American Embassy Djakarta to Department of State, November 26, 1965, POL 23-9 INDON, NARA.
14 "Mati Sjahid," *Angkatan Bersendjata*, November 2, 1965.
15 Sukarno speech, October 16, 1965, quoted in Harold Crouch, *The Army and Politics in Indonesia* (Ithaca, NY: Cornell University Press, 1978), 162.
16 *Berita Yudha*, October 19, 1965.
17 *Angkatan Bersendjata*, October 14, 1965.
18 Airgram A-15, US Consulate Medan to American Embassy Djakarta, November 18, 1965, POL 2 INDON, NARA.
19 Telegram 755a, American Embassy Djakarta to Department of State, November 20, 1965, POL 23-9 INDON, NARA.
20 Telegram 1566, American Embassy Jakarta to State Department, November 26, 1965, POL 23-9 INDON, NARA.
21 "Kontrev 'G.30.S' takut RPKAD," *Suara Indonesia*, December 9, 1965.
22 Telegram A-512, American Embassy Djakarta to Department of State, February 11, 1966, DEF INDO 13, NARA.
23 "Musuh Revolusi adalah musuh agama jang paling garang," *Suara Indonesia*, October 7, 1965.
24 "Pengakuan seorang ketua Gerwani. Diperintahkan mendjual diri kepada anggota2 ABRI," *Suara Indonesia*, November 21, 1965.

**Part IV: The Fact-Finding Commission**

1 Fact Finding Commission Komando Operasi Tertinggi, *Laporan tentang Fact Finding Commission KOTI*, Jakarta, January 10, 1966, 1.
2 Telegram 957A, American Embassy Djakarta to Department of State, December 28, 1965, POL 23-9 INDON, NARA.
3 John Hughes, *Indonesian Upheaval* (New York: David McKay, 1967), 185.
4 Ita F. Nadia, "Partini: Perempuan eks-tapol sampah segala sampah," in *Suara perempuan korban tragedi '65* (Yogyakarta: Galang, 2009), 60–61.
5 Josepha Sukartiningsih, "Ketika perempuan menjadi Tapol," in *Tahun yang tak pernah berahkir: Memahami pengalaman korban 65*, ed. John Roosa, Ayu Ratih, and Hilmar Farid (Jakarta: Elsam, 2004), 96.

**Part V: The Struggle for Power**

1 Telegram 137A, American Embassy Djakarta to Department of State, January 5, 1966, POL INDO, NARA.
2 Quoted in Harold Crouch, *The Army and Politics in Indonesia* (Ithaca, NY: Cornell University Press, 1978), 166–67.
3 Quoted in Crouch, *Army and Politics*, 167.
4 Airgram A-474, American Embassy Djakarta to Department of State, January 25, 1966, POL 2-1 INDON, NARA.
5 Telegram 724A, American Embassy Djakarta to Department of State, December 20, 1965, POL 23-9, NARA.
6 Quoted in Telegram 459A, American Embassy Djakarta to Department of State, February 17, 1966, POL 23 INDON, NARA.
7 Quoted in Airgram A-474, American Embassy Djakarta to Department of State, January 25, 1966, POL 2-1 INDON, NARA.
8 Ambassador Harald Edelstam, telegram to Nilsson (Foreign Minister), February 21, 1966, UA/HP 1/XI, Riksarkivet, National Archives of Sweden.
9 Ambassador Gilchrist, telegram to Foreign Office, February 23, 1966, DH 1011/66, FO 371/186028, UK National Archives.
10 Airgram A-641, American Embassy Djakarta to Department of State, April 15, 1966, POL 2 INDON, NARA.
11 Airgram A-550, American Embassy Djakarta to Department of State, March 4, 1966, POL 2 INDON, NARA.
12 Airgram A-551, American Embassy Djakarta to Department of State, March 4, 1966, POL 2 INDON, NARA.
13 John Legge, *Sukarno: A Political Biography* (Sydney: Allen & Unwin, 1990), 402.
14 Telegram 702A, American Embassy Djakarta to Department of State, March 19, 1966, 017926, NARA.
15 Telegram 426A, American Embassy Djakarta to Department of State, March 12, 1966, POL 23-9 INDON, NARA.

**Part VI: Allegiances and Suspicions**

1 Telegram 1263A, American Embassy Djakarta to Secretary of State, Washington, DC, October 27, 1965, [POL] INDON, NARA.
2 Telegram 981A, American Embassy Djakarta to Department of State, March 19, 1966, POL INDO, NARA.
3 Telegram 1014A, American Embassy Djakarta to Secretary of State, Washington, DC, March 29, 1966, AID US/INDO, NARA.

4 Telegram A-665, American Embassy Djakarta to Department of State, April 27, 1966, POL 12 INDON, NARA.
5 Telegram 173A, American Embassy Djakarta to Department of State, June 4, 1966, POL 15-1 INDON, NARA.
6 Telegram A-641, American Embassy Jakarta to Department of State, Washington, DC, April 15, 1966, POL 2 INDON, NARA.
7 Letter dated April 3, 1966, in Airgram A-25, US Consulate Surabaya to Department of State, April 14, 1966, POL 12 INDON, NARA.
8 Peking NCNA International Service in English, 05.00 GMT, April 12, 1966, in Central Intelligence Agency, *Daily Report Foreign Radio Broadcasts*, April 12, 1966.
9 Telegram 615, American Embassy Djakarta to Department of State, April 22, 1966, POL 23-8 INDON, NARA.
10 "One Reported Dead in Indonesia Clash," *New York Times*, May 31, 1966.
11 Suwondo Budiardjo, "Salemba: Cuplikan Kecil Derita Nasional," unpublished manuscript, September 1990, 17.
12 Telegram 1063A, American Embassy Djakarta to Department of State, December 30, 1965, AID (US) 15-10 INDON, NARA.
13 Telegram 1654, American Embassy Djakarta to Department of State, December 5, 1965, POL 1[?]-1 INDON, NARA.
14 Telegram 159A, American Embassy Djakarta to Department of State, July 11, 1966, [INDON], NARA.
15 Airgram A453, American Embassy Djakarta to Department of State, January 14, 1966, POL 2-3 INDON, NARA.
16 Speech translated in Airgram A-89, American Embassy Djakarta to Department of State, August 24, 1966, POL 15-1 INDON, NARA.

**Part VII: The New Order Emerges**

1 Airgram A-60, American Embassy Djakarta to Department of State, July 30, 1966, POL 15-1 INDON, NARA.
2 Telegram 1223, American Embassy Djakarta to Department of State, September 13, 1966, POL 15-1 INDON, NARA.
3 Airgram A-145, American Embassy Djakarta to Department of State, September 24, 1966, POL 2 INDON, NARA.
4 Telegram 1802, American Embassy Djakarta to Department of State, October 13, 1966, POL 2 INDON, NARA.
5 Harold Crouch, *The Army and Politics in Indonesia* (Ithaca, NY: Cornell University Press, 1978), 211.
6 Quoted in R. E. Elson, *Suharto: A Political Biography* (Cambridge: Cambridge University Press, 2001), 157.
7 Marshall Green, *Indonesia: Crisis and Transformation, 1965–68* (New York: Compass, 1990), 103, 105.
8 Green, *Indonesia*, 110.
9 Green, *Indonesia*, 117.
10 Quoted in *Kronik '65: Catatan hari per hari peristiwa G30S sebelum ingga setelahnya (1963–1971)* (Yogyakarta: Media Pressindo, 2014), 665.
11 "Penumpasan terhadap gerombolan Tjina Komunis di daerah Kalbar," unpublished and undated manuscript, 5.
12 Soemadi, *Peranan Kalimantan Barat dalam menghadapi subversi Komunis Asia Tenggara* (Pontianak: Yayasan Tanjungpura, 1974), 96.
13 Telegram 18R, US Consulate Surabaya to Department of State, November 21, 1965, POL 23-8 INDON, NARA.
14 "Reds in Indonesia Renew Campaign," *New York Times*, August 11, 1968.
15 *Sukarno: An Autobiography*, as told to Cindy Adams (Hong Kong: Gunung Agung, 1966), 312.

**Part VIII: Long-Term Detention**

1 Quoted in Justus M. van der Kroef, "Indonesia's Political Prisoners," *Pacific Affairs* 49 (1976): 626.
2 Herb Feith, "Dayak Legacy," *Far Eastern Economic Review*, January 25, 1968.
3 Peter Schumacher, personal communication with the authors, December 20, 2017, English-language excerpts from *Ogenblikken van Genezing* (The Netherlands: van Gennep, 1996).
4 Carmel Budiardjo, *Surviving Indonesia's Gulag* (London: Cassell, 1996), 29.

# Bibliographic Essay

Scholarship on the actors, events, and dynamics considered in this book is uneven: extremely rich on some subjects but almost nonexistent on others. It has also emerged slowly, with only a handful of significant books and articles published in the thirty years after the alleged coup, followed by an avalanche of new work after 1998 when President Suharto was finally forced to step down. In large part, that divergence in research and published scholarship reflects the simple fact that while the military remained in power, it was simply too dangerous to investigate, speak, or write about these events. One important consequence of the ending of authoritarian rule in 1998 is that the new scholarship has increasingly been undertaken not by foreign scholars but by Indonesians, and published in the Indonesian language. While most of the works listed here are in English, we include some examples of Indonesian-language contributions.

It should also be noted that while we focus here on secondary materials that should be readily available to most readers, serious scholarship on this period requires access to a variety of archives. Although many documents remain secret, rich collections of declassified government documents can be found in the national archives of the United States, the United Kingdom, Australia, Sweden, Germany, the Netherlands, and other countries. While most official Indonesian records either have been destroyed or remain classified, in recent years some researchers have gained access to local archives where they have discovered materials that add new layers to our understanding of this history.

There are very few scholarly works expressly concerned with the visual record of the mass violence against the Indonesian Left, but four items are worthy of special mention. In 1977, the Indonesian State Secretariat produced an illustrated commemorative work titled *30 tahun Indonesia merdeka*, the last volume of which includes ninety pages on the years 1965–67. Two years later, the Indonesian Army's History Bureau issued a 286-page coffee-table book titled *Lukisan pemberontakan PKI di Indonesia dan penumpasannya*

(Bandung: Disjarahad-AD, 1979), which, produced in limited numbers, was clearly intended for internal military consumption rather than the general public. On the academic front, far and away the best source for understanding the history and impact of photography in modern Indonesia is Karen Strassler's *Refracted Visions: Popular Photography and National Modernity in Java* (Durham, NC: Duke University Press, 2010). Finally, the Indonesian journal *Historia*, founded by Bonnie Triyana, has run extensive coverage of the destruction of the PKI, including important visual materials.

## Part I. Sukarno's Indonesia

The decade preceding the cataclysm of 1965 was dominated politically by President Sukarno and the Indonesian Left. While there has been scant attention paid to these years in the most recent scholarship, works from an earlier era remain indispensable. These include Herbert Feith, *The Decline of Constitutional Democracy in Indonesia* (Ithaca, NY: Cornell University Press, 1962); J. D. Legge, *Sukarno: A Political Biography* (Sydney: Allen & Unwin, 1990); Ann Booth, *The Indonesian Economy: A History of Missed Opportunities* (London: Macmillan, 1998); and Harold Crouch, *The Army and Politics in Indonesia* (Ithaca, NY: Cornell University Press, 1978). On Indonesia's foreign policy in these years, the most reliable source is Franklin B. Weinstein, *Indonesian Foreign Policy and the Dilemma of Dependence: From Sukarno to Soeharto* (Ithaca, NY: Cornell University Press, 1976).

For the history and politics of the Indonesian Left, the best works are Ruth McVey, *The Rise of Indonesian Communism* (Ithaca, NY: Cornell University Press, 1965); Rex Mortimer, *Indonesian Communism under Sukarno: Ideology and Politics, 1959–1965* (Ithaca, NY: Cornell University Press, 1974); Rex Mortimer, *The Indonesian Communist Party and Land Reform, 1954–1965* (Clayton, Victoria: Monash University Centre for Southeast Asian Studies, 1972); and Margot Lyon, *Bases of Conflict in Rural Java* (Berkeley, CA: Center for South and Southeast Asian Studies, 1970). Sukarno's 1926 essay *Nationalism, Islam, and Marxism*, Translation Series No. 48 (Ithaca, NY: Modern Indonesia Project, Cornell University, 1984) provides invaluable insight into his distinctive political thought and rhetorical style. Many of his later speeches have been gathered in Budi Setyono and Bonnie Triyana, eds., *Revolusi belum selesai: Kumpulan pidato Presiden Sukarno 30 September 1965—pelengkap Nawaksara* (Jakarta: Serambi Ilmu Semesta, 2014).

## Part II. Crisis in Jakarta

October 1, 1965, has been the subject of a substantial body of scholarship and debate. The key issues at stake have been, first, who was responsible for the kidnapping and murder of the generals that morning, and second, what the event should be called. The earliest intervention was Benedict Anderson and Ruth McVey, *A Preliminary Analysis of the October 1, 1965 "Coup" in Indonesia*, completed and distributed in mimeograph form to colleagues in January 1966 but not published until 1971 (Ithaca, NY: Cornell Modern Indonesia Project, 1971). Challenging the Indonesian Army's contention that the plot was an attempted PKI coup, Anderson and McVey argued that it was more likely an internal army affair that the army then blamed on the PKI.

The army commissioned a number of books to buttress its version of events, the most notable of which are Nugroho Notosusanto's hurriedly written *40 hari kegagalan "G-30-S" 1 Oktober–10 November* (Jakarta: Pusat Sedjarah Angkatan Bersendjata, 1965); Boerhan and Soebekti, *Gerakan 30 September* (Jakarta: Lembaga Pendidikan Ilmu Pengetahuan dan Kebudajaan Kosgoro, 1966); and Nugroho Notosusanto and Ismail Saleh, *The Coup Attempt of the "September 30 Movement" in Indonesia* (Jakarta: Pembimbing Massa, 1968). A useful discussion of variation and contradictions in the official army accounts is John Roosa, "The September 30th Movement: The Aporias of the Official Narratives," in *The Contours of Mass Violence in Indonesia, 1965–68*, ed. Douglas Kammen and Katharine McGregor, ASAA Southeast Asia Publications Series (Singapore: NUS Press, 2012), 25–49. Later works challenged the official position on a variety of fronts. In 1970, the Dutch scholar W. F. Wertheim, in "Suharto and the Untung Coup—the Missing Link," *Journal of Contemporary Asia* 1, no. 2 (Winter 1970): 50–57, argued that it was not the PKI but General Suharto himself who had masterminded the October 1 plot.

The army's dubious claims received additional support from the US Central Intelligence Agency, which in 1968 published *Indonesia—1965: The Coup That Backfired* (Washington, DC: CIA, 1968), echoing the official Indonesian account's version of events. Four decades later, the former CIA analyst Helen-Louise Hunter, the principal author of the 1968 book, published *Sukarno and the Indonesian Coup* (Westport, CT: Praeger Security International, 2007).

Meanwhile, a number of works began to draw attention to the role of foreign actors. These included Peter Dale Scott, "The United States and the Overthrow of Sukarno, 1965–1967," *Pacific Affairs* 58, no. 2 (Summer 1985): 239–64; Bradley Simpson, *Economists with Guns: Authoritarian Development and U.S.-Indonesian Relations, 1960–1968* (Stanford, CA: Stanford University Press, 2008); Baskara T. Wardaya, *Bung Karno menggugat! Dari Marhaen, CIA, pembantaian massal '65 hingga G30S* (Yogyakarta: Galang, 2009); and Geoffrey Robinson, *The Killing Season: A History of the Indonesian Massacres, 1965–66* (Princeton, NJ: Princeton University Press, 2018), all of which argue that the US and its allies played a significant role in creating the conditions for the plot and the army takeover. On Chinese involvement, see Taomo Zhou, *Migration in the Time of Revolution: China, Indonesia and the Cold War* (Ithaca, NY: Cornell University Press, 2019). Former US ambassador Marshall Green's memoir, *Indonesia: Crisis and Transformation, 1965–1968* (Washington, DC: Compass, 1990) sought to exonerate both the army and the United States by pointing the finger of blame squarely at the PKI.

These debates are thoroughly reviewed and evaluated in John Roosa, *Pretext for Mass Murder: The September 30th Movement and Suharto's Coup d'État in Indonesia* (Madison: University of Wisconsin Press, 2006); and Asvi Warman Adam, *1965: Orang-orang di balik tragedi* (Yogyakarta: Galang, 2009). Also valuable in understanding this period is the massive chronology compiled under the leadership of Kuncoro Hadi, *Kronik 65: Catatan hari per hari peristiwa G30S sebelum hingga setelahnya (1963–1971)* (Yogyakarta: Media Pressindo, 2017).

## Part III. Onslaught

Among the earliest attempts to understand the mass violence of 1965–67 and to chart its geographical and social variations was Robert Cribb's edited volume *The Indonesian Killings, 1965–1966: Studies from Java and Bali* (Clayton, Victoria: Monash Papers on Southeast Asia, 1990). That work was followed by a handful of regional studies that traced the historical origins and patterns of the violence, including Ann Laura Stoler, *Capitalism and Confrontation in Sumatra's Plantation Belt, 1870–1979* (New Haven, CT: Yale University Press, 1985); Geoffrey Robinson, *The Dark Side of Paradise: Political Violence in Bali* (Ithaca, NY: Cornell University Press, 1995); and Iwan Gardono Sudjatmiko, "The Destruction of the Indonesian Communist Party: A Comparative Study of East Java and Bali" (PhD diss., Harvard University, 1992).

With the fall of Suharto in 1998, the mass violence became a major focus of scholarly inquiry. Notable general works from this period include the contributions in Kammen and McGregor, *Contours of Mass Violence*; Robinson, *Killing Season*; Katharine McGregor, Jess Melvin, and Annie Pohlman, eds., *The Indonesian Genocide of 1965: Causes, Dynamics and Legacies* (Cham: Palgrave Macmillan, 2018); and John Roosa, *Buried Histories: The Anticommunist Massacres of 1965–1966 in Indonesia* (Madison: University of Wisconsin Press, 2020).

In addition to such general accounts, excellent regional studies have been published in the past two decades, including Leslie Dwyer and Degung Santikarma, "'When the World Turned to Chaos': 1965 and Its Aftermath in Bali, Indonesia," in *The Specter of Genocide: Mass Murder in Historical Perspective*, ed. Robert Gellately and Ben Kiernan (Cambridge: Cambridge University Press, 2003), 289–305; Jamie Davidson and Douglas Kammen, "Indonesia's Unknown War and the Lineages of Violence in West Kalimantan," *Indonesia* 73 (April 2002): 53–87; Gerry Van Klinken, *The Making of Middle Indonesia: Middle Classes in Kupang Town, 1930s–1980s* (Leiden: Brill, 2014); and Jess Melvin, *The Army and the Indonesian Genocide: Mechanics of Mass Murder* (New York: Routledge, 2018). Melvin's work, based on the discovery of an important trove of military documents in Aceh, extends Robert Cribb's argument that the campaign of violence against the PKI was a genocide. Siddharth Chandra has pioneered a demographic approach to the mass killings in Java in a series of journal articles, starting with "New Findings on the Indonesia Killings of 1965–66," *Journal of Asian Studies* 76, no. 4 (November 2017): 1059–86.

Valuable research has been done on the experience of women and on gender-based violence. Notable examples include Saskia Wieringa, *Sexual Politics in Indonesia* (New York: Palgrave, 2002); Ita F. Nadia, *Suara perempuan korban tragedi '65* (Yogyakarta: Galang, 2009); and Annie Pohlman, *Women, Sexual Violence, and the Indonesian Killings of 1965–66* (New York: Routledge, 2015).

Another important development since 1998 has been the publication of survivor testimonies. These include John Roosa, Ayu Ratih, and Hilmar Farid, eds., *Tahun yang tak pernah berakhir: Pengalaman korban 1965; Esai-esai sejarah lisan* (Jakarta: Elsam, 2004); Baskara Wardaya, ed., *Truth Will Out: Indonesian Accounts of the 1965 Mass Violence* (Clayton, Victoria: Monash University Press, 2013); Putu Oka Sukanta, ed., *Breaking the Silence: Survivors Speak about the 1965–1966 Violence in Indonesia* (Clayton, Victoria: Monash University Press, 2014); Mary Kolimon, Liliya Wetangterah, and Karen Campbell-Nelson, eds., *Forbidden Memories: Women's Experiences of 1965 in Eastern Indonesia* (Clayton, Victoria: Monash University Press, 2015); and Soe Tjen Marching, ed., *The End of Silence: Accounts of the 1965 Genocide in Indonesia* (Amsterdam: Amsterdam University Press, 2019). These personal testimonies complement the moving accounts we have from an earlier period, such as Marni, "I Am a Leaf in the Storm," *Indonesia* 47 (April 1989): 49–60; Pipit Rochijat, "Am I PKI or Non-PKI?," *Indonesia* 40 (October 1985): 37–56; and Harry Aveling, ed., *From Surabaya to Armageddon: Indonesian Short Stories* (Singapore: Heinemann Educational Books, 1976), a collection of short stories about the events of 1965–67.

## Part IV. The Fact-Finding Commission

To our knowledge, there has been no serious study of the Fact-Finding Commission established by Sukarno in December 1965 as part of his effort to recapture the political momentum from his critics. Our understanding of the commission must therefore be gleaned from the contents of the report itself, from the available photographic record, and from passing references to the commission in other works. Those include a tantalizing exchange between commission member, and later political prisoner, Oei Tjoe Tat and the journalist John Hughes in *Indonesian Upheaval* (New York: David McKay, 1967). A fuller account of the commission, and of the political machinations of the time, can be found in Oei's memoir, *Memoar Oei Tjoe Tat: Pembantu Presiden Soekarno*, eds. Pramoedya Ananta Toer and Stanley Adi Prasetyo (Jakarta: Hasta Mitra, 1995).

## Part V. The Struggle for Power, and Part VI. Allegiances and Suspicions

In contrast to the wealth of material now available about the "coup" and the mass violence, scholarship on the *political* struggles of this period is remarkably sparse. The best account of those struggles is still Crouch, *Army and Politics in Indonesia*. The posture of Muslim organizations and leaders is well articulated in Greg Fealy and Katharine McGregor, "East Java and the Role of Nahdlatul Ulama in the 1965–66 Anti-Communist Violence," in Kammen and McGregor, *Contours of Mass Violence*, 104–30. The pivotal role of university students and their relationship with the army is recounted in Christianto Wibisono's *Sejarah demonstrasi mahasiswa 1966: Aksi-aksi Tritura* (Jakarta: Yayasan

Management Informasi, 1980). On the state of the Indonesian economy and the transformation initiated at this time, see Guy Pauker, *Indonesia's Convalescence* (Santa Monica, CA: RAND Corporation, 1967); Anne Booth, *The Indonesian Economy: A History of Missed Opportunities* (London: Macmillan, 1998); and Hal Hill, *The Indonesian Economy since 1966: Southeast Asia's Emerging Giant* (New York: Cambridge University Press, 1996). On the delicate position of Chinese Indonesians and the relationship with China, the best sources are Charles A. Coppel, *Indonesian Chinese in Crisis* (Kuala Lumpur: Oxford University Press, 1983); Robert Cribb and Charles A. Coppel, "A Genocide That Never Was: Explaining the Myth of Anti-Chinese Massacres in Indonesia, 1965–66," *Journal of Genocide Research* 11, no. 4 (December 2009): 447–65; and Zhou, *Migration in the Time of Revolution*.

## Part VII. The New Order Emerges

As for the earlier period, Crouch's *Army and Politics in Indonesia* provides the most complete account of the emergence of the New Order from mid-1966 through 1968. R. E. Elson's *Suharto: A Political Biography* (Cambridge: Cambridge University Press, 2001) recounts Suharto's rise to power. More critical assessments, which highlight the New Order's deep entanglement with international capital, are provided in Simpson, *Economists with Guns*; and Robinson, *Killing Season*. The high-profile political show trials of Subandrio, Supardjo, Omar Dhani, Sudisman, and others in 1966–67 are described in Amnesty International's 1977 report, *Indonesia: An Amnesty International Report* (London: Amnesty International Publications). Valuable analyses of the trial documents include John Roosa's study of the Supardjo record in *Pretext for Mass Murder*; and Benedict Anderson's analysis of Sudisman's defense oration, "Analysis of Responsibility" (Melbourne, Victoria: Works Co-operative, 1975). Finally, several recent works examine the regime's campaigns to crush what it claimed to be a resurgent Communism in 1967 and 1968. Notable works in this vein include Bonnie Triyana, "Peristiwa Purwodadi: Kasus pembunuhan massal anggota dan simpatisan Partai Komunis Indonesia di Kabupaten Grobogan tahun 1965–1969" (BA thesis, Universitas Diponegoro, 2003); Vannessa Hearman, *Unmarked Graves: Death and Survival in the Anti-Communist Violence in East Java, Indonesia*, ASAA Southeast Asia Publications Series (Singapore: NUS Press, 2018); and Grace Leksana, "Embedded Remembering: Memory Culture of the 1965 Violence in Rural East Java" (PhD diss., Leiden University, 2020).

## Part VIII. Long-Term Detention

The first comprehensive accounts of Indonesia's long-term political detainees emerged in the late 1970s in the context of an international campaign calling for their release. Among the earliest and still most useful studies were Justus Van der Kroef, "Indonesia's Political Prisoners," *Pacific Affairs* 49 (1976): 625–47; Amnesty International, *Indonesia*; and TAPOL, *Treatment of Indonesian Political*

*Prisoners: Forced Labour and Transmigration* (London: TAPOL, 1978). Also see Greg Fealy, *The Release of Indonesia's Political Prisoners: Domestic versus Foreign Policy, 1975–1979* (Clayton, Victoria: Monash University Centre for Southeast Asian Studies, 1995). These accounts, together with the international campaign, stimulated a lively public debate about the events of 1965 and the fate of the detainees, including an animated exchange between former US embassy official Francis Galbraith and the then secretary general of Amnesty International, Martin Ennals ("What Happened in Indonesia? An Exchange," *New York Review of Books*, February 9, 1978). Visits by domestic and foreign journalists, though heavily restricted, also resulted in a number of journalistic exposés, including Djamal Marsudi, *Laporan pertama dari Pulau Buru* (Jakarta: Intibuku Utama, 1971).

More recently, our understanding of the system of long-term detention has been enriched by the publication of memoirs and testimonials by former political prisoners. Among the first and most notable was the memoir of the renowned Indonesian author Pramoedya Ananta Toer, who was held without charge or trial for thirteen years: *The Mute's Soliloquy* (New York: Hyperion East, 1999). Others soon followed, including Col. Abdul Latief, *Pledoi Kol. A. Latief: Soeharto terlibat G30S* (Jakarta: Institut Studi Arus Informasi, 2000); Hersri Setiawan, *Aku eks Tapol* (Yogyakarta: Galang, 2003); and Tan Swie Ling, *G30S 1965, perang dingin & kehancuran nasionalisme: Pemikiran Cina jelata korban Orba* (Jakarta: Komunitas Bambu, 2010). The memoirs of women political detainees have been especially valuable. Among the first was the memoir of Carmel Budiardjo, an English woman held without trial for more than three years: *Surviving Indonesia's Gulag* (London: Cassell, 1996). Since 1998, works by and about women detainees have included Sumiyarsi Simirini C., *Plantungan: Pembuangan Tapol perempuan* (Yogyakarta: Pusat Sejarah dan Etika Politik, Universitas Sanata Dharma, 2010); and Amurwani Dwi Lestariningsih, *Gerwani: Kisah Tapol wanita di Kamp Plantungan*, 2nd ed. (Jakarta: Kompas, 2011), a collection of testimonials.

## Part IX. Epilogue

Suharto's fall in 1998 set in motion a period of reflection on the events of 1965 and their aftermath. That reflection has taken many forms, including scholarly studies, works of investigative journalism, judicial initiatives, memoirs, and creative interventions of all kinds. Valuable scholarly contributions include Mary Zurbuchen, ed., *Beginning to Remember: The Past in the Indonesian Present* (Seattle: University of Washington Press, 2005); and Martijn Eickhoff, Gerry van Klinken, and Geoffrey Robinson, eds., "1965 Today: Living with the Indonesian Massacres," special issue, *Journal of Genocide Research* 19, no. 3 (2017). Among the more notable journalistic efforts is the collection of perpetrator testimonies in Kurniawan, ed., *Pengakuan algojo: Investigasi Tempo perihal Pembantaian 1965* (Jakarta: Tempo, 2012), published in English as *The Massacres: Coming to Terms with the Trauma of 1965* (Jakarta: Tempo, 2015).

In the judicial field, the proceedings of International People's Tribunal for 1965, held in The Hague in 2015, marked a major milestone, as ably explored in Saskia Wieringa, Jess Melvin, and Annie Pohlman, eds., *The International People's Tribunal for 1965 and the Indonesian Genocide* (Abingdon, Oxon: Routledge, 2019). The number and range of creative works reflecting on the legacies of 1965 is vast, but the most influential have arguably been the films of Joshua Oppenheimer—*The Act of Killing* (2013) and *The Look of Silence* (2016)—which fundamentally altered the memory landscape of "1965" in Indonesia and abroad.

# Index of Place Names

# Index of Personal Names

# Index of Parties, Organizations, and Institutions